**PRACTICE
MAKES
PERFECT**

Statistics

W9-CAD-729

PRACTICE MAKES PERFECT

Statistics

Sandra McCune, Ph.D.

New York Chicago San Francisco Lisbon London Madrid Mexico City
Milan New Delhi San Juan Seoul Singapore Sydney Toronto

The *McGraw·Hill* Companies

Copyright © 2010 by The McGraw-Hill Companies, Inc. All rights reserved. Printed in
the United States of America. Except as permitted under the United States Copyright
Act of 1976, no part of this publication may be reproduced or distributed in any form
or by any means, or stored in a database or retrieval system, without the prior written
permission of the publisher.

1 2 3 4 5 6 7 8 9 10 11 12 13 14 15   WDQ/WDQ   1 9 8 7 6 5 4 3 2 1 0

ISBN   978-0-07-163818-0
MHID   0-07-163818-0

LIBRARY OF CONGRESS CONTROL NUMBER: 2009941937

Trademarks: McGraw-Hill, the McGraw-Hill Publishing logo, Practice Makes Perfect
and related trade dress are trademarks or registered trademarks of The McGraw-Hill
Companies and/or its affiliates in the United States and other countries, and may not be
used without written permission. All other trademarks are the property of their respective
owners. The McGraw-Hill Companies is not associated with any product or vendor
mentioned in this book.

Interior design by Village Bookworks, Inc.
Interior illustrations by Glyph International

McGraw-Hill books are available at special quantity discounts to use as premiums and
sales promotions or for use in corporate training programs. To contact a representative,
please e-mail us at bulksales@mcgraw-hill.com.

This book is printed on acid-free paper.

To my beloved parents
Joe and Kathryne Luna

Contents

Introduction

Practice Makes Perfect Statistics is designed as a tool for review and practice in statistics for the beginner or intermediate learner of statistics. It is not intended to introduce concepts, but rather it is meant to reinforce what already has been presented to readers. The topics offered are those that a competent user of statistics needs to know. To that end, this practice workbook is a useful supplementary text for introductory courses in statistics. It can also serve as a refresher text for readers who need to review previously learned statistical concepts and techniques.

Like most topics worth knowing, learning statistics requires diligence and hard work. The foremost purpose of *Practice Makes Perfect Statistics* is as a source of solved statistics problems. I believe that the best way to develop understanding, while, at the same time, acquiring accuracy and speed in statistics is to work numerous practice exercises. This book has more than 500 practice exercises from beginning to end. A variety of exercises and levels of difficulty are presented to provide reinforcement of statistical concepts. In each unit, a concept discussion followed by example problems precedes each set of exercises to serve as a concise review for readers already familiar with the topics covered. Concepts are broken into basic components to provide ample practice of fundamental skills.

To use *Practice Makes Perfect Statistics* in the most effective way, it is important that you work through every exercise. After working a set of exercises, use the worked-out solutions to check your understanding of the concepts. I sincerely hope that this book will help you acquire greater competence and confidence in using statistics in your future endeavors.

Sandra Luna McCune, Ph.D.

DESCRIPTIVE STATISTICS

Descriptive statistics is the branch of statistics that focuses on describing, summarizing, and organizing information. Part I discusses various aspects of descriptive statistics.

Classification of data

Data is a term used to describe information that derives from some form of measurement (counting, using a standard scale, sorting into categories, rank ordering, and so on). You can classify data in several ways according to various qualities. You might classify data as quantitative or qualitative; discrete or continuous; or nominal, ordinal, interval, or ratio level. This chapter describes these different ways of classifying data.

Quantitative or qualitative data

You can classify data as either quantitative or qualitative. **Quantitative data** are counts or measurements for which representation on a numerical scale is naturally meaningful. **Qualitative data** consist of labels, category names, ratings, rankings, and such for which representation on a numerical scale is not naturally meaningful. Distinguishing data as quantitative or qualitative is an important skill in statistics.

PROBLEMS   For a–e, classify the data as quantitative or qualitative.
a. Daytime temperature readings (in degrees Fahrenheit) in a 30-day period
b. Heights (in centimeters) of plants in a plot of land
c. Satisfaction ratings (on a scale from "not satisfied" to "very satisfied") by users of a website
d. Number (0, 1, 2, or so on) of people attending a conference
e. Party affiliation (Republican, Democrat, Libertarian, or so on) of voters

SOLUTIONS   a. Quantitative, because representation of temperature readings (in degrees Fahrenheit) on a numerical scale is naturally meaningful
b. Quantitative, because representation of heights (in centimeters) on a numerical scale is naturally meaningful
c. Qualitative, because representation of satisfaction ratings (on a scale from "not satisfied" to "very satisfied") on a numerical scale is not naturally meaningful
d. Quantitative, because number (0, 1, 2, or so on) of people is count data
e. Qualitative, because representation of party affiliation (Republican, Democrat, Libertarian, or so on) on a numerical scale is not naturally meaningful

EXERCISE
1·1

For each exercise, classify the data as quantitative or qualitative.

1. Eye colors (blue, brown, or so on) of babies

2. Distances (in miles) traveled by students commuting to school

3. Heights (in inches) of girls in a classroom

4. Number (0, 1, 2, or so on) of students in a classroom

5. Number (0, 1, 2, or so on) of teachers in favor of school uniforms

6. Names (first and last) of a group of students who took an exam

7. Ages (in months) of children in a preschool

8. Ten-digit Social Security numbers of a group of citizens

9. Foremost colors (red, yellow, orange, or so on) of flowers in a garden

10. Sex (male or female) of users of a website

Discrete or continuous data

You can further classify quantitative data as discrete or continuous. **Discrete data** are quantitative data that are countable using a finite count, such as 0, 1, 2, and so on. **Continuous data** are quantitative data that can take on any value within a range of values on a numerical scale in such a way that there are no gaps, jumps, or other interruptions. Recognizing quantitative data as discrete or continuous is another useful skill in statistics.

PROBLEMS   For each of the quantitative data sets described in a–d, classify the data as discrete or continuous.
a. Number (0, 1, 2, or so on) of people attending a conference
b. Ages (in years) of participants in a survey
c. Number (0, 1, 2, or so on) of male children in a family
d. Heights (in inches) of plants in a plot of land

SOLUTIONS   a. Discrete, because number (0, 1, 2, or so on) of people is count data.
b. Continuous, because ages (in years) can assume any value within a range of values on a numerical scale. For example, a person could be $5\frac{1}{2}$ years old or 35.67 years old.
c. Discrete, because number (0, 1, 2, or so on) of male children is count data.
d. Continuous, because heights (in inches) can assume any value within a range of values on a numerical scale.

EXERCISE
1·2

For each exercise, classify the data as discrete or continuous.

1. Lengths (in inches) of newborn babies

2. Distances (in miles) traveled by students commuting to school

3. Heights (in inches) of girls in a classroom

4. Number (0, 1, 2, or so on) of students in a classroom

5. Number (0, 1, 2, or so on) of female teachers at a school

6. Lengths (in meters) of broad jumps

7. Weights (in pounds) of male police officers

8. Number (0, 1, 2, or so on) of correct answers on a 20-item quiz

9. Number (0, 1, 2, or so on) of heads in 100 tosses of a coin

10. Daytime temperatures (in degrees Fahrenheit) over a 30-day period

Levels of measurement

Determining the level of measurement of a set of data is commonly the first step in a statistical process. The four levels of measurement are nominal, ordinal, interval, and ratio. These levels are hierarchical, ranging from nominal level, the lowest level of measurement, to ratio level, the highest level of measurement—and with higher levels subsuming the characteristics of lower levels. Thus, the characteristics associated with a certain level of measurement apply to data that achieve that level and to all data that achieve a level higher than that particular level. Following are the characteristics associated with each level:

* **Nominal level:** When the highest level of a data set is nominal level, the data consist of categories (names, labels, colors, gender, geographic location, etc.) only. Standard mathematical operations (addition, subtraction, multiplication, and division) are not defined when applied to data that are strictly nominal-level data.
* **Ordinal level:** When the highest level of a data set is ordinal level, the data consist of categories that can be arranged in some meaningful order according to their relative size or quality, but differences between data values are meaningless. For example, customer ratings of a service might be 1, 2, or 3, where 3 is "excellent" and 1 is "unacceptable." Standard mathematical operations (addition, subtraction, multiplication, and division) are not defined when applied to data that reach only ordinal level.
* **Interval level:** When the highest level of a data set is interval level, both ordering and computing differences can be meaningfully applied to the data. However, the zero point on a strictly interval level scale does not correspond to the absence of the quantity being measured, so ratios for data that reach only interval level are not considered meaningful. For instance, scores on subject content exams are interval-level data. A person who scores zero on a subject content exam does not necessarily have zero knowledge about the subject being tested by the exam.
* **Ratio level:** When the highest level of a data set is ratio level, the data can be meaningfully ordered, both arithmetic differences and ratios are meaningful, and the scale has a meaningful zero. For instance, the weights of individuals are ratio-level data. A person who weighs 200 pounds is twice as heavy as a person who weighs 100 pounds, and zero pounds represents no weight.

When summarizing, organizing, or analyzing a data set, it is important that you determine the highest level of measurement that can be attributed to the data.

For a–e, determine the highest level of measurement that can be attributed to the data set described.

a. Daytime temperature readings (in degrees Fahrenheit) in a 30-day period

b. Heights (in centimeters) of plants in a plot of land

c. Satisfaction ratings (on a scale from "not satisfied" to "very satisfied") by users of a website

d. Number (0, 1, 2, or so on) of people attending a conference

e. Party affiliation (Republican, Democrat, Libertarian, or so on) of voters

SOLUTIONS

a. Interval level, because temperature readings (in degrees Fahrenheit) can be meaningfully ordered, and the arithmetic difference between any two temperature readings is meaningful. However, the zero point on a Fahrenheit scale does not correspond to the absence of temperature (average kinetic energy).

b. Ratio level, because heights (in centimeters) can be meaningfully ordered, and both arithmetic differences and ratios are meaningful.

c. Ordinal level, because satisfaction ratings (on a scale from "not satisfied" to "very satisfied") can be arranged in some meaningful order, but differences between data values are meaningless.

d. Ratio level, because number (0, 1, 2, or so on) of people can be meaningfully ordered, and both arithmetic differences and ratios are meaningful.

e. Nominal level, because party affiliation (Republican, Democrat, Libertarian, or so on) consists of categories only.

EXERCISE 1·3

For each exercise, determine the highest level of measurement that can be attributed to the data set described.

1. Rankings (1st, 2nd, etc.) of universities

2. Distances (in miles) traveled by students commuting to school

3. Heights (in inches) of girls in a classroom

4. Thermostat settings (in degrees Fahrenheit) in a home

5. Number (0, 1, 2, or so on) of teachers in favor of school uniforms

6. Scores on a mathematics exam

7. Ages (in months) of children in a preschool

8. Ten-digit Social Security numbers of a group of citizens

9. Customer satisfaction ratings of an Internet store

10. Sex (male or female) of users of a website

Organizing quantitative data

After collecting data, you need to organize it so that you can more readily glean information from it and, perhaps, statistically analyze it. This chapter describes three useful ways to organize quantitative data: stem-and-leaf plots, frequency distributions, and histograms.

Stem-and-leaf plots

A **stem-and-leaf plot** is a visual display of data in which each data value is separated into two parts: a stem and a leaf. For a given data value, the leaf is usually the last digit, and the stem is the remaining digits. For example, for the data value 238, 23 is the stem and 8 is the leaf. When you create a stem-and-leaf plot, you should include a **legend** that explains what is represented by the stem and leaf so that the reader can interpret the information in the plot; for example, 23|8 = 238. Note that a feature of a stem-and-leaf plot is that the original data are retained and displayed in the plot.

Here are typical attributes of a stem-and-leaf plot:

1. The data are recorded in two columns. The column on the left is labeled "Stem" and the column on the right is labeled "Leaves."

2. The stems are listed vertically, from smallest to largest, in the column labeled "Stem."

3. The leaves are listed horizontally under the column labeled "Leaves." Each leaf is listed to the right of its corresponding stem and as many times as it occurs in the original data set. Usually, the leaves are listed from smallest to largest in the row of their corresponding stem.

4. The plot has a legend to guide the reader in interpreting the information displayed.

Reading information from a stem-and-leaf plot is a matter of interpreting the stems and leaves of the plot.

Ages in Years of 44 U.S. Presidents at Inauguration

Stem	Leaves
4	2 3 6 6 7 7 8 9 9
5	0 0 1 1 1 1 2 2 4 4 4 4 4 5 5 5 5 6 6 6 7 7 7 7 8
6	0 1 1 1 2 4 4 5 8 9

Legend: 5|7 = 57

Answer the following questions based on the stem-and-leaf plot shown above.
a. What is the youngest age at which a President was inaugurated?
b. What is the oldest age at which a President was inaugurated?
c. The majority of the 44 U.S. Presidents were in what age decade (40s, 50s, or 60s) when they were inaugurated?
d. How many of the 44 U.S. Presidents were 65 or older at inauguration?

SOLUTIONS a. The youngest age at which a President was inaugurated is 42.
b. The oldest age at which a President was inaugurated is 69.
c. The majority of the 44 U.S. Presidents were in their 50s when they were inaugurated.
d. Three of the 44 U.S. Presidents were 65 or older at inauguration.

EXERCISE 2·1

Answer 1–10 based on the stem-and-leaf plot shown below.

Pre-Weights in Pounds of 35 Female Students Participating in a Weight Loss Program

Stem	Leaves
12	3 8 8
13	1 3 4 4 5 6 8
14	0 0 2 4 5 5 7 7 7 8 9
15	0 1 3 3 5 6 7 8 9 9
16	1 2 2 9

Legend: 12|3 = 123

1. What is the weight of the lightest female participant?

2. What is the weight of the heaviest female participant?

3. How many of the 35 female participants weigh exactly 134 pounds?

4. How many of the 35 female participants weigh exactly 150 pounds?

5. Which weight occurs most often?

6. How many of the 35 female participants have a weight less than 130 pounds?

7. How many of the 35 female participants have a weight less than 110 pounds?

8. How many of the 35 female participants weigh at least 150 pounds?

9. How many of the 35 female participants weigh more than 160 pounds?

10. How many of the 35 female participants weigh more than 170 pounds?

Frequency distributions and histograms

A **frequency distribution** is a tabular display that shows **classes** (or categories) of values, along with the **frequency** (or count) of the number of data values that fall into each class. **Class boundaries** are the numbers used to separate the data into non-overlapping classes. **Class width** is the difference between the upper and lower class boundaries. A frequency distribution gives an overview of the data in a clear and concise format.

Here are typical attributes of a frequency distribution:

1. The data are recorded in a two-column table. The column on the left names the classes and the column on the right is labeled "Frequency."

2. The class boundaries are listed (in order) in the left column.

3. Generally, the class width is the same for all classes.

4. Each of the original data values must fall into one and only one class.

5. The sum of the class frequencies equals the number of original data values.

Understanding the information presented in a frequency distribution involves reading the frequencies associated with each class.

Prices (in U.S. Dollars) of 20 Large-Screen Televisions

Price (in U.S. Dollars)	Frequency
800.00–1099.99	3
1100.00–1399.99	5
1400.00–1699.99	8
1700.00–1999.99	4

PROBLEMS   Answer the following questions based on the frequency distribution shown above.
    a. How many of the 20 large-screen televisions fall in the $1100.00 to $1399.99 price range?
    b. How many of the 20 large-screen televisions cost less than $1400.00?
    c. How many of the 20 large-screen televisions cost more than $2000.00?

SOLUTIONS   a. Five of the 20 large-screen televisions fall in the $1100.00 to $1399.99 price range.
    b. Eight (5 + 3) of the 20 large-screen televisions cost less than $1400.00.
    c. None of the 20 large-screen televisions cost more than $2000.00.

A **relative frequency distribution** shows the frequency of each class as a proportion or percentage of the whole data set. The total of all relative frequencies should be 1.00 or 100 percent, but instead might be close to 1.00 or 100 percent, due to round-off error. Relative frequencies are useful because percentages make it easier to consider portions of the data compared to the whole. Relative frequency distributions might have two columns, one for the class list and one for the relative frequencies; or they might have three columns: one for the class list, one for the frequencies, and one for the relative frequencies. Here is the relative frequency distribution for the frequency distribution given in the first example:

Prices (in U.S. Dollars) of 20 Large-Screen Televisions

Price (in U.S. Dollars)	Frequency	Relative Frequency
800.00–1099.99	3	20/3 ≃ 15%
1100.00–1399.99	5	20/5 ≃ 25%
1400.00–1699.99	8	20/8 ≃ 40%
1700.00–1999.99	4	20/4 ≃ 20%

20

As you can see from the relative frequency distribution, 40 percent of the 20 large-screen televisions fall in the $1400.00 to $1699.99 price range.

The graphical display of a frequency distribution or a relative frequency distribution is called a **histogram**. In a histogram, the frequency or relative frequency of occurrence of the data values within a class interval is represented by a rectangular (or vertical) column. The height (or length) of the column is proportional to the frequency or relative frequency of data values within that interval. To read a histogram, examine the frequency or relative frequency scale to determine the number or percent corresponding to the space between tick marks (or grid lines). Then determine where the heights or lengths of the bars fall relative to the scale. Figure 2.1 shows the relative frequency histogram representation for the relative frequency distribution for the data in the first example.

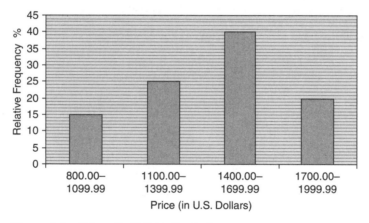

Figure 2.1 Prices (in U.S. Dollars) of 20 large-screen televisions.

The relative frequency histogram shows that 15 percent of the 20 large-screen televisions fall in the $800.00 to $1099.99 price range.

EXERCISE
2·2

Answer 1–5 based on the frequency distribution shown below.

Heights (in Inches) of 25 Male Students in a Gymnastics Class

Height (in Inches)	Frequency
55–59	1
60–64	5
65–69	12
70–74	7

1. How many of the 25 male students in the gymnastics class are shorter than 5 feet (60 inches)?

2. How many of the 25 male students in the gymnastics class are taller than 5 feet 4 inches (64 inches)?

3. How many of the 25 male students in the gymnastics class fall in the 70- to 74-inch height class?

4. Which height class has the highest frequency?

5. How many of the 25 male students in the gymnastics class are no more than 5 feet 4 inches (64 inches) tall?

Answer 6–10, based on the relative frequency histogram shown below. (Note that the vertical axis is marked in increments of 2 percentage points.)

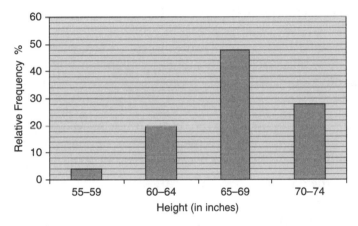

Heights (in inches) of 25 male students in a gymnastics class.

6. Which height class for the male students in the gymnastics class has the highest percentage?

7. What percent of the 25 male students in the gymnastics class are shorter than 4 feet 7 inches (55 inches)?

8. What percent of the 25 male students in the gymnastics class are no more than 5 feet 4 inches (64 inches)?

9. What percent of the 25 male students in the gymnastics class fall in the 60- to 64-inch height class?

10. What percent of the 25 male students in the gymnastics class are at least 5 feet 5 inches (65 inches) tall?

Measures of central tendency

A **measure of central tendency** is a numerical value that describes a data set by attempting to provide a "central" or "typical" value of the data set. Measures of central tendency should have the same units as those of the data values from which they are determined. If no units are specified for the data values, no units are specified for the measures of central tendency. This chapter describes three common measures of central tendency: mean, median, and mode. Each of these measures is a way to typify a central value of a set of data.

Mean

The **mean** of a data set is another name for the arithmetic average of the data values in the data set. Thus, the mean $= \dfrac{\text{sum of the data values}}{\text{number of data values}}$. This definition can be expressed as the following formula: mean $= \dfrac{\sum x}{n}$, where $\sum x$ represents the sum of all the data values, and n represents the number of data values in the data set.

PROBLEMS   Find the mean for each of the following data sets.
a. 25, 43, 40, 60, 12
b. –7, 22, –7, 8, 16, 1
c. 6.7, 7.6, 7.5, 6.9, 9.3, 6.7, 7.6, 8.5

SOLUTIONS   a. mean $= \dfrac{\sum x}{n} = \dfrac{25+43+40+60+12}{5} = \dfrac{180}{5} = 36$

b. mean $= \dfrac{\sum x}{n} = \dfrac{-7+22-7+8+16+1}{6} = \dfrac{33}{6} = 5.5$

c. mean $= \dfrac{\sum x}{n} = \dfrac{6.7+7.6+7.5+6.9+9.3+6.7+7.6+8.5}{8}$

$= \dfrac{60.8}{8} = 7.6$

A **weighted mean** is a mean computed by assigning weights to the data values using the following formula: weighted mean $= \dfrac{\sum w_i x_i}{\sum w_i}$, where x_i is the ith data value, with respective assigned weight, w_i.

PROBLEM   A student scores 50, 40, and 96 on three exams. Find the weighted mean of the student's three scores, where the score of 50 counts 20 percent, the score of 40 counts 30 percent, and the score of 96 counts 50 percent.

SOLUTION $$\text{weighted mean} = \frac{\sum w_i x_i}{\sum w_i} = \frac{20\%(50)+30\%(40)+50\%(96)}{20\%+30\%+50\%} = 70$$

Note: For reasons having to do with statistical techniques used in Part IV Basic Inferential Statistics, there is a distinction made when the mean is computed from a whole group, or **population**, as opposed to when it is computed from a subset, or **sample**, from a population. The formula for computing the mean of a population is exactly the same as the formula for computing the mean of a sample, but the symbolism for each is different. The symbol for the mean of a population is the Greek letter μ (pronounced "mew"), while the symbol for the mean of a sample is $\bar{x}$ (read "x bar").

EXERCISE
3·1

For 1–9, find the mean of the given data set.

1. 15, 33, 30, 50, 0

2. −4, 25, −4, 11, 19, 4

3. 4.7, 5.6, 2.5, 4.9, 7.3, 4.7, 5.6, 6.5

4. −10, 0 , 3, 3, 6, 16

5. 150, 330, 300, 500, 0

6. 0, 0, 0, 100, 100, 100

7. 50, 50, 50, 50, 50, 50, 50

8. 30, 40, 50, 50, 60, 70

9. −30, −40, −50, −50, −60, −70

For 10, solve the problem presented.

10. A student scores 80, 90, and 70 on three exams. Find the weighted mean of the student's three scores, where the score of 80 counts 10 percent, the score of 90 counts 30 percent, and the score of 70 counts 60 percent.

Median

The **median** is the middle value or the arithmetic average of the two middle values in an *ordered set* of data. You find the median of a data set using a two-step process:

1. Put the data values in order from least to greatest (or greatest to least).

2. Locate the middle data value. If there is no single middle data value, compute the arithmetic average of the two middle data values.

PROBLEMS   Find the median for each of the following data sets.
a. 25, 43, 40, 60, 12
b. −7, 22, −7, 8, 16, 1
c. 6.7, 7.6, 7.5, 6.9, 9.3, 6.7, 7.6, 8.5

a. 1. Order the numbers: 12, 25, 40, 43, 60.

    2. The median is 40, the middle number.

b. 1. Order the numbers: −7, −7, 1, 8, 16, 22.

    2. The median is $\dfrac{1+8}{2} = 4.5$, the arithmetic average of the two middle numbers, 1 and 8.

c. 1. Order the numbers: 6.7, 6.7, 6.9, 7.5, 7.6, 7.6, 8.5, 9.3.

    2. The median is $\dfrac{7.5+7.6}{2} = 7.55$, the arithmetic average of the two middle numbers, 7.5 and 7.6.

EXERCISE

3·2

Find the median for each of the following data sets.

1. 15, 33, 30, 50, 0

2. −4, 25, −4, 11, 19, 4

3. 4.7, 5.6, 2.5, 4.9, 7.3, 4.7, 5.6, 6.5

4. −10, 0, 3, 3, 6, 16

5. 150, 330, 300, 500, 0

6. 0, 0, 0, 100, 100, 100

7. 50, 50, 50, 50, 50, 50, 50

8. 30, 40, 50, 50, 60, 70

9. −30, −40, −50, −50, −60, −70

10. 1, 1, 4, 4, 4, 10, 10, 10

Mode

The **mode** is the data value (or values) that occurs with the greatest frequency in a data set. A data set in which each data value occurs the same number of times has **no mode**. If only one data value occurs with the greatest frequency, the data set is **unimodal**; that is, it has one mode. If exactly two data values occur with the same frequency that is greater than any of the other frequencies, the data set is **bimodal**; that is, it has two modes. If more than two data values occur with the same frequency that is greater than any of the other frequencies, the data set is **multimodal**; that is, it has more than two modes.

PROBLEMS   Find the mode, if any, for each of the following data sets. For the data sets that have modes, state whether the data set is unimodal, bimodal, or multimodal.

a. 25, 43, 40, 60, 12

b. −7, 22, −7, 8, 16, 1

c. 6.7, 7.6, 7.5, 6.9, 9.3, 6.7, 7.6, 8.5

SOLUTIONS   a. There is no mode because each data value occurs only once.
             b. The number -7 is the mode because it is the value that occurs most often. The data set is unimodal.
             c. The numbers 6.7 and 7.6 are both modes because they occur with the same frequency that is greater than any of the other frequencies. The data set is bimodal.

Find the mode, if any, for each of the following data sets. For the data sets that have modes, state whether the data set is unimodal, bimodal, or multimodal.

1. 15, 33, 30, 50, 0

2. −4, 25, −4, 11, 19, 4

3. 4.7, 5.6, 2.5, 4.9, 7.3, 4.7, 5.6, 6.5

4. −10, 0, 3, 3, 6, 16

5. 150, 330, 300, 500, 0

6. 0, 0, 0, 100, 100, 100

7. 50, 50, 50, 50, 50, 50, 50

8. 30, 40, 50, 50, 60, 70

9. −30, −40, −50, −50, −60, −70

10. 1, 1, 4, 4, 4, 10, 10, 10

Measures of variability

A **measure of variability** is a value that describes the spread or dispersion of a data set about its central value. The interpretation of measures of central tendency for a data set is enhanced when the variability about the central value is known. This chapter describes three common measures of variability: the range, standard deviation, and variance.

Range

The **range** for a data set is the difference between the **maximum value** (greatest value) and the **minimum value** (least value) in the data set; that is, range = maximum value − minimum value. The range should have the same units as those of the data values from which it is computed. If no units are specified, the range will not specify units.

PROBLEMS   Find the range for each of the following data sets.
a. 25, 43, 40, 60, 12
b. −7, 22, −7, 8, 16, 1
c. 6.7, 7.6, 7.5, 6.9, 9.3, 6.7, 7.6, 8.5

SOLUTIONS   a. range = maximum value − minimum value = 60 − 12 = 48
b. range = maximum value − minimum value = 22 − (−7) = 29
c. range = maximum value − minimum value = 9.3 − 6.7 = 2.6

EXERCISE 4·1

Find the range for each of the following data sets.

1. 15, 33, 30, 50, 0

2. −4, 25, −4, 11, 19, 4

3. 4.7, 5.6, 2.5, 4.9, 7.3, 4.7, 5.6, 6.5

4. −10, 0 , 3, 3, 6, 16

5. 150, 330, 300, 500, 0

6. 0, 0, 0, 100, 100, 100

7. 50, 50, 50, 50, 50, 50, 50

8. 30, 40, 50, 50, 60, 70

9. −30, −40, −50, −50, −60, −70

10. 1, 1, 4, 4, 4, 10, 10, 10

Variance and standard deviation

The **variance** and **standard deviation** are widely used measures of variability. They provide a measure of the variability of a set of data values about the *mean* of the data set. If there is no variability in a data set, each data value equals the mean, so both the variance and standard deviation for the data set are zero. The more the data values vary from the mean, the greater are the variance and standard deviation.

The relationship between the variance and standard deviation measures is quite simple. The standard deviation is the square root of the variance. The standard deviation should have the same units as those of the data values from which it is computed. If no units are specified, the standard deviation will not specify units.

As with the mean, the symbols used for the population variance and standard deviation are different from those used for the sample variance and standard deviation. Furthermore, the formulas for computing population variance and standard deviation are different from those for computing sample variance and standard deviation. Following is a summary of the distinctions:

1. The symbol for the population variance is σ^2.

2. The symbol for the sample variance is s^2.

3. The symbol for the population standard deviation is σ.

4. The symbol for the sample standard deviation is s.

5. The formula for the population variance is $\sigma^2 = \dfrac{\sum (x_i - \mu)^2}{N}$, where x_i is the ith data value from the population, μ is the population mean, and N is the size of the population.

6. The formula for the sample variance is $s^2 = \dfrac{\sum (x_i - \bar{x})^2}{n-1}$, where x_i is the ith data value from the sample, $\bar{x}$ is the sample mean, and n is the size of the sample.

7. The formula for the population standard deviation is $\sigma = \sqrt{\sigma^2} = \sqrt{\dfrac{\sum (x_i - \mu)^2}{N}}$.

8. The formula for the sample standard deviation is $s = \sqrt{s^2} = \sqrt{\dfrac{\sum (x_i - \bar{x})^2}{n-1}}$.

Generally for your work in statistics, you will be dealing with sample data. For that reason, hereafter use the formulas for the sample variance and standard deviation unless specifically directed otherwise.

PROBLEMS   Find the (a) sample variance and (b) sample standard deviation for the following data set: 25, 43, 40, 60, 12.

(a) mean $= \bar{x} = \dfrac{\sum x}{n} = \dfrac{25+43+40+60+12}{5} = \dfrac{180}{5} = 36$

$$\text{variance} = s^2 = \frac{\sum(x_i - \bar{x})^2}{n-1}$$

$$= \frac{(25-36)^2 + (43-36)^2 + (40-36)^2 + (60-36)^2 + (12-36)^2}{4}$$

$$= \frac{(-11)^2 + (7)^2 + (4)^2 + (24)^2 + (-24)^2}{4} = \frac{1338}{4} = 334.5$$

(b) standard deviation $= s = \sqrt{s^2} = \sqrt{334.5} = 18.2893$

EXERCISE
4·2

Find the (a) sample variance and (b) sample standard deviation for each of the following data sets. Round standard deviations to four decimal places.

1. 15, 33, 30, 50, 0

2. −4, 25, −4, 11, 19, 4

3. 4.7, 5.6, 2.5, 4.9, 7.3, 4.7, 5.6, 6.5

4. −10, 0, 3, 3, 6, 16

5. 150, 330, 300, 500, 0

6. 0, 0, 0, 100, 100, 100

7. 50, 50, 50, 50, 50, 50, 50

8. 30, 40, 50, 50, 60, 70

9. −30, −40, −50, −50, −60 −70

10. 1, 1, 4, 4, 4, 10, 10, 10

Interquartile range and the five-number summary ·5·

This chapter presents two additional ways to describe quantitative data sets: the interquartile range and the five-number summary.

Interquartile range

The **interquartile range** is another measure of the spread of a data set. To compute the interquartile range, you first compute the first and third quartiles of the data set. **Quartiles** are values that divide an ordered data set into four parts that each contain approximately one-fourth of the data values. Twenty-five percent of the data values fall at or below the **first quartile** (Q_1), 50 percent of the data values fall at or below the **second quartile** (Q_2) (which is the same value as the median), and 75 percent of the data values fall at or below the **third quartile** (Q_3).

PROBLEM   In a set of students' test scores, the third quartile is 68. What percent of the students scored above 68?

SOLUTION   Since 68 is the third quartile, 75% of the scores are at or below 68. Thus, 100% − 75% = 25% of the scores are above 68.

The **interquartile range (IQR)** is the difference between the first and third quartiles; that is, $IQR = Q_3 - Q_1$. The *IQR* contains the center 50 percent of the data. It gives you an indication of how much the data values stretch from the center of the data.

PROBLEM   Find the interquartile range for a data set for which $Q_1 = 18.5$ and $Q_3 = 51.5$.

SOLUTION $IQR = Q_3 - Q_1 = 51.5 - 18.5 = 33$

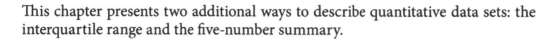
EXERCISE
5·1

1. In a set of students' test scores, the first quartile is 52. What percent of the students scored at or below 52?

2. On a set of scores from a standardized exam, the second quartile is 450. What is the median for the set of scores?

3. The third quartile for salaries at a company is $60,000. How many employees make more than $60,000?

4. Find the interquartile range for a data set for which $Q_1 = 21$ and $Q_3 = 45$.

5. Find the interquartile range for a data set for which $Q_1 = 124.5$ and $Q_3 = 316.5$.

Five-number summary

Sometimes it's difficult to make sense of large data sets. One helpful way to make it easier to harvest information from the data is to "summarize" it using the five-number summary. For a data set, the five-number summary is a set of five measures:

1. The minimum data value, Min

2. The first quartile, Q_1

3. The median of the data set, Med

4. The third quartile, Q_3

5. The maximum data value, Max

Generally, these five measures divide an ordered data set into four groups, each having approximately the same number of data values. Knowing these five measures provides you with useful information.

PROBLEMS   For a–c, answer based on the data set that has the five-number summary:
Min = 23, $Q_1 = 37$, Med = 77.5, $Q_3 = 105.5$, Max = 122.
a. What is the range of the data set?
b. What percent of the data values are at or below 105.5?
c. What is the *IQR*?

SOLUTIONS   a. range = Max − Min = 122 − 23 = 99
b. 75 percent
c. $IQR = Q_3 - Q_1 = 105.5 - 37 = 68.5$

You can graphically represent the five-number summary for a data set using a **box-and-whiskers plot** as shown in Figure 5.1.

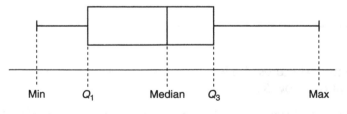

Figure 5.1   Box-and-whiskers plot.

PROBLEM What is the *IQR* of the data set whose box-and-whiskers plot is shown below?

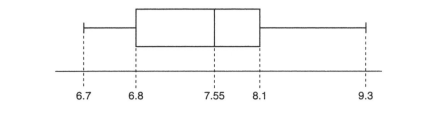

6.7   6.8   7.55   8.1   9.3

SOLUTION $IQR = Q_3 - Q_1 = 8.1 - 6.8 = 1.3$

EXERCISE

5·2

For 1–3, answer based on the data set that has the five-number summary: Min = 11, $Q_1 = 51$, Med = 73, $Q_3 = 81.5$, Max = 88.

1. What is the range of the data set?

2. What percent of the data values are at or below 51?

3. What is the *IQR*?

For 4–5, answer the question presented.

4. What is the median of the data set whose box-and-whiskers plot is shown below?

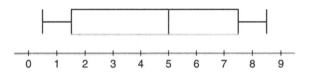

    0   1   2   3   4   5   6   7   8   9

5. What is the range of the data set whose box-and-whiskers plot is shown below?

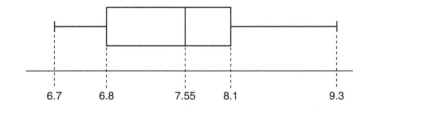

6.7   6.8   7.55   8.1   9.3

FUNDAMENTALS OF
CLASSICAL PROBABILITY

Counting techniques

Classical probability depends on being able to count the number of ways various occurrences can happen. This chapter will discuss commonly used counting techniques.

The fundamental counting principle

The **Fundamental Counting Principle** states that if a first task can be done in any one of m different ways and, after that task is completed, a second task can be done in any one of n different ways, then both tasks can be done, in the order given, in $m \cdot n$ different ways.

PROBLEM   How many different meals consisting of one sandwich and one drink are possible from a selection of 10 different sandwiches and 6 different drinks?

SOLUTION   This problem consists of two tasks: selecting a sandwich and then selecting a drink. You have 10 ways to select a sandwich; following that selection, you have 6 ways to select a drink. Therefore, you have $10 \cdot 6 = 60$ different meals that consist of one sandwich and one drink.

This counting principle can be extended to any number of tasks. Thus, in general, for a sequence of k tasks, if a first task can be done in any one of n_1 different ways and, after that task is completed, a second task can be done in any one of n_2 different ways, and, after the first two tasks have been completed, a third task can be done in any one of n_3 different ways, and so on to the kth task, which can be done in any one of n_k different ways, then the total number of different ways the sequence of k tasks can be done is $n_1 \cdot n_2 \cdot n_3 \cdots \cdot n_k$.

PROBLEM   A code for a home alarm system consists of four digits that must be entered in a specific order. Each of the digits zero through nine may be used in the code, and repetition of digits is allowed. How many different four-digit codes are possible?

SOLUTION   This problem consists of four tasks. You have 10 ways to select the first digit, 10 ways to select the second digit, 10 ways to select the third digit, and 10 ways to select the fourth digit. Therefore, you have $10 \cdot 10 \cdot 10 \cdot 10 = 10,000$ different possible codes.

PROBLEM   There are 20 separate candidates for three vice-president (VP) positions at a university. Assuming all 20 candidates are qualified to be selected for any one of the three VP positions, how many different ways can the positions be filled?

SOLUTION   This problem consists of three tasks. You have 20 candidates available to fill the first VP position; after filling that position, you have 19 candidates remaining that are available to fill the second VP position, and after filling the first and second VP positions, you have 18 candidates remaining to fill the third VP position. Therefore, you can fill the three VP positions in $20 \cdot 19 \cdot 18 = 6840$ different ways.

Note that this counting technique yields results in which the *order of the elements determines different outcomes*. For example, the codes 2413 and 3124 for a home alarm system consist of the same digits, but are considered different codes because the order in which the digits appear is different.

EXERCISE

6·1

1. How many meals consisting of one sandwich, one drink, and one type of chips are possible from a selection of eight different sandwiches, five different drinks, and seven different types of chips?

2. A code for a locking briefcase consists of five digits that must be entered in a definite order. Each of the digits zero through nine may be used in the code, and repetition of digits is allowed. How many different five-digit codes are possible?

3. There are 30 separate candidates for three vice-president positions at a university. Assuming all 30 candidates are qualified to be selected for any one of the three VP positions, how many different ways can the positions be filled?

4. Suppose a high school issues a student identification number (ID) that consists of two letters followed by six digits (zero through nine) to each student. Assuming repetition of letters and digits is allowed, how many unique student ID numbers are possible?

5. In a certain state, a car license plate number consists of three letters followed by three digits (zero through nine). For that state, how many different car license plate numbers are possible if repetition of digits and letters is allowed?

6. In the area code 936, how many seven-digit telephone numbers that begin with 564- are possible if repetition of digits is allowed?

7. Suppose a code is dialed by means of three disks, each of which is stamped with 15 letters. How many three-letter codes are possible using the three disks?

8. How many three-digit codes are possible using only the digits one and zero if repetition of digits is allowed?

9. In how many different ways is it possible to seat three people in three chairs?

10. How many different ways can you arrange the five letters in the word *chair* if you use all five letters each time?

Permutations

A **permutation** is an ordered arrangement of a set of distinctly different items. For example, two permutations of the numbers one through five are 12345 and 53142. For permutations, different orderings of the same items are counted as distinctly different permutations. Thus, when the order of the items in an arrangement is important in a problem, you have a permutation problem.

Through a direct application of the Fundamental Counting Principle, the number of permutations of n distinct items is given by

$$n! = n(n-1)(n-2)\cdots(2)(1)$$

where the notation $n!$ is read "n factorial." A factorial is the product of all positive integers less than or equal to a given positive integer. Exception: By definition $0! = 1$.

PROBLEM   Six separate people are to be seated in six chairs that are placed in a straight row. How many different arrangements of the six people in the six chairs are possible?

SOLUTION   Since the order in which the people are seated is important in the problem, this is a permutation problem. The number of different possible arrangements of the six people in the six chairs is $6! = 6 \cdot 5 \cdot 4 \cdot 3 \cdot 2 \cdot 1 = 720$.

Sometimes, when you have n items, you might want to count the number of different possible arrangements of some, instead of all, of the items. The number of permutations of r items selected from n distinctly different items is denoted by $_nP_r$ and is equal to $_nP_r = \dfrac{n!}{(n-r)!}$.

When you apply the formula $_nP_r$, you need to make sure that (1) the n items from which you select are n *mutually different* items (that is, none are alike), (2) the r items that you select from the n items are selected *without replacement*, and (3) different orderings of the same r items are counted *separately*.

PROBLEM   Six separate people are to be seated in four chairs that are placed in a straight row. How many different arrangements of the six people in the four chairs are possible?

SOLUTION   Since the order in which the people are seated is important, this is a permutation problem. The number of different possible arrangements of the six people in the four chairs is given by

$$_6P_4 = \frac{6!}{(6-4)!} = \frac{6!}{2!} = 6 \cdot 5 \cdot 4 \cdot 3 = 360.$$

When you want to count the number of different possible arrangements of n items, but some of the n items are identical to each other, you use a formula that adjusts for the like items. The number of permutations of n items for which n_1 of the n items are alike, n_2 of the n items are alike,..., n_k of the n items are alike is $\dfrac{n!}{n_1!n_2!\cdots n_k!}$.

PROBLEM   How many different ways can you arrange the six letters in the word *banana* if you use all six letters each time?

SOLUTION   Since the order in which the letters appear is important, this is a permutation problem. The word *banana* consists of six letters: one b, three a's, and two n's. Since the six items (that is, the letters) to be arranged are not all mutually different items, the number of arrangements is given by

$$\frac{n!}{n_1!n_2!\cdots n_k!} = \frac{6!}{3!2!} = \frac{6 \cdot 5 \cdot 4}{2 \cdot 1} = 60.$$

Note: Some situations that indicate you might have a permutation problem are the following: creating codes, passwords, or license plates; making words; assigning roles; filling positions; making ordered arrangements of things (people, objects, colors, and so on); selecting persons or things as first, second, third, and so on; flipping several coins and observing head or tail on each coin; distributing items among several objects or people; and similar situations.

EXERCISE 6·2

For 1–10, calculate the given expression.

1. $0!$

2. $5!$

3. $\dfrac{5!}{0!}$

4. $\dfrac{7!}{5!}$

5. $\dfrac{100!}{99!}$

6. $\dfrac{8!}{(8-5)!}$

7. $\dfrac{7!}{1!3!2!}$

8. $_{10}P_0$

9. $_6P_2$

10. $_{100}P_1$

For 11–15, solve the problem presented.

11. Five separate people are to be seated in five chairs that are placed in a straight row. How many different arrangements of the five people in the five chairs are possible?

12. Ten separate people are to be seated in eight chairs that are placed in a straight row. How many different arrangements of the ten people in the eight chairs are possible?

13. How many different 10-letter arrangements of the 10 letters in the word *statistics* are possible?

14. How many different ways can a club of 25 members select a president, vice-president, and secretary from its membership if no person holds more than one office and all members are eligible for any one of the three positions?

15. How many six-digit (zero through nine) passwords are possible if repetition of digits is not allowed?

Combinations

A **combination** is an arrangement of a set of distinct items in which different orderings of the same items are considered the same. For example, the set of vowels *a, e, i, o,* and *u* is the same as the set of vowels *i, a, u, o,* and *e.* That is, in a combination problem (unlike a permutation problem), different orderings of the same items are *not* counted as separate results. Thus, when the order in which the items are arranged is not important in the problem, you have a combination problem.

The number of combinations of *r* items selected from *n* distinct items is denoted by $_nC_r$ and is equal to $_nC_r = \dfrac{n!}{r!(n-r)!}$.

Note: The notation $_nC_r$ is also written $\binom{n}{r}$.

PROBLEM   How many different ways can a club of 25 members select a 3-member officer-nominating committee from its membership if all members are eligible to serve on the committee?

SOLUTION   Since the order in which the committee members are arranged is not important in the problem, this is a combination problem. The number of different possible 3-member committees that can be formed from the 25 club members is given by

$$_{25}C_3 = \frac{25!}{3!(25-3)!} = \frac{25!}{3!22!} = \frac{25 \cdot 24 \cdot 23}{3 \cdot 2 \cdot 1} = 2300$$

When you apply the formula $_nC_r$, you need to make sure that (1) the n items from which you select are n *distinct* items, (2) the r items that you select from the n items are selected *without replacement*, and (3) different orderings of the same r items are not distinguished as being different from each other.

Sometimes, the combination formula is used in conjunction with the Fundamental Counting Principle to determine the number of possible outcomes, as shown in the following problem.

PROBLEM   A shopper will buy 6 shirts, 3 pairs of slacks, and 2 pairs of shoes from a selection of 10 different shirts, 7 different pairs of slacks, and 5 different pairs of shoes. How many different ways can the shopper make the purchase?

SOLUTION   Thinking in terms of the Fundamental Counting Principle, the shopper has three tasks to do: Select 6 of the 10 shirts, select 3 of the 7 pairs of slacks, and select 2 of the 5 pairs of shoes. Since the order of selection of the clothing items is not important in the problem, the number of ways to select each of the clothing items can be determined using the combination formula. Then, following those calculations, the Fundamental Counting Principle can be used to determine the total number of different ways the shopper can make the purchase. Thus, the number of different ways the shopper can make the purchase equals (the number of ways to select 6 of 10 shirts) × (the number of ways to select 3 of 7 pairs of slacks) × (the number of ways to select 2 of 5 pairs of shoes) = $_{10}C_6 \cdot _7C_3 \cdot _5C_2 =$

$$\frac{10!}{6!(10-6)!} \cdot \frac{7!}{3!(7-3)!} \cdot \frac{5!}{2!(5-2)!} = \frac{10!}{6!4!} \cdot \frac{7!}{3!4!} \cdot \frac{5!}{2!3!} = 210 \cdot 35 \cdot 10 = 73,500.$$

Note: Some situations that indicate you might have a combination problem are the following: making a collection of things (books, coins, and so on), selecting a committee, choosing questions from a test, counting the number of subsets of a given size from a set, dealing hands from a deck of cards, selecting pizza toppings, listing the combinations from a set of items, choosing students for groups, and similar situations.

EXERCISE
6·3

For 1–10, calculate the given expression.

1. $\dfrac{8!}{0!8!}$

2. $\dfrac{5!}{3!(5-3)!}$

3. $\dfrac{6!}{4!2!}$

4. $\dfrac{10!}{9!1!}$

5. $\dfrac{13!}{5!8!}$

6. $_{10}C_0$

7. $_5C_3$ 8. $_{13}C_5$

9. $_{20}C_3$ 10. $_{100}C_1$

For 11–15, solve the problem presented.

11. How many different ways can a club of 20 members select a 3-member officer-nominating committee from its membership if all members are eligible to serve on the committee?

12. How many 5-card hands are possible from a standard deck of 52 playing cards if the cards are drawn without replacement?

13. How many ways can 3 pizza toppings be selected from a choice of 12 toppings if each topping can be chosen only once?

14. How many ways can 7 out of 15 patients with the same illness be randomly selected to receive an experimental drug?

15. How many different ways can 5 out of 8 different shirts, 4 out of 10 different pairs of slacks, and 3 out of 6 different ties be selected?

Basic probability concepts ◆·7·◆

Probability is ongoing in everyday life. It is used in determining casino gaming payoffs, weather predictions, tables of life expectancy, airline baggage loss expectations, and numerous other chance occurrences. This chapter will introduce the basic terminology and concepts that you must know in order to understand and calculate probabilities.

Sample spaces

A **random experiment** is a process that gives a single result that cannot be determined beforehand. Examples of simple random experiments are tossing a fair die one time and observing the up face; flipping a fair coin one time and observing the up face; and drawing one card at random from a well-shuffled deck of cards and observing which card was drawn. Each of these experiments yields a single result that occurs randomly. In each case, you can expect one of a number of possible results. Each individual possible result is called an **outcome** of the experiment. For instance, in the random experiment of tossing a fair die one time and observing the up face, the six possible outcomes are the following: one dot is on the up face, two dots are on the up face, three dots are on the up face, four dots are on the up face, five dots are on the up face, and six dots are on the up face.

A **sample space**, S, is the set of all possible outcomes of an experiment. Each member of S is called an **outcome** (or simple event, sample point, or elementary outcome). For instance, for the random experiment of tossing a fair die, $S = \{1, 2, 3, 4, 5, 6\}$, where "1" represents the elementary outcome "the die shows one dot on the up face," "2" represents the outcome "the die shows two dots on the up face," and so on.

Note: A sample space can be finite or infinite. For this practice book, only finite sample spaces are considered.

Sometimes an experiment consists of several stages. For instance, consider the experiment of flipping three fair coins and observing the up face on each. You can think of this experiment as having three stages: flipping the first coin and observing the up face, flipping the second coin and observing the up face, and flipping the third coin and observing the up face. From the Fundamental Counting Principle, you know there are $2 \cdot 2 \cdot 2 = 8$ outcomes for this experiment. The sample space for this experiment is {HHH, HHT, HTH, HTT, THH, THT, TTH, TTT}, where "H" in the first position means "Heads on the first coin," "H" in the second position means "Heads on the second coin," "H" in the third position means "Heads on the third coin," "T" in the first position means "Tails on the first coin," and so on.

For some experiments, listing and counting the outcomes in the sample space is easy, as in the previous examples. In other experiments, especially those consisting of several stages, you will have to rely on counting techniques to determine the number of outcomes in the sample space.

PROBLEM   A standard deck of 52 playing cards consists of four suits: clubs (♣), spades (♠), hearts (♥), and diamonds (♦). Clubs and spades are black-colored suits; hearts and diamonds are red-colored suits. Each suit has 13 cards consisting of 3 face cards (king, queen, and jack) and number cards from 1 (ace) to 10, as shown in Figure 7.1.

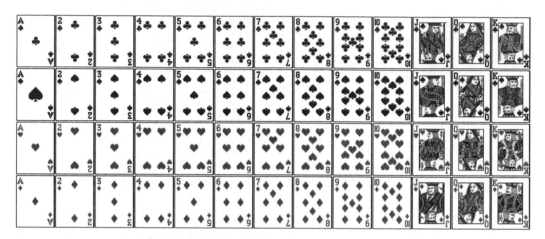

Figure 7.1   A standard deck of 52 playing cards.

Consider the experiment of drawing 5 cards at random from a well-shuffled deck of 52 playing cards. How many outcomes are in the sample space of this experiment?

SOLUTION   Since the order in which the five cards are arranged after they are drawn is not important in the problem, this is a combination problem. You want to know how many different 5-card combinations are possible when drawing from a deck of 52 playing cards. Therefore, you need to calculate the combination of 5 items

selected from 52 distinct items $= {}_{52}C_5 = \dfrac{52!}{5!(52-5)!} = \dfrac{52!}{5!47!} = \dfrac{52 \cdot 51 \cdot 50 \cdot 49 \cdot 48}{\cdot 5 \cdot 4 \cdot 3 \cdot 2 \cdot 1} =$

2,598,960. Thus, in the experiment of drawing 5 cards from a standard deck of 52 playing cards, the number of outcomes in the sample space is 2,598,960.

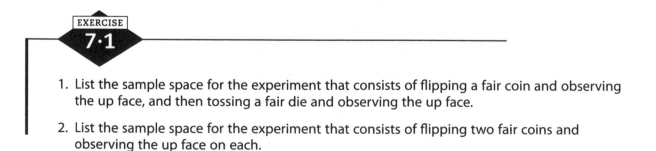

EXERCISE
7·1

1. List the sample space for the experiment that consists of flipping a fair coin and observing the up face, and then tossing a fair die and observing the up face.

2. List the sample space for the experiment that consists of flipping two fair coins and observing the up face on each.

3. List the sample space for the experiment that consists of tossing a pair of fair dice and observing the up face on each.

4. Two cards are drawn at random from a well-shuffled standard deck of 52 playing cards. Determine the number of outcomes in the sample space of this experiment if the first card is replaced before the second card is drawn.

5. Four marbles are drawn at random from an urn containing 7 black marbles and 10 red marbles. Determine the number of outcomes in the sample space of this experiment if the marbles are drawn without replacement.

Classical probability

A **probability measure** on a sample space, S, is a function that assigns to each outcome in S a real number between 0 and 1, inclusive, so that the values assigned to the outcomes in S sum to 1. The value assigned to an outcome in S is called the **probability** of that outcome. For instance, for $S = \{1, 2, 3, 4, 5, 6\}$, the sample space for the experiment of tossing a fair die one time and observing the up face, the probability of each outcome in S is $\frac{1}{6}$ (since each number has an equal chance of showing on the up face). The sum of the probabilities of the outcomes in S is $P(1) + P(2) + P(3) + P(4) + P(5) + P(6) = \frac{1}{6} + \frac{1}{6} + \frac{1}{6} + \frac{1}{6} + \frac{1}{6} + \frac{1}{6} = \frac{6}{6} = 1$, where $P(1)$ is the probability of the outcome 1, $P(2)$ is the probability of the outcome 2, and so on.

An **event**, E, is a collection of outcomes from a sample space S; that is, an event E is a subset of the sample space S. An event E is said to **occur** if a member of E occurs when the experiment is performed. For example, if the sample space is the set of outcomes from the experiment of tossing a fair die and observing the up face, and E is the event that the die shows a number less than 3, then $S = \{1, 2, 3, 4, 5, 6\}$ and $E = \{1, 2\}$.

Note: By convention, capital letters are used to designate events, with the word *event* being omitted in cases where the meaning is clear.

The **probability of an event E**, denoted $P(E)$, is the sum of the probabilities of the individual outcomes that are members of the event E. The probability of an event is a numerical value between 0 and 1, inclusive, that quantifies the chance or likelihood that the event will occur. For instance, given the sample space $S = \{1, 2, 3, 4, 5, 6\}$, the set of outcomes from the die-tossing experiment, and $E = \{1, 2\}$, the event that the die shows a number less than 3, you have $P(E) = P(1) + P(2) = \frac{1}{6} + \frac{1}{6} = \frac{2}{6} = \frac{1}{3}$.

Outcomes are **equally likely** if each outcome is as likely to occur as any other outcome. If all outcomes in the sample space are equally likely, the probability of an event E is given by:

$$P(E) = \frac{\text{Number of outcomes favorable to } E}{\text{Total number of outcomes in the sample space}}$$

For example, for the die-tossing experiment and the event E that the die shows a number less than 3, $P(E) = \frac{\text{Number of outcomes favorable to } E}{\text{Total number of outcomes in the sample space}} = \frac{2}{6} = \frac{1}{3}$.

Note: When using the formula for the probability of an event, the denominator always will be *larger than* or *equal to* the numerator, so check for this when you plug into the formula.

Probabilities can be expressed as fractions, decimals, or percents. In the example given, the probability that the up face of the die is a number less than 3 can be expressed as $\frac{1}{3}$, .$33\frac{1}{3}$, or $33\frac{1}{3}$ percent.

Keep in mind that the formula for probability in which the outcomes are equally likely will *not* apply to sample spaces in which the events are not equally likely. For instance, the sample space for spinning a spinner that is one-fourth red, one-fourth yellow, and one-half green is $S = \{R, Y, G\}$, where "R" means "the spinner lands on red," "Y" means "the spinner lands on yellow," and "G" means "the spinner lands on green." The probabilities for the three different outcomes are the following: $P(\text{red}) = \frac{1}{4}$, $P(\text{yellow}) = \frac{1}{4}$, and $P(\text{green}) = \frac{1}{2}$.

An event is **certain** to occur if and only if the probability of the event is 1. An event is **impossible** if and only if the probability of the event is 0. The probability of any event is a number between 0 and 1, inclusive. Thus, the lowest probability you can have is 0, and the highest probability you can have is 1. All other probabilities fall between 0 and 1. The closer the probability of an event is to 1, the more likely the event is to occur; the closer the probability of an event is to zero, the less likely the event is to occur.

EXERCISE
7·2

1. Find the probability that a number greater than or equal to 4 appears on the up face in a single toss of a fair die.

2. Find the probability that an even number appears on the up face in a single toss of a fair die.

3. Find the probability that heads appears on the up face in a single toss of a fair coin.

4. Find the probability that at least one head appears when two fair coins are flipped and the up face on each is observed.

5. Find the probability that the number of dots on the up faces sum to 7 when a pair of fair dice is tossed and the up face on each is observed.

6. Find the probability of drawing a face card when a single card is drawn at random from a well-shuffled standard deck of 52 playing cards.

7. Find the probability of drawing a diamond when a single card is drawn at random from a well-shuffled standard deck of 52 playing cards.

8. Find the probability of drawing a red marble when a single marble is drawn at random from an urn containing 7 black marbles, 6 green marbles, and 10 red marbles. (Assume the marbles are identical except for color).

9. A multiple-choice question has four possible answer choices (A, B, C, or D), one of which is correct. Suppose that an unprepared student does not read the question, but simply makes a random guess for the question. What is the probability that the student will guess the correct answer?

10. A box contains 30 identical-looking items of which 3 are defective. If one item is selected at random, what is the probability that the item is defective?

The complement rule for probability

The **complement of an event E**, denoted $\overline{E}$ (or E^c), is the event that E does not occur. The probability of the complement of an event E is given by $P(\overline{E}) = 1 - P(E)$.

$$\text{If } P(E) = \frac{1}{3}, \text{ then } P(\overline{E}) = 1 - P(E) = 1 - \frac{1}{3} = \frac{2}{3}.$$

PROBLEM   Suppose a single card is drawn at random from a well-shuffled standard deck of 52 playing cards. What is the probability that the card is not a diamond?

SOLUTION   There are 13 diamonds in the deck, so $P(\text{diamond}) = \dfrac{13}{52}$; thus, the probability that the card is not a diamond $= 1 - \dfrac{13}{52} = \dfrac{39}{52} = \dfrac{3}{4}$.

EXERCISE 7·3

For 1–5, find the probability of the complement of the event E that has the given probability.

1. $P(E) = \dfrac{3}{8}$

2. $P(E) = \dfrac{5}{100}$

3. $P(E) = 30\%$

4. $P(E) = 0.25$

5. $P(E) = \dfrac{1}{2}$

For 6–10, find the probability of the complement of the event described.

6. A number greater than or equal to 4 appears on the up face in a single toss of a fair die.

7. An even number appears on the up face in a single toss of a fair die.

8. A heads appears on the up face in a single toss of a fair coin.

9. At least one head appears when two fair coins are flipped and the up face on each is observed.

10. The number of dots on the up faces sum to 7 when a pair of fair dice is tossed and the up face on each is observed.

For 11–15, use the definition of the complement of an event to find the given probability.

11. Find the probability of not drawing a face card when a single card is drawn at random from a well-shuffled standard deck of 52 playing cards.

12. Find the probability of not drawing a diamond when a single card is drawn at random from a well-shuffled standard deck of 52 playing cards.

13. A single marble is drawn at random from an urn containing 7 black marbles, 6 green marbles, and 10 red marbles. (Assume the marbles are identical except for color.) What is the probability that the marble drawn is not red?

14. A multiple-choice question has four possible answer choices (A, B, C, or D), one of which is correct. Suppose that an unprepared student does not read the question, but simply makes a random guess for the question. What is the probability that the student will guess incorrectly?

15. A box contains 30 identical-looking items of which 3 are defective. If one item is selected at random, what is the probability that the item is not defective?

The addition rule for probability and mutually exclusive events

A **compound event** is a combination of two or more events. For two events A and B, a compound event that is important in probability is the compound event A **or** B. Note that in mathematics, the word *or* is used in the inclusive sense. Therefore, the compound event A or B is the event that A occurs or B occurs or that both occur simultaneously on one trial of an experiment.

The **addition rule** states that $P(A \text{ or } B) = P(A) + P(B) - P(A \text{ and } B \text{ occur simultaneously})$. Keep in mind that this rule applies to *one* trial of an experiment.

PROBLEM   Suppose one card is drawn at random from a standard deck of 52 playing cards; find the probability that the card is a jack or a diamond.

SOLUTION   There are 4 jacks in the deck, so $P(\text{jack}) = \dfrac{4}{52}$. There are 13 diamonds, so $P(\text{diamond}) = \dfrac{13}{52}$. There is one jack of diamonds card, so $P(\text{jack and diamond occur simultaneously}) = \dfrac{1}{52}$. Thus, $P(\text{jack or diamond}) = P(\text{jack}) + P(\text{diamond}) - P(\text{jack and diamond occur simultaneously}) = \dfrac{4}{52} + \dfrac{13}{52} - \dfrac{1}{52} = \dfrac{16}{52} = \dfrac{4}{13}$.

For most problems, an efficient way to find $P(A \text{ or } B)$ is to sum the number of ways that A can occur and the number of ways that B can occur, *being sure to add in such a way that no outcome is counted twice*, and then divide by the total number of outcomes in the sample space.

Applying this strategy to the previous example, there are 4 jacks and there are 12 diamonds that are *not* jacks. Thus, there are $4 + 12 = 16$ distinct cards favorable to the event "jack or diamond." Therefore, $P(\text{jack or diamond}) = \dfrac{4+12}{52} = \dfrac{16}{52} = \dfrac{4}{13}$.

Two events are **mutually exclusive** if they cannot occur at the same time; that is, they have no outcomes in common. For instance, if you randomly draw one card from a deck of cards, the event of drawing a red card and the event of drawing a club are mutually exclusive.

When two events A and B are mutually exclusive, $P(A \text{ or } B) = P(A) + P(B)$.

PROBLEM   One card is randomly drawn from a well-shuffled standard deck of 52 playing cards. Find the probability that the card drawn is a jack or a queen.

SOLUTION   There are four jacks in the deck, so $P(\text{jack}) = \dfrac{4}{52}$. There are four queens in the deck, so $P(\text{queen}) = \dfrac{4}{52}$. The event of drawing a queen and the event of drawing a jack are mutually exclusive (since you cannot draw both at the same time on one draw from the deck), so $P(\text{jack or queen}) = P(\text{jack}) + P(\text{queen}) = \dfrac{4}{52} + \dfrac{4}{52} = \dfrac{8}{52} = \dfrac{2}{13}$.

For 1–5, state whether the given events are mutually exclusive.

1. Drawing a red card and drawing a jack on one draw from a standard deck of 52 playing cards

2. Rolling a 3 and rolling a number greater than 4 on one toss of a fair die

3. Drawing a red marble and drawing a green marble in one draw from an urn containing 7 black marbles, 6 green marbles, and 10 red marbles

4. Rolling an odd number and rolling a number less than 3 on one roll of a fair die

5. Drawing a face card and drawing a king on one draw from a standard deck of 52 playing cards

For 6–10, use the information given to calculate P(A or B) = P(A) + P(B) − P(A and B).

6. $P(A) = .5, P(B) = .3, P(A \text{ and } B) = .06$

7. $P(A) = .4, P(B) = .1, P(A \text{ and } B) = .05$

8. $P(A) = .65, P(B) = .22, P(A \text{ and } B) = .08$

9. $P(A) = \dfrac{4}{52}, P(B) = \dfrac{13}{52}, P(A \text{ and } B) = \dfrac{1}{52}$

10. $P(A) = \dfrac{3}{8}, P(B) = \dfrac{5}{8}, P(A \text{ and } B) = 0$

For 11–15, find the indicated probability.

11. What is the probability of rolling an odd number or a number less than 3 on one roll of a fair die?

12. One card is randomly drawn from a well-shuffled standard deck of 52 playing cards. Find the probability that the card drawn is an ace or either a spade or a diamond.

13. Three fair coins are flipped and the up face on each is observed. Find the probability that at least two heads are observed or the number of heads observed is an odd number.

14. Three fair coins are flipped and the up face on each is observed. Find the probability that all heads or all tails are observed.

15. Find the probability of drawing a red marble or a green marble when a single marble is drawn at random from an urn containing 7 black marbles, 6 green marbles, and 10 red marbles. (Assume the marbles are identical except for color.)

Conditional probability, independence, and the multiplication rule

The probability of an event B, given that an event A has already occurred, is called a **conditional probability** and is denoted $P(B|A)$ [read "Probability B given A"]. For the conditional probability, $P(B|A)$, you must compute the probability of event B by taking into account that the event A has already occurred.

PROBLEM	Suppose that you draw 2 marbles from a box containing 10 red marbles and 5 blue marbles.
	(a) Find the probability of drawing a blue marble on the second draw given that a red marble was drawn *without replacement* on the first draw.
SOLUTION	After the red marble is drawn without replacement, there are 9 red marbles and 5 blue marbles in the box. Therefore, $P(\text{blue} \mid \text{red drawn without replacement}) = \dfrac{5}{14}$.
PROBLEM	(b) Find the probability of drawing a blue marble on the second draw given that a red marble was drawn *with replacement* on the first draw.
SOLUTION	After the red marble is drawn with replacement, there are 10 red marbles and 5 blue marbles in the box. Therefore, $P(\text{blue} \mid \text{red drawn with replacement}) = \dfrac{5}{15} = \dfrac{1}{3}$.

For two events A and B, the compound event **A and B** is the event that A occurs on the first trial and B occurs on the second trial of an experiment. The **multiplication rule** states that $P(A \text{ and } B) = P(A)\, P(B \mid A)$.

An efficient way to find the probability that event A occurs on the first trial and event B occurs on the second trial is to multiply the probability of event A times the probability of event B, where you have determined the probability of B by taking into account that the event A has already occurred.

PROBLEM	Two cards are drawn at random without replacement from a well-shuffled standard deck of 52 playing cards. What is the probability of drawing a queen on the first draw and an ace on the second draw?
SOLUTION	First draw: There are 4 queens in the deck of 52 cards, so the probability of a queen on the first draw is $\dfrac{4}{52}$. Second draw: After the first card is drawn without replacement, there are 4 aces in the remaining deck of 51 cards, so $P(\text{ace on 2nd draw}) = \dfrac{4}{51}$. Therefore, $P(\text{queen on 1st draw and ace on 2nd draw}) = \dfrac{4}{52} \cdot \dfrac{4}{51} = \dfrac{1}{13} \cdot \dfrac{4}{51} = \dfrac{4}{663}$.

Two events A and B are **independent** if the occurrence of one does not affect the probability of the occurrence of the other. For instance, if a box contains 10 red marbles and 5 blue marbles, the event of drawing a red marble *with replacement* on the first draw and the event of drawing a blue marble on the second draw are independent events. If events A and B are not independent, they are said to be **dependent**. For example, if a box contains 10 red marbles and 5 blue marbles, the event of drawing a red marble *without replacement* on the first draw and the event of drawing a blue marble on the second draw are dependent.

In terms of conditional probability, when two events are independent, $P(A) = P(A \mid B)$ and $P(B) = P(B \mid A)$. Thus, if A and B are independent events, $P(A \text{ and } B) = P(A)P(B)$.

PROBLEM	Two cards are drawn at random with replacement from a well-shuffled standard deck of 52 playing cards. What is the probability of drawing a diamond on the first draw and a jack on the second draw?
SOLUTION	Since the two cards are drawn with replacement, the two draws are independent because the second event is not affected by the outcome of the first event. Thus, $P(\text{diamond on 1st draw and jack on 2nd draw}) = P(\text{diamond})\, P(\text{jack}) = \dfrac{13}{52} \cdot \dfrac{4}{52} = \dfrac{1}{52}$.

For 1–5, use the information given to determine whether the events A and B are independent.

1. $P(A) = \dfrac{1}{2}$, $P(B) = \dfrac{1}{2}$, $P(A \text{ and } B) = \dfrac{1}{4}$

2. $P(A) = .35$, $P(B) = .63$, $P(A \text{ and } B) = .32$

3. $P(A) = \dfrac{1}{2}$, $P(B) = \dfrac{21}{55}$, $P(A \text{ and } B) = \dfrac{3}{22}$

4. $P(A) = .7$, $P(A|B) = .7$

5. $P(A) = .7$, $P(A|B) = .9$

For 6–10, find the indicated probability.

6. What is the probability of rolling an odd number and then a number less than 3 on two rolls of a fair die?

7. Two cards are randomly drawn without replacement from a well-shuffled standard deck of 52 playing cards. Find the probability that the first card drawn is an ace and the second card drawn is a face card.

8. Three fair coins are flipped and the up face on each is observed. Find the probability of observing all heads.

9. Two cards are randomly drawn with replacement from a well-shuffled standard deck of 52 playing cards. Find the probability that the first card drawn is a face card and the second card drawn is a number that is greater than 7 but less than 10.

10. Suppose that you draw 2 marbles from a box containing 8 red marbles and 6 blue marbles. Find the probability of drawing a blue marble on the second draw given that a red marble was drawn with replacement on the first draw. (Assume the marbles are identical except for color.)

THE BINOMIAL AND NORMAL DISTRIBUTIONS

A **random variable** is a function that assigns a real number to each outcome of a random experiment (see "Sample Spaces" in Chapter 7 for a discussion of random experiment). Random variables are divided into two types: discrete random variables and continuous random variables.

A **discrete random variable** can assume only a countable number of distinct values such as 0, 1, 2, 3, ... For instance, the number of heads obtained when a coin is tossed 20 times is a discrete random variable. A **continuous random variable** potentially can assume any numerical value; for any two values that it might assume, there is another value between them that is possible. For example, the height of a randomly selected male university student is a continuous random variable.

A **probability distribution** consists of a chart, table, graph, or formula that specifies all the values that the random variable can assume along with the probability of those values occurring. In statistics, the most important discrete probability distribution is the **binomial (probability) distribution**, and the most important continuous probability distribution is the **normal (probability) distribution**. Part III presents these two well-known and versatile distributions.

The binomial distribution

Binomial distributions are important because they allow you to deal with random situations that result in only two relevant outcomes, such as yes–no, pass–fail, defective–nondefective, correct–incorrect, or male–female. This chapter covers this very useful discrete distribution.

Introduction to the binomial distribution

Consider n independent trials of an experiment where at each trial there are exactly two possible outcomes: success with probability p that is constant from trial to trial and failure with probability $1 - p$. Let X equal the number of successes out of the n repeated trials. The random variable X is called a **binomial random variable**, and its probability distribution is called a **binomial distribution**. To summarize, a binomial distribution results from a process that has the following characteristics:

1. There are a fixed number n of identical trials.

2. Each trial results in exactly one of only two outcomes, which, by convention, are labeled "success" and "failure."

3. The probability of success, denoted p, on a single trial remains the same from trial to trial.

4. The trials are independent.

5. The binomial random variable X is the number of successes out of the n repeated trials.

To determine whether the binomial distribution is an appropriate model for the probability distribution of a given experiment, you check whether these five characteristics are satisfied.

Determine whether the binomial distribution is an appropriate model for the probability distribution of the given experiment.

PROBLEM   Flip a fair coin 20 times and count the number of times heads shows on the up face of the coin.

SOLUTION   The binomial distribution is an appropriate model for the probability distribution of this experiment because (1) there are n identical trials: 20 flips of the coin; (2) each trial (flip) results in only two outcomes: heads or tails, where the outcome heads will denote "success;" (3) p, the probability of success (heads) on a single trial (flip) remains the same from trial to trial; (4) the trials (flips) are independent since the outcome of one flip of the coin

PROBLEM   does not affect the outcome of any other flip; and (5) the random variable of interest is the number of successes (heads) out of the 20 repeated trials (flips).

PROBLEM   Randomly select 20 student names without replacement from a list containing 100 student names along with their respective ages, and record whether the age of the student is 40 years or older.

SOLUTION   The binomial distribution is not an appropriate model for the probability distribution of this experiment because p, the probability of success (the age of the student is 40 years or older), changes from trial to trial since the selections are made without replacement.

Often, in real life, a binomial distribution can serve as a satisfactory model for the probability distribution of an experiment if *for all practical purposes* the experiment satisfies the properties of a binomial experiment. For these situations, you must use your own judgment when checking whether the five characteristics for a binomial distribution are satisfied.

Determine whether the binomial distribution is an appropriate model for the probability distribution of the given experiment.

PROBLEM   Each student in a random sample of 100 students from a certain university is interviewed and asked whether he or she favors construction of a new athletic facility, and the number of yes responses is recorded. Assume that none of the students interviewed refuses to answer the question.

SOLUTION   The binomial distribution is an appropriate model for the probability distribution of this experiment because (1) there are n identical trials: 100 interviews, all the same; (2) each trial (interview) results in only two outcomes: yes or no, where the outcome yes will denote "success;" (3) p, the probability of success (yes) on a single trial (interview) remains the same (for all practical purposes) from trial to trial; (4) the trials are independent since the outcome of one interview does not affect the outcome of any other interview; and (5) the random variable of interest is the number of successes (yes responses) out of the 100 repeated trials (interviews).

PROBLEM   Each student in a sample consisting of 50 music majors and 50 kinesiology majors from a certain university is interviewed and asked whether he or she favors construction of a new athletic facility, and the number of yes responses is recorded. Assume that none of the students interviewed refuses to answer the question.

SOLUTION   The binomial distribution is not an appropriate model for the probability distribution of this experiment because the characteristic of independent trials likely would not be satisfied since you can expect that responses of students from the same major will tend to be similar. For instance, most likely the kinesiology majors would tend to be in favor of a new athletic facility.

Note: The word *success* as used to characterize a binomial distribution is not intended to convey the message that the targeted success outcome is something you would ordinarily consider successful, good, or even desirable. It is simply used to designate whichever outcome is being counted in the n trials. Either outcome may be named the "success" outcome. However, once the success outcome is identified, its probability of occurrence is designated as p.

EXERCISE
8·1

Determine whether the binomial distribution is an appropriate model for the probability distribution of the given experiment.

1. Toss a fair die five times and record whether the up face of the die shows four dots.

2. Randomly draw 10 cards without replacement from a well-shuffled deck of 52 playing cards and observe whether each card is a diamond.

Note: A standard deck of 52 playing cards consists of four suits: clubs, spades, hearts, and diamonds. Each suit has 13 cards.

3. Randomly interview 200 students about whether they favor a campus issue and count the number of yes responses. Assume that none of the students interviewed refuses to answer the question.

4. Test 100 male subjects who were given an experimental drug to prevent a certain flu strain and count the number of subjects who show symptoms consistent with that particular flu strain.

5. Randomly test 25 pine trees in a forest and count the number of trees that are infested by the pine beetle.

Properties of the binomial distribution

The binomial distribution has the following properties:

1. It has parameters n and p.

2. Its mean is given by $\mu = np$.

3. Its variance is given by $\sigma^2 = np(1-p)$.

4. Its standard deviation is given by $\sigma = \sqrt{np(1-p)}$.

PROBLEM A quiz consists of five multiple-choice questions, each with four possible answer choices (A, B, C, or D), one of which is correct. Suppose that an unprepared student does not read the question, but simply makes one random guess for each question. Let the random variable X equal the number of correct guesses the student makes for the five questions.
  a. Is the binomial distribution an appropriate model for the probability distribution of the random variable X? Yes or no? Justify your answer.
  If your answer to part a is "Yes," do the following:
  b. Identify n and p.
  c. Calculate μ, σ^2, and σ.

SOLUTION Yes, the binomial distribution is an appropriate model for the probability distribution of the given process because (1) there are n identical trials: five random guesses; (2) each trial (guess) results in only two outcomes: correct or incorrect, where the outcome correct will denote "success;" (3) p, the probability of success (correct) on a single trial (guess) is one out of four or 0.25 and is the same from trial to trial; (4) the trials (guesses) are independent since the outcome of one guess does not affect the outcome of any other; and (5) the random variable of interest is the number of successes (correct guesses) in the five trials (guesses).
  b. $n = 5$ and $p = 0.25$

  c. $\mu = np = 5(0.25) = 1.25$, $\sigma^2 = np(1-p) = 5(.25)(.75) = 0.9375$,

  $\sigma = \sqrt{np(1-p)} = \sqrt{5(.25)(.75)} \approx 0.9682$

  Calculate μ, σ^2, and σ for a binomial distribution with n repeated trials and probability p of success as indicated.

PROBLEM $n = 10$, $p = 0.2$
SOLUTION $\mu = np = 10(0.2) = 2$, $\sigma^2 = np(1-p) = 10(.2)(.8) = 1.6$,

  $\sigma = \sqrt{np(1-p)} = \sqrt{10(.2)(.8)} \approx 1.265$

PROBLEM $n = 20, p = 0.7$

SOLUTION $\mu = np = 20(0.7) = 14, \sigma^2 = np(1-p) = 20(.7)(.3) = 4.2,$
$\sigma = \sqrt{np(1-p)} = \sqrt{20(.7)(.3)} \approx 2.05$

PROBLEM $n = 4, p = 0.25$

SOLUTION $\mu = np = 4(0.25) = 1, \sigma^2 = np(1-p) = 4(.25)(.75) = 0.75,$
$\sigma = \sqrt{np(1-p)} = \sqrt{4(.25)(.75)} \approx 0.866$

EXERCISE

8·2

1. A quality control inspector randomly draws a sample of 15 light bulbs from a recent production lot. Suppose it is known that 10 percent of the bulbs in the lot are defective. Let the random variable X be the number of defective light bulbs in the sample. Assume that the population from which the random drawings are made is very large so that the percent of defective items remains approximately constant.

   a. Is the binomial distribution an appropriate model for the probability distribution of X? Yes or no? Justify your answer.

   If your answer to part a is "Yes," do the following:

   b. Identify n and p.
   c. Calculate μ, σ^2, and σ.

For 2–10, calculate μ, σ^2, and σ for a binomial distribution with n repeated trials and probability p of success as indicated.

2. $n = 8, p = 0.2$

3. $n = 15, p = 0.9$

4. $n = 3, p = 0.25$

5. $n = 100, p = 0.5$

6. $n = 20, p = 0.15$

7. $n = 150, p = 0.9$

8. $n = 300, p = 0.25$

9. $n = 475, p = 0.55$

10. $n = 800, p = 0.7$

Calculating binomial probabilities by formula

Let the random variable X denote the number of successes in n trials of a binomial experiment. Then X has a binomial distribution and the **formula for the probability of observing exactly x successes in n trials** is given by

$$P(X = x) = \binom{n}{x} p^x q^{n-x} \text{ for } x = 0, 1, 2, ..., n$$

where

n = number of trials

x = number of successes among n trials

p = probability of success on a single trial

$q = 1 - p$

$$\binom{n}{x} = {_nC_x} = \frac{n!}{x!(n-x)!}$$

PROBLEM   Toss a fair die five times and record the number of dots on the up face of the die. What is the probability that four dots on the up face occurs exactly three times?

SOLUTION $n = 5$

$x = 3$

p = probability four dots appears on the up face of the die $= \dfrac{1}{6}$

$q = 1 - \dfrac{1}{6} = \dfrac{5}{6}$

$P(X = 3) = \dfrac{5!}{3!(5-3)!}\left(\dfrac{1}{6}\right)^3\left(\dfrac{5}{6}\right)^{5-3} = (10)(0.00463)(0.6944) \approx 0.03215$

PROBLEM   Flip a fair coin six times and record the up face of the coin. What is the probability that heads shows on the up face fewer than three times?

SOLUTION $n = 6$

$x = 3$

p = probability head appears on the up face of the coin $= \dfrac{1}{2} = .5$

$q = 1 - .5 = .5$

$P(X < 3) = P(X = 0) + P(X = 1) + P(X = 2)$

$$= \frac{6!}{0!(6-0)!}(.5)^0(.5)^{6-0} + \frac{6!}{1!(6-1)!}(.5)^1(.5)^{6-1} + \frac{6!}{2!(6-2)!}(.5)^2(.5)^{6-2}$$

$$= 0.015625 + 0.09375 + 0.234375 = 0.34375$$

For a binomial random variable X, find the indicated probabilities.

PROBLEM $P(X < 1)$ when $n = 4$, $p = .2$

SOLUTION $P(X < 1) = P(X = 0) = \dfrac{4!}{0!(4-0)!}(.2)^0(.8)^{4-0} = 0.4096$

PROBLEM $P(X \leq 1)$ when $n = 4$, $p = .2$

SOLUTION $P(X \leq 1) = P(X = 0) + P(X = 1) = \dfrac{4!}{0!(4-0)!}(.2)^0(.8)^{4-0} + \dfrac{4!}{1!(4-1)!}(.2)^1(.8)^{4-1}$

$$= 0.4096 + 0.4096 = 0.8192$$

PROBLEM $P(X > 6)$ when $n = 8$, $p = .7$

SOLUTION $P(X > 6) = P(X = 7) + P(X = 8) = \dfrac{8!}{7!(8-7)!}(.7)^7(.3)^{8-7} + \dfrac{8!}{8!(8-8)!}(.7)^8(.3)^{8-8}$

$$\approx 0.19765 + 0.057648 \approx 0.255298$$

PROBLEM $P(X \geq 6)$ when $n = 8, p = .7$

SOLUTION $p(X \geq 6) = p(X = 6) + p(X = 7) + p(X = 8)$

$$= \frac{8!}{6!(8-6)!}(.7)^6(.3)^{8-6} + \frac{8!}{7!(8-7)!}(.7)^7(.3)^{8-7} + \frac{8!}{8!(8-8)!}(.7)^8(.3)^{8-8}$$

$$\approx 0.296475 + 0.19765 + 0.057648 \approx 0.551773$$

1. Toss a fair die five times and record the number of dots on the up face of the die. What is the probability that six dots on the up face occurs exactly three times?

2. Flip a fair coin three times and record the up face of the coin. What is the probability that heads shows on the up face fewer than two times?

3. Suppose researchers determine that a new drug has a 40 percent chance of preventing a certain flu strain. If the drug is administered to 10 male subjects, what is the probability that the drug will be effective in preventing the flu strain for exactly 8 of the male subjects?

4. Suppose researchers determine that the chances a pine tree in a particular forest is infected by the pine beetle is 10 percent. If five randomly selected pine trees are tested for infection by the pine beetle, what is the probability that exactly two are infected by the pine beetle?

5. A quiz consists of five multiple-choice questions, each with four possible answer choices (A, B, C, or D), one of which is correct. Suppose that an unprepared student does not read the question, but simply makes one random guess for each question. What is the probability that the student will get exactly five questions correct?

For exercises 6–15, find the indicated probabilities for a binomial random variable X.

6. $P(X < 1)$ when $n = 5, p = .2$

7. $P(X \leq 1)$ when $n = 5, p = .2$

8. $P(X > 8)$ when $n = 10, p = .5$

9. $P(X < 1)$ when $n = 10, p = .5$

10. $P(X = 2)$ when $n = 3, p = .7$

11. $P(X < 2)$ when $n = 3, p = .7$

12. $P(X \leq 2)$ when $n = 3, p = .7$

13. $P(X > 2)$ when $n = 3, p = .7$

14. $P(X \geq 2)$ when $n = 3, p = .7$

15. $P(X = 5)$ when $n = 6, p = .4$

Calculating binomial probabilities using a table

In some cases, an efficient way to calculate binomial probabilities is to refer to a table of binomial probabilities, like Table A shown in the Appendix. This table gives binomial probabilities (rounded to three decimal places) for $P(X = x)$ for various values of n, p, and x. Part of the table is reproduced in Table 8.1.

To use Table A, first locate n and read down to find the row in which the corresponding value of x appears. Now read across that row to the desired value for p. For example, from Table A, when $n = 4$ and $p = .7$, $P(X = 3) = 0.412$.

Table 8.1 Binomial Probabilities for Selected Values of n and p

n	x	0.1	0.2	0.3	0.4	0.5	0.6	0.7	0.8	0.9
1	0	0.900	0.800	0.700	0.600	0.500	0.400	0.300	0.200	0.100
	1	0.100	0.200	0.300	0.400	0.500	0.600	0.700	0.800	0.900
2	0	0.810	0.640	0.490	0.360	0.250	0.160	0.090	0.040	0.010
	1	0.180	0.320	0.420	0.480	0.500	0.480	0.420	0.320	0.180
	2	0.010	0.040	0.090	0.160	0.250	0.360	0.490	0.640	0.810
3	0	0.729	0.512	0.343	0.216	0.125	0.064	0.027	0.008	0.001
	1	0.243	0.384	0.441	0.432	0.375	0.288	0.189	0.096	0.027
	2	0.027	0.096	0.189	0.288	0.375	0.432	0.441	0.384	0.243
	3	0.001	0.008	0.027	0.064	0.125	0.216	0.343	0.512	0.729
4	0	0.656	0.410	0.240	0.130	0.062	0.026	0.008	0.002	0.000
	1	0.292	0.410	0.412	0.346	0.250	0.154	0.076	0.026	0.004
	2	0.049	0.154	0.265	0.346	0.375	0.346	0.265	0.154	0.049
	3	0.004	0.026	0.076	0.154	0.250	0.346	0.412	0.410	0.292
	4	0.000	0.002	0.008	0.026	0.062	0.130	0.240	0.410	0.656

For a binomial random variable X, use Table A to find the indicated probabilities when $n = 3$, and $p = .1$.

PROBLEM $\quad P(X = 2)$

SOLUTION $\quad$ Using Table A, $P(X = 2) = 0.027$

PROBLEM $\quad P(X \geq 2)$

SOLUTION $\quad P(X \geq 2) = P(X = 2) + P(X = 3) = 0.027 + 0.001 = 0.028$

Sometimes, certain key phrases, such as "at least," "at most," "less than," "greater than," and so forth, are used in probability problems, including binomial probability distribution problems. To work the problem correctly, you must know how to correctly express the problem using mathematical symbolism. Table 8.2 shows a list of some commonly used phrases and the mathematical symbolism that corresponds to each.

PROBLEM $\quad$ Flip a fair coin four times and record the up face of the coin. Use Table A to find the probability that heads shows on the up face no more than two times.

SOLUTION $\quad$ The symbol for "is no more than" is $\leq$, so you must find $P(X \leq 2)$ when $n = 4$ and $p = .5$. You have $P(X \leq 2) = P(X = 0) + P(X = 1) + P(X = 2) = 0.062 + 0.250 + 0.375 = 0.687$.

Table 8.2 Commonly Used Phrases and Their Corresponding Mathematical Symbolism

Phrase	Translation
"is equal to" or "equals"	=
"is exactly" or "exactly equals"	=
"is less than" or "is fewer than"	<
"is less than or equal to"	≤
"is at most"	≤
"is not more than" or "is no more than"	≤
"is greater than"	>
"is more than"	>
"exceeds"	>
"is at least"	≥
"is not less than" or "is no less than"	≥

EXERCISE 8·4

Use Table A to find the following probabilities.

1. Toss a fair die five times and record the number of dots on the up face of the die. What is the probability that an even number on the up face occurs exactly four times?

2. Flip a fair coin three times and record the up face of the coin. What is the probability that heads shows on the up face no more than two times?

3. Suppose researchers determine that a new drug has a 40 percent chance of preventing a certain flu strain. If the drug is administered to 10 male subjects, what is the probability that the drug will be effective in preventing the flu strain for exactly 8 of the male subjects?

4. Suppose researchers determine that the chances a pine tree in a particular forest is infected by the pine beetle is 10 percent. If 20 randomly selected pine trees are tested for infection by the pine beetle, what is the probability that fewer than 2 are infected by the pine beetle?

5. A quiz consists of 10 multiple-choice questions, each with five possible answer choices (A, B, C, D, or E), one of which is correct. Suppose that an unprepared student does not read the question, but simply makes one random guess for each question. What is the probability that the student will get at least seven questions correct?

For exercises 6–15, find the indicated probabilities for a binomial random variable X.

6. $P(X$ is less than 1) when $n = 15$, $p = .2$

7. $P(X$ is not less than 8) when $n = 10$, $p = .9$

8. $P(X$ exceeds 8) when $n = 10$, $p = .5$

9. $P(X$ is less than or equal to 3) when $n = 12$, $p = .2$

10. $P(X$ is exactly 17) when $n = 19$, $p = .8$

11. $P(X$ is at most 2) when $n = 11$, $p = .4$

12. $P(X$ is no less than 6) when $n = 9$, $p = .7$

13. $P(X$ is greater than 18) when $n = 20$, $p = .9$

14. $P(X$ is no more than 1) when $n = 15$, $p = .2$

15. $P(X$ is at least 15) when $n = 16$, $p = .7$

The normal distribution  ·9·

The most prevalent and, by far, the most important continuous distribution is the normal (probability) distribution or normal curve. The normal distribution is so prevalent because it can be used as a model for the distributions of many naturally occurring phenomena, such as heights, weights, IQs, and so on. This distribution and its characteristics are introduced in this chapter.

Properties of the normal distribution

A random variable X is said to be normally distributed with mean μ and standard deviation σ if the graph of its probability distribution, called its **density curve**, is

a bell-shaped curve defined by the equation $y = f(x) = \dfrac{e^{-\frac{1}{2}\left(\frac{x-\mu}{\sigma}\right)^2}}{\sigma\sqrt{2\pi}}$, where $-\infty < x < \infty$,

with the graph depicted as shown in Figure 9.1.

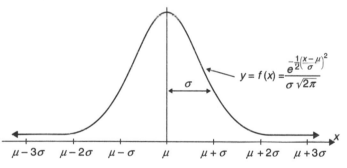

Figure 9.1 Normal curve with mean μ and standard deviation σ.

The density curve must satisfy the following two properties:

1. The total area under the curve, bounded by the horizontal axis, is 1.

2. Every point on the curve must have a vertical height greater than or equal to 0.

The **normal curve** or **normal distribution** is the name given to the family of distributions of normal random variables. Normal distributions have the following properties in common:

1. The equation for the graph of the distribution is given by $y = \dfrac{e^{-\frac{1}{2}\left(\frac{x-\mu}{\sigma}\right)^2}}{\sigma\sqrt{2\pi}}$.

2. The distribution is completely defined by two parameters: its mean μ and standard deviation σ.

3. The distribution is bell-shaped and symmetric about its mean μ.

4. The standard deviation σ is the distance from a vertical line at μ to where the curvature of the graph changes on either side.

5. The distribution is continuous, extending from $-\infty$ to ∞.

6. The x-axis is a horizontal asymptote for the curve (meaning the graph never touches the x-axis).

7. The total area bounded by the curve and the horizontal axis is 1, with 0.5 area to the left of μ and 0.5 area to the right of μ.

8. The mean, median, and mode coincide.

The mean μ of a normal distribution is a *location* parameter because it determines where the *center* of the distribution is located along the horizontal axis. Figure 9.2 shows three normal curves with identical standard deviations but different means.

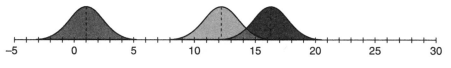

Figure 9.2 Normal curves with identical standard deviations but different means.

The standard deviation is a measure of the *variability* (or spread) of the distribution. You can think of σ as a *shape* parameter because it determines whether the distribution is tall and thin (corresponding to small values of σ) or short and wide (corresponding to large values of σ). Figure 9.3 shows three normal curves with identical means but different standard deviations.

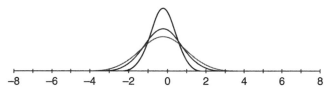

Figure 9.3 Normal curves with identical means but different standard deviations.

The bell shape of the curve means that most of the data will fall in the middle of the distribution, with the amount of data tapering off evenly in both directions as you move away from the center of the distribution. This characteristic of normal distributions can be expressed in a more accurate way, which (for convenience) you can call the **68.26-95.44-99.74 Property**, as follows: About 68.26 percent of the values of a random variable that is normally distributed fall within one standard deviation of the mean, about 95.44 percent fall within two standard deviations of the mean, and about 99.74 percent fall within three standard deviations of the mean, as shown in Figure 9.4.

In other words, about 68.26 percent of the values of a normal random variable fall between $\mu - 1\sigma$ and $\mu + 1\sigma$, 95.44 percent fall between $\mu - 2\sigma$ and $\mu + 2\sigma$, and 99.74 percent fall between $\mu - 3\sigma$ and $\mu + 3\sigma$.

In addition, because the normal curve is symmetric about its mean, the area under the curve is distributed as shown in Figure 9.5.

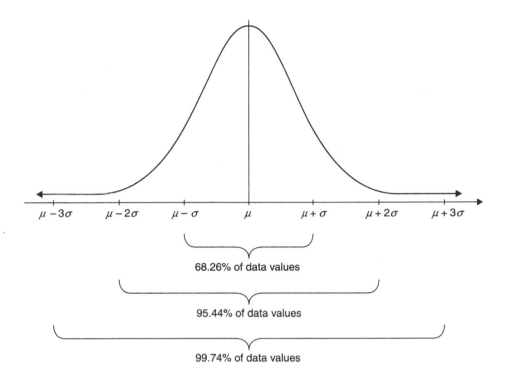

Figure 9.4   Normal curve areas about the mean, μ.

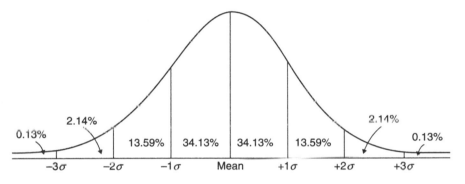

Figure 9.5   Distribution of area under a normal curve about its mean.

PROBLEM
Express the 68.26-95.44-99.74 Property in terms of a normal random variable with mean $\mu = 100$ and standard deviation $\sigma = 15$.

SOLUTION
According to the 68.26-95.44-99.74 Property, about 68.26 percent of the values will fall between $100 - 1(15)$ and $100 + 1(15)$, 95.44 percent will fall between $100 - 2(15)$ and $100 + 2(15)$, and 99.74 percent will fall between $100 - 3(15)$ and $100 + 3(15)$. Thus, for a normal random variable with mean $\mu = 100$ and standard deviation $\sigma = 15$: About 68.26 percent of the values fall between 85 and 115, about 95.44 percent fall between 70 and 130, and about 99.74 percent fall between 55 and 145.

Because the total area bounded by the curve and the horizontal axis is 1, *the area over a particular interval along the horizontal axis equals the probability that the normal random variable will assume a value in that interval.* Therefore, for any random variable X, you have the following probabilities:

1. $P(\mu - 1\sigma < X < \mu + 1\sigma) = 0.6826$

2. $P(\mu - 2\sigma < X < \mu + 2\sigma) = 0.9544$

3. $P(\mu - 3\sigma < X < \mu + 3\sigma) = 0.9974$

Considering that, geometrically, area is a region, the "area" above a point on the horizontal axis of a normal distribution is zero. Therefore, *the probability that a normal random variable assumes any particular exact value is zero.* Thus, in probability statements for normal random variables, the probability is unchanged when the symbols "<" and "≤" are interchanged or the symbols ">" and "≥" are interchanged.

PROBLEM   The normal random variable X has mean $\mu = 200$ and standard deviation $\sigma = 10$. Find the probability that X assumes a value within one standard deviation of $\mu = 200$.

SOLUTION   Since $\mu = 200$ is the mean, the probability that X assumes a value within one standard deviation of its mean equals $P(\mu - 1\sigma < X < \mu + 1\sigma) = P(200 - 1\cdot10 < X < 200 + 1\cdot10) = P(190 < X < 210) = 0.6826$

PROBLEM   The normal random variable X has mean $\mu = 200$ and standard deviation $\sigma = 10$. Find the probability that X assumes a value more than three standard deviations from its mean.

SOLUTION   The probability that X assumes a value within three standard deviations of its mean equals $P(\mu - 3\sigma < X < \mu + 3\sigma) = P(200 - 3\cdot10 < X < 200 + 3\cdot10) = P(270 < X < 230) = 0.9974$. Since the total area under the normal curve is 1, the probability that X assumes a value more than three standard deviations from its mean $= 1 - 0.9974 = 0.0026$.

PROBLEM   The normal random variable X has mean $\mu = 200$ and standard deviation $\sigma = 10$. Find $P(180 < X < 220)$.

SOLUTION $P(180 < X < 220) = P(200 - 2(10) < X < 200 + 2(10))$
$= P(\mu - 2\sigma < X < \mu + 2\sigma) = 0.9544$

PROBLEM   The normal random variable X has mean $\mu = 200$ and standard deviation $\sigma = 10$. Find $P(X \le 200)$.

SOLUTION   According to Property 7 for normal distributions on page 52, the area to the left of μ is 0.5. Thus, since $\mu = 200$, $P(X \le 200) = 0.5$

EXERCISE 9·1

For 1–5, express the 68.26-95.44-99.74 Property in terms of a normal distribution with the following parameters:

1. mean $\mu = 25$ and standard deviation $\sigma = 3$

2. mean $\mu = 300$ and standard deviation $\sigma = 50$

3. mean $\mu = 75$ and standard deviation $\sigma = 5$

4. mean $\mu = 4.5$ and standard deviation $\sigma = 0.2$

5. mean $\mu = 0$ and standard deviation $\sigma = 1$

For 6–10, consider the normal random variable X with mean $\mu = 75$ and standard deviation $\sigma = 5$.

6. Find the probability that X assumes a value within one standard deviation of $\mu = 75$.

7. Find the probability that X assumes a value within two standard deviations of $\mu = 75$.

8. Find the probability that X assumes a value more than one standard deviation from $\mu = 75$.

9. Find the probability that X assumes a value more than two standard deviations from $\mu = 75$.

10. Find the probability that X assumes a value more than three standard deviations from $\mu = 75$.

For 11–15, find the indicated probabilities for the normal random variable X with mean $\mu = 300$ and standard deviation $\sigma = 20$.

11. $P(260 < X < 340)$

12. $P(240 < X < 360)$

13. $1 - P(260 < X < 340)$

14. $P(X < 300)$

15. $P(X > 300)$

For 15–20, find the indicated probabilities for the normal random variable X with mean $\mu = 0$ and standard deviation $\sigma = 1$.

16. $P(-1 < X < 1)$

17. $P(-2 < X < 2)$

18. $P(-3 < X < 3)$

19. $P(X \leq 0)$

20. $P(X \geq 0)$

The standard normal distribution

The **standard normal distribution**, denoted **Z**, is the special normal distribution that has mean $\mu = 0$ and standard deviation $\sigma = 1$. Due to its unique parameters, a point z along the horizontal axis of a standard normal distribution expresses the position of the value relative to the mean, with negative values lying to the left of the mean and positive values lying to the right of the mean. Furthermore, the z value is in terms of standard deviations. For instance, the z value -1 is one standard deviation below the mean, and the z value 1 is one standard deviation above the mean. Similarly, the z value -1.58 is 1.58 standard deviations below the mean, while the z value 2.45 is 2.45 standard deviations above the mean.

PROBLEM   Describe the location of the point $z = -2.34$ along the horizontal axis of a standard normal distribution in terms of standard deviations from the mean.

SOLUTION   The point $z = -2.34$ is 2.34 standard deviations below the mean.

PROBLEM   Describe the location of the point $z = 1.25$ along the horizontal axis of a standard normal distribution in terms of standard deviations from the mean.

SOLUTION   The point $z = 1.25$ is 1.25 standard deviations above the mean.

PROBLEM   Describe the location of the point $z = 0$ along the horizontal axis of a standard normal distribution in terms of standard deviations from the mean.

SOLUTION   The point $z = 0$ is zero standard deviations from the mean; that is, its location is the mean.

PROBLEM   For the standard normal distribution, find the probability that z assumes a value between -3 and 3.

SOLUTION   Since the standard normal distribution has mean $\mu = 0$ and standard deviation $\sigma = 1$, $P(-3 < Z < 3) = P(\mu - 3\sigma < Z < \mu + 3\sigma) = 0.9974$.

For 1–10, describe the location of the point z along the horizontal axis of a standard normal distribution in terms of standard deviations from the mean.

1. $z = -2$

2. $z = -1.5$

3. $z = 2.33$

4. $z = -1.99$

5. $z = 3.05$

6. $z = -1.04$

7. $z = -1.96$

8. $z = 1.96$

9. $z = 2$

10. $z = -2.1$

For 11–15, find the indicated probabilities for the standard normal random variable X with mean $\mu = 0$ and standard deviation $\sigma = 1$.

11. $P(-1 < Z < 1)$

12. $P(-2 < Z < 2)$

13. $P(-3 < Z < 3)$

14. $P(Z \leq 0)$

15. $P(Z \geq 0)$

Finding probabilities for the standard normal distribution

A number of different tables give areas corresponding to intervals for the standard normal distribution. Regardless of the table used, the results are the same. A relatively easy table to use is Table B in the Appendix. This table gives the cumulative area bounded by the curve and the horizontal axis all the way from negative infinity ($-\infty$) up to a vertical cut-off line at a specific z value, as shown in Figure 9.6.

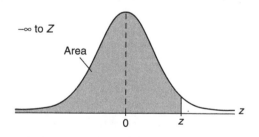

Figure 9.6 Table B area for a value z of the standard normal distribution.

In other words, the entry in Table B corresponding to a particular z value is the area under the curve all the way to the left of that z value. This type of table is called a cumulative table.

The area given in Table B can be interpreted as the probability that the standard normal random variable Z assumes a value less than (or less than or equal to) the z value corresponding to that area. Symbolically, the entry corresponding to a particular z value is $P(Z < z) = P(Z \leq z)$. When using Table B to find probabilities, keep the following points in mind:

1. Table B gives left-tail probabilities for the *standard* normal distribution.

2. Table B has two parts: Table B1, which has negative z values up to $z =$ zero, and Table B2, which starts at $z = 0$ and continues with positive z values.

3. If z is negative, the Table B1 entry for z will be less than 0.5 (because z lies to the left of the mean); if z is positive, the Table B2 entry for z will be greater than 0.5 (because z lies to the right of the mean).

4. Table B displays $P(Z < z) = P(Z \leq z)$ for z values that may be written as decimals up to *hundredths* only.

5. The entries in Table B, because they are probabilities (or areas), are all *nonnegative* and range between 0 and 1, inclusive.

To find the Table B entry for a particular z value, say $z = 1.96$, write the z value as a number that has exactly two decimal places, if needed. Next, split the z value into two parts: the first part will be the number to the tenth's place, and the second part will be the hundredths part of the number. For $z = 1.96$, the first part is 1.9 and the hundredths part is 0.06. Now, look in Table B2 (because $z = 1.96$ is positive) for the intersection of the row labeled 1.9 and the column labeled 0.06. Thus, $P(Z < 1.96) = P(Z \leq 1.96) = 0.9750$, as shown in the following excerpt from Table B2:

Table 9.1

z	0.00	0.01	0.02	0.03	0.04	0.05	0.06	0.07	0.08	0.09
⋮	⋮	⋮	⋮	⋮	⋮	⋮	⋮	⋮	⋮	⋮
1.9	0.9713	0.9719	0.9726	0.9732	0.9738	0.9744	**0.9750**	0.9756	0.9761	0.9767

Use Table B to find the following probabilities.

PROBLEM	$P(Z < -2)$
SOLUTION	$P(Z < -2) = P(Z < -2.00) = 0.0228$
PROBLEM	$P(Z \leq -1.5)$
SOLUTION	$P(Z \leq -1.5) = P(Z \leq -1.50) = 0.0668$
PROBLEM	$P(Z \leq 3.05)$
SOLUTION	$P(Z \leq 3.05) = 0.9989$

Although Table B is designed so that the entry corresponding to a particular z value is $P(Z < z) = P(Z \leq z)$, you also can use Table B to find probabilities for other probability statements as well. Following is a list of four types of probability statements you might encounter, along with the procedure for determining the probability when using Table B:

1. For any z value, z_0, the probability that Z equals z_0 is given by $P(Z = z_0) = 0$.

PROBLEM	Find $P(Z = -2.25)$.
SOLUTION	$P(Z = -2.25) = 0$

2. For any z value, z_0, the probability that Z is less than z_0 is given by $P(Z < z_0) =$ the Table B entry for z_0.

PROBLEM   Use Table B to find $P(Z < -2)$.

SOLUTION $P(Z < -2) = P(Z < -2.00) = 0.0228$

3. For any z value, z_0, the probability that Z is greater than z_0 is given by $P(Z > z_0) = 1.0000$ minus the Table B entry for z_0.

PROBLEM   Use Table B to find $P(Z > -2)$.

SOLUTION $P(Z > -2) = 1.0000 - P(Z < -2.00) = 1.0000 - 0.0228 = 0.9772$

4. For any two z values, z_1 and z_2, the probability that Z lies between z_1 and z_2 is given by $P(z_1 < Z < z_2) =$ Table B entry for z_2 minus Table B entry for z_1.

PROBLEM   Use Table B to find $P(-1.5 < Z < 3.05)$.

SOLUTION $P(-1.5 < Z < 3.05) = P(Z < 3.05) - P(Z < -1.50) = 0.9989 - 0.0668 = 0.9321$

Note: In probability statements 2–4, the symbols < and > can be replaced with ≤ (less than or equal to) and ≥ (greater than or equal to), respectively, without any change in the probability.

EXERCISE

9·3

Use Table B to find the following probabilities.

1. $P(Z = 2.23)$

2. $P(Z < 0.08)$

3. $P(Z < 2.33)$

4. $P(Z \le -1.99)$

5. $P(Z \le -0.05)$

6. $P(Z < -1.04)$

7. $P(Z < 2.8)$

8. $P(Z < -1.96)$

9. $P(Z < -3)$

10. $P(Z < 3)$

11. $P(Z \le 0)$

12. $P(Z > 2.33)$

13. $P(Z \ge -1.99)$

14. $P(Z \ge 0)$

15. $P(0 < Z < 1.65)$

16. $P(-1 < Z < 1)$

17. $P(-2 < Z < 2)$

18. $P(-3 < Z < 3)$

19. $P(-2.28 < Z < -1.45)$

20. $P(1.28 < Z < 1.95)$

Finding percentiles for the standard normal distribution

The kth **percentile** is a value at or below which k percent of the data fall. For example, the median is the 50th percentile because 50 percent of the data fall at or below the median. Since for any z value, z_0, Table B shows the left-tail probability for z_0, every z value in Table B is a percentile! For instance, $z = 1.96$ is the 97.5th percentile because $0.9750 = 97.5\%$ of the distribution lies to the left of $z = 1.96$.

State the percentile corresponding to each of the following z values.

PROBLEM $z = -2$

SOLUTION   The Table B entry for $z = -2$ is 0.0228. Therefore, $z = -2$ is the 2.28th percentile.

PROBLEM $z = -1.5$

SOLUTION   The Table B entry for $z = -1.5$ is 0.0668. Therefore, $z = -1.5$ is the 6.68th percentile.

PROBLEM $z = 3.05$

SOLUTION   The Table B entry for $z = 3.05$ is 0.9989. Therefore, $z = 3.05$ is the 99.89th percentile.

Now consider a problem in which you must find the z value corresponding to a given percentile. For instance, suppose you need to find the 99th percentile for the standard normal distribution. Symbolically, you are to find z_0 such that $P(Z \le z_0) = 99\% = 0.9900$. You will scan the entries in Table B until you find 0.9900 or an entry that is very close to 0.9900. The closest entry is 0.9901. Next, read the table "in reverse" to determine that $z_0 = 2.33$ is approximately the 99th percentile.

PROBLEM   Find the 80th percentile for the standard normal distribution.

SOLUTION   You need to find z_0 such that $P(Z \le z_0) = 80\% = 0.8000$. The closest entry in Table B is 0.7995. Thus, $z_0 = 0.84$ is approximately the 80th percentile.

PROBLEM   Find the 10th percentile for the standard normal distribution.

SOLUTION   You need to find z_0 such that $P(Z \le z_0) = 10\% = 0.1000$. The closest entry in Table B is 0.1003. Thus, $z_0 = -1.28$ is approximately the 10th percentile.

Sometimes, you might simply be asked to find z_0 such that $P(Z < z_0)$ or $P(Z \le z_0)$ is a given probability. You work these problems the same way as you work percentile problems.

PROBLEM   Find z_0 such that $P(Z < z_0) = 0.3410$.

SOLUTION   The closest entry in Table B is 0.3409. Therefore, $z_0 = -0.41$.

PROBLEM   Find z_0 such that $P(Z \le z_0) = 0.9720$.

SOLUTION   The closest entry in Table B is 0.9719. Therefore, $z_0 = 1.91$.

EXERCISE
9·4

For 1–5, state the percentile corresponding to the given z value.

1. $z = -2.5$

2. $z = 2.5$

3. $z = -1.49$

4. $z = 1.64$

5. $z = 1.65$

For 6–10, find the following percentiles for the standard normal distribution.

6. 90th

7. 20th

8. 14th

9. 60th

10. 3rd

For 11–15, find z_0 corresponding to the indicated probability.

11. $P(Z < z_0) = 0.8771$

12. $P(Z \leq z_0) = 0.0124$

13. $P(Z \leq z_0) = 0.9936$

14. $P(Z < z_0) = 0.025$

15. $P(Z \leq z_0) = 0.881$

Finding probabilities for a normally distributed random variable

The z-score is used to transform any normal random variable with mean μ and standard deviation σ into a standard normal random variable. The z-score, denoted z, for a given x value is given by the formula

$$z = \frac{x - \mu}{\sigma}$$

This transformation formula allows you to find probabilities for any normally distributed random variable. You simply convert x values to z-scores. Under the transformation, the problem is then represented using the standard normal distribution with mean $\mu = 0$ and standard deviation $\sigma = 1$.

PROBLEM   Find the probability that a normal random variable X with mean $\mu = 25$ and standard deviation $\sigma = 5$ is less than 32.

SOLUTION $P(X < 32) = P\left(Z < \dfrac{32 - 25}{5} \right) = P(Z < 1.40) = 0.9192$

PROBLEM   Find the probability that a normal random variable X with mean $\mu = 25$ and standard deviation $\sigma = 5$ lies between 15 and 25.

SOLUTION $P(15 < X < 25) = P\left(\dfrac{15 - 25}{5} < Z < \dfrac{25 - 25}{5} \right) = P(-2 < Z < 0)$

$$= 0.5000 - 0.0228 = 0.4772$$

PROBLEM   Suppose that scores on a national exam are normally distributed with mean $\mu = 500$ and standard deviation $\sigma = 100$. Find the probability that a randomly selected test taker will score greater than 800.

SOLUTION $P(X > 800) = P\left(Z > \dfrac{800 - 500}{100} \right) = P(Z > 3.00) = 1.0000 - 0.9987 = 0.0013$

PROBLEM   A local deli chain makes a signature sandwich. Suppose that the amount of fat grams in the signature sandwich are normally distributed, with mean $\mu = 16$ grams and standard deviation $\sigma = 1.5$ grams. Find the probability that a randomly selected signature sandwich will have no more than 12 fat grams.

SOLUTION $P(X \leq 12) = P\left(Z \leq \dfrac{12 - 16}{1.5} \right) = P(Z \leq -2.67) = 0.0038$

PROBLEM A plumbing company has found that the length of time, in minutes, for installing a bathtub is normally distributed, with mean $\mu = 160$ minutes and standard deviation $\sigma = 25$ minutes. What percent of the bathtubs are installed within 204 minutes by the company?

SOLUTION $P(X \leq 204) = P\left(Z \leq \dfrac{204 - 160}{25}\right) = P(Z \leq 1.76) = 0.9608$

For 1–5, find the indicated probabilities when X is a normally distributed random variable with mean $\mu = 60$ and standard deviation $\sigma = 10$.

1. $P(X = 60)$

2. $P(X \leq 60)$

3. $P(50 \leq X \leq 70)$

4. $P(40 \leq X \leq 80)$

5. $P(30 \leq X \leq 90)$

For 6–20, find the indicated probabilities.

6. Find the probability that a normal random variable X with mean $\mu = 25$ and standard deviation $\sigma = 5$ is less than 20.

7. Find the probability that a normal random variable X with mean $\mu = 300$ and standard deviation $\sigma = 50$ lies between 150 and 250.

8. Find the probability that a normal random variable X with mean $\mu = 30$ and standard deviation $\sigma = 6$ is at least 40.5.

9. Find the probability that a normal random variable X with mean $\mu = 120$ and standard deviation $\sigma = 15$ is no less than 100.

10. Find the probability that a normal random variable X with mean $\mu = 1600$ and standard deviation $\sigma = 200$ is at most 1900.

11. Find the probability that a normal random variable X with mean $\mu = 1600$ and standard deviation $\sigma = 200$ is at least 1900.

12. IQ scores for adults are normally distributed with mean $\mu = 100$ and standard deviation $\sigma = 15$. What percent of adults have IQ scores greater than 130?

13. Suppose that scores on a national exam are normally distributed with mean $\mu = 500$ and standard deviation $\sigma = 100$. Find the probability that a randomly selected test taker will score at least 750 on the exam.

14. A local deli chain makes a signature sandwich. Suppose that the amount of fat grams in the signature sandwich are normally distributed with mean $\mu = 16$ grams and standard deviation $\sigma = 1.5$ grams. Find the probability that a randomly selected signature sandwich will have no more than 19 fat grams.

15. A plumbing company has found that the length of time, in minutes, for installing a bathtub is normally distributed with mean $\mu = 160$ minutes and standard deviation $\sigma = 25$ minutes. What percent of the bathtubs are installed within 189 minutes by the company?

16. The weights of newborn baby girls born at a local hospital are normally distributed with mean $\mu = 100$ ounces and standard deviation $\sigma = 8$ ounces. If a newborn baby girl born at the local hospital is randomly selected, what is the probability that the child's weight will be at least 105 ounces?

17. The weights of newborn baby boys born at a local hospital are normally distributed with mean $\mu = 118$ ounces and standard deviation $\sigma = 9.5$ ounces. What percent of the baby boys born at the local hospital weigh between 100 and 120 ounces?

18. Suppose the caloric content of a 12-ounce can of a certain diet drink is normally distributed with mean $\mu = 5$ calories and standard deviation $\sigma = 0.5$ calories. What is the probability that a randomly selected 12-ounce can of the diet drink contains no more than 6 calories?

19. A coffee machine outputs a mean of 8 ounces. The machine's output is normally distributed with a standard deviation of 1 ounce. If the coffee cups hold 9.5 ounces, find the probability that the machine will overfill a cup.

20. The lifetime for a certain brand of incandescent light bulbs is normally distributed with a mean lifetime of 480 hours and standard deviation of 40 hours. What percent of these light bulbs last at least 500 hours?

Finding percentiles for a normally distributed random variable

Suppose you need to determine the kth percentile for a normal random variable X with mean μ and standard deviation σ. Symbolically, you need to find x_0 such that $P(X \le x_0) = k\%$. You can work this problem using methods with which you are already familiar.

Observe that for any normal variable X with mean μ and standard deviation σ, the formula for finding a z-score may be rewritten to express the value, x_0, of X in terms of the number (z_0) of standard deviations (σ) that it is above or below the mean (μ) to yield the formula

$$x_0 = \mu + z_0 \sigma$$

As a result, you can find x_0 such that $P(X \le x_0) = k\%$ for a normal random variable X with mean μ and standard deviation σ using the following two-step process:

Step 1. Find z_0 such that $P(Z \le z_0) = k\%$.

Step 2. Convert the z_0 obtained to the appropriate x value using $x_0 = \mu + z_0 \sigma$.

PROBLEM   Find the 99th percentile for the normal random variable X with mean $\mu = 300$ and standard deviation $\sigma = 50$.

SOLUTION   You need to find x_0 such that $P(X \le x_0) = 99\% = 0.9900$.

Step 1. Find z_0 such that $P(Z \le z_0) = 99\% = 0.9900$; $z_0 = 2.33$.

Step 2. $x_0 = \mu + z_0 \sigma = 300 + (2.33)(50) = 416.5$

PROBLEM   Find the 10th percentile for the normal random variable X with mean $\mu = 500$ and standard deviation $\sigma = 100$.

SOLUTION   You need to find x_0 such that $P(X \le x_0) = 10\% = 0.1000$.

Step 1. Find z_0 such that $P(Z \le z_0) = 10\% = 0.1000$; $z_0 = -1.28$.

Step 2. $x_0 = \mu + z_0\sigma = 500 + (-1.28)(100) = 372$

Sometimes, you might simply be asked to find x_0 such that $P(X < x_0)$ or $P(X \le x_0)$ is a given probability. You work these problems the same way as you work percentile problems.

PROBLEM   For the random variable X with mean $\mu = 25$ and standard deviation $\sigma = 5$, find x_0 such that $P(X < x_0) = 0.341$.

SOLUTION   You need to find x_0 such that $P(X \le x_0) = 0.3410$.

Step 1. Find z_0 such that $P(Z < z_0) = 0.3410$; $z_0 = -0.41$.

Step 2. $x_0 = \mu + z_0\sigma = 25 + (-0.41)(5) = 22.95$

PROBLEM   IQ scores are normally distributed, with mean $\mu = 100$ and standard deviation $\sigma = 15$. Find an IQ score such that 97.5 percent of IQ scores are lower.

SOLUTION   You need to find x_0 such that $P(X \le x_0) = 97.5\% = 0.9750$.

Step 1. Find z_0 such that $P(Z \le z_0) = 0.9750$; $z_0 = 1.96$.

Step 2. $x_0 = \mu + z_0\sigma = 100 + (1.96)(15) = 129.4$

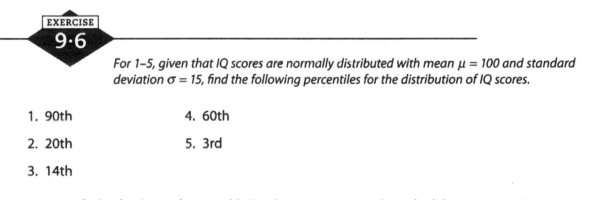

EXERCISE
9·6

For 1–5, given that IQ scores are normally distributed with mean $\mu = 100$ and standard deviation $\sigma = 15$, find the following percentiles for the distribution of IQ scores.

1. 90th   4. 60th

2. 20th   5. 3rd

3. 14th

For 6–10, find x_0 for the random variable X with mean $\mu = 500$ and standard deviation $\sigma = 100$ corresponding to the indicated probability.

6. $P(X < x_0) = 0.8771$

7. $P(X \le x_0) = 0.0124$

8. $P(X \le x_0) = 0.9936$

9. $P(X < x_0) = 0.025$

10. $P(X \le x_0) = 0.881$

11. Suppose that scores on a national exam are normally distributed with mean $\mu = 500$ and standard deviation $\sigma = 100$. Ninety percent of test takers will score less than what score on the exam?

12. A local deli chain makes a signature sandwich. Suppose that the amount of fat grams in the signature sandwich is a normally distributed random variable with mean $\mu = 16$ grams and standard deviation $\sigma = 1.5$ grams. Find an amount of fat grams such that 50 percent of the sandwiches have no more than that many fat grams.

13. A plumbing company has found that the length of time, in minutes, for installing a bathtub is normally distributed with mean $\mu = 160$ minutes and standard deviation $\sigma = 25$ minutes. Eighty percent of the bathtubs are installed by the company within how many minutes?

14. The weights of newborn baby girls born at a local hospital are normally distributed with mean $\mu = 100$ ounces and standard deviation $\sigma = 8$ ounces. Find the weight for a newborn baby girl born at the local hospital at which 25 percent of the newborn baby girls weigh less.

15. The lifetime for a certain brand of incandescent light bulbs is normally distributed with a mean lifetime of 480 hours and standard deviation of 40 hours. Find a lifetime for this brand of incandescent light bulbs at which the probability is 0.9505 that a randomly selected incandescent light bulb of this brand will last at least that long.

·IV·

BASIC INFERENTIAL STATISTICS

Part IV presents basic procedures used in inferential statistics. **Inferential statistics** is the branch of statistics wherein you use sample data to make informed decisions about a population. For instance, a university recruiter might want to estimate the mean SAT Reasoning Test mathematics section (SAT math) score of students who have enrolled in the recruiter's university in the past five years. The **population** is the set of all persons or things of interest to you. A **sample** is a subset of the population. For example, the university recruiter might look at a sample of 25 SAT math scores from the population of SAT math scores of all students who have enrolled in the recruiter's university in the past five years. Numerical descriptions of a population are called **parameters**. The mean SAT math score of all students who have enrolled in the recruiter's university in the past five years is a population parameter. Numerical descriptions of a sample are called **statistics**. The mean SAT math score of the 25 students in the sample is a sample statistic.

When you find it is impractical or impossible to obtain the value of parameters directly from an entire population, you collect the corresponding statistics from **a random sample** of the population. You use a random sample so that it will be representative of the population from which it is selected and, therefore, provide meaningful results. The powerful techniques of inferential statistics allow you to take the sample data and draw conclusions about the entire population based on the data from the sample. Of course, a degree of uncertainty is involved because your data is not from the entire population. Fortunately, the degree of uncertainty is measurable and can be expressed numerically using statistical formulas.

Estimation

·10·

Estimation is the statistical process in which sample statistics are used to estimate population parameters. In this chapter, the central limit theorem and confidence intervals for estimating unknown population parameters are discussed and explained.

The central limit theorem

When you sample from a population, the numerical value of the mean of the sample is a random variable $\bar{X}$ that estimates the population mean. The value of $\bar{X}$ will vary because the sample data varies from sample to sample. Like all random variables, $\bar{X}$ has a probability distribution. This distribution is called the **sampling distribution** of $\bar{X}$. It is the distribution of the means of all the possible samples of a given size that can be drawn from the population.

The **central limit theorem** states that when sampling repeatedly from a population with mean μ and finite standard deviation σ using a fixed sample size n, the sampling distribution of $\bar{X}$ will approach a normal distribution with mean μ and standard deviation $\dfrac{\sigma}{\sqrt{n}}$ (called the **standard error** of $\bar{X}$) as the sample size n becomes large (generally, for the central limit theorem to apply, a sample of at least 30 is considered large enough; that is, $n \geq 30$).

Some important points to keep in mind about the central limit theorem are the following:

1. Two distributions are involved in the statement of the central limit theorem: (1) the distribution of the population that is being sampled and (2) the sampling distribution of $\bar{X}$.

2. Usually you do not know whether the distribution of the population is or is not normally distributed.

3. The central limit theorem is noteworthy because it states that if the sample size is large enough ($n \geq 30$), the sampling distribution of $\bar{X}$ is approximately normal, *regardless* of the distribution of the population.

4. The mean of all the sample means is μ, the population mean.

5. The standard deviation of all the sample means is $\dfrac{\sigma}{\sqrt{n}}$, the population standard deviation divided by the square root of the sample size.

6. The sampling distribution of $\overline{X}$ is a theoretical concept, meaning that in practice, *only one sample is taken and one sample mean is calculated.*

It is important to note that if the population itself has a *normal* distribution, then the sampling distribution of $\overline{X}$ is *normal for any sample size n.*

PROBLEM A random sample of size $n = 49$ is obtained from a population with $\mu = 75$ and $\sigma = 14$. Describe the sampling distribution of $\overline{X}$ in terms of its shape, mean, and standard deviation.

SOLUTION Because the sample size $n = 49$ is large (≥ 30), by the central limit theorem, the sampling distribution of $\overline{X}$ is approximately normal with mean $\mu = 75$ and standard deviation $\dfrac{\sigma}{\sqrt{n}} = \dfrac{14}{\sqrt{49}} = 2$.

The central limit theorem allows you to solve a wide variety of practical problems that deal with sampling using methods that apply to normal distributions.

PROBLEM A random sample of size $n = 49$ is obtained from a population with $\mu = 75$ and $\sigma = 14$. Find the probability that the mean $\overline{x}$ of the sample will be greater than 78.92.

SOLUTION Because the sample size $n = 49$ is large (≥ 30), by the central limit theorem, the random variable $\overline{X}$ has an approximately normal distribution. Therefore, the methods from chapter 9 in the section "Finding Probabilities for a Normally Distributed Random Variable" for dealing with normal distributions can be applied to problems such as this one, which involves the central limit theorem. In that section, you were dealing with an *individual* value from a normally distributed population. You used μ as the mean of the normal random variable X, σ as its standard deviation, and $z = \dfrac{x - \mu}{\sigma}$ as the z-score for a given x value.

Here, you are working with a *mean* from a sample of 49 data values (not just one individual value). By the central limit theorem, you use μ as the mean of the normal distribution associated with the random variable $\overline{X}$, $\dfrac{\sigma}{\sqrt{n}}$ for its standard deviation (not σ), and $z = \dfrac{\overline{x} - \mu}{\sigma/\sqrt{n}}$ as the z-score for a given $\overline{x}$ value. You proceed as follows:

According to the central limit theorem, the distribution of the sample means is approximately normally distributed with mean $\mu = 75$ and standard deviation $\dfrac{\sigma}{\sqrt{n}} = \dfrac{14}{\sqrt{49}} = 2$. Thus, you need to find $P(\overline{X} > 78.92) = P\left(Z > \dfrac{\overline{x} - \mu}{\sigma/\sqrt{n}} \right) =$

$P\left(Z > \dfrac{78.92 - 75}{14/\sqrt{49}} \right) = P\left(Z > \dfrac{78.92 - 75}{2} \right) = P(Z > 1.96) = 1.0000 - 0.9750 = 0.025$.

PROBLEM IQ scores for adults are normally distributed, with mean $\mu = 100$ and standard deviation $\sigma = 15$. If a random sample of 25 adults is selected, find the probability that the mean IQ of the sample will be less than or equal to 94.

SOLUTION   Since the population has a normal distribution, the sampling distribution of $\bar{X}$ has a normal distribution with mean $\mu = 100$ and standard deviation $\dfrac{\sigma}{\sqrt{n}} =$

$\dfrac{15}{\sqrt{25}} = 3$. Thus, you need to find $P(\bar{X} \le 94) = P\left(Z \le \dfrac{\bar{x} - \mu}{\sigma/\sqrt{n}}\right) = P\left(Z \le \dfrac{94 - 100}{15/\sqrt{25}}\right) =$

$P\left(Z \le \dfrac{94 - 100}{3}\right) = P(Z \le -2.00) = 0.0228$

PROBLEM   The lifetime for a certain brand of incandescent light bulbs is normally distributed, with a mean lifetime of 480 hours and standard deviation of 40 hours. What is the probability that a random sample of 10 incandescent light bulbs will have a mean lifetime of at least 500?

SOLUTION   Since the population has a normal distribution, the sampling distribution of $\bar{X}$ has a normal distribution, with mean $\mu = 480$ and standard deviation $\dfrac{\sigma}{\sqrt{n}} = \dfrac{40}{\sqrt{10}} \approx$

12.649. Thus, you need to find $P(\bar{X} \ge 500) = P\left(Z \ge \dfrac{\bar{x} - \mu}{\sigma/\sqrt{n}}\right) = P\left(Z \ge \dfrac{500 - 480}{40/\sqrt{10}}\right) =$

$P(Z > 1.58) = 1.0000 - 0.9429 = 0.0571$

EXERCISE 10·1

For 1–5, describe the sampling distribution of $\bar{X}$ In terms of its shape, mean, and standard deviation.

1. A random sample of size $n = 100$ is obtained from a population with $\mu = 300$ and $\sigma = 50$.

2. A random sample of size $n = 35$ is obtained from a population with $\mu = 60$ and $\sigma = 10$.

3. A random sample of size $n = 9$ is obtained from a normally distributed population with $\mu = 25$ and $\sigma = 6$.

4. A random sample of size $n = 36$ is obtained from a population with $\mu = 30$ and $\sigma = 12$.

5. A random sample of size $n = 225$ is obtained from a population with $\mu = 120$ and $\sigma = 27$.

For 6–15, find the indicated probabilities.

6. A random sample of size $n = 100$ is obtained from a population with $\mu = 300$ and $\sigma = 50$. What is the probability that the sample mean will fall between 299 and 301?

7. A random sample of size $n = 36$ is obtained from a population with $\mu = 60$ and $\sigma = 15$. What is the probability that the sample mean will be at least 58?

8. A random sample of size $n = 9$ is obtained from a normally distributed population with $\mu = 25$ and $\sigma = 6$. What is the probability that the sample mean will exceed 26.7?

9. A random sample of size $n = 36$ is obtained from a population with $\mu = 30$ and $\sigma = 12$. Find the probability that the sample mean will be no more than 26.08.

10. A random sample of size $n = 225$ is obtained from a population with $\mu = 120$ and $\sigma = 27$. Find the probability that the sample mean will lie between 122 and 124.

11. A random sample of size $n = 25$ is obtained from a normally distributed population with $\mu = 120$ and $\sigma = 15$. Find the probability that the sample mean will be no more than 126.

12. A random sample of size $n = 100$ is obtained from a population with $\mu = 1200$ and $\sigma = 250$. Find the probability that the sample mean will lie between 1200 and 1250.

13. IQ scores for adults are normally distributed, with mean $\mu = 100$ and standard deviation $\sigma = 15$. If a random sample of 16 adults is selected, find the probability that the average IQ score in the sample will be at least 92.5.

14. Suppose that scores on a national exam are normally distributed, with mean $\mu = 500$ and standard deviation $\sigma = 100$. If a random sample of 200 test takers is selected, find the probability that the average score of the sample will be between 500 and 520.

15. A local deli chain makes a signature sandwich. Suppose that the amount of fat grams in the signature sandwich are normally distributed, with mean $\mu = 16$ grams and standard deviation $\sigma = 1.5$ grams. If a random sample of four signature sandwiches is selected, find the probability that the average amount of fat grams will be no more than 17 fat grams.

Large-sample confidence interval estimate of μ

A **confidence interval** is a range of values believed to include an unknown population parameter. Associated with the interval is a level of confidence (such as 95 percent) that the interval does indeed contain the parameter of interest. The level of confidence gives the success rate of the process that is used to construct the confidence interval.

A $(1 - \alpha)100\%$ confidence interval for μ when σ is known and sampling is done from a normal population or with a large sample ($n \geq 30$) is given by

$$\bar{x} \pm z_{\alpha/2} \frac{\sigma}{\sqrt{n}} = (\bar{x} - E, \bar{x} + E)$$

where

$(1 - \alpha)$ = the **confidence coefficient**
$(1 - \alpha)100\%$ = the **level of confidence**
α = the **error probability**
$\bar{x}$ = the mean of the sample
σ = the standard deviation of the population
n = the sample size
$z_{\alpha/2}$ = the **critical value** = the z value that cuts off a right-tail area of $\dfrac{\alpha}{2}$ under the standard normal curve; that is, $1 - P\left(Z < z_{\alpha/2}\right) = \alpha/2$

$z_{\alpha/2} \dfrac{\sigma}{\sqrt{n}} = E$, the **margin of error**

Note: When you construct a $(1 - \alpha)100\%$ confidence interval for μ, you can say that you are $(1 - \alpha)100\%$ confident that μ lies between $1 - E$ and $1 + E$.

Confidence coefficients used in real-life applications usually range from .90 to .99. Table 10.1 contains the most commonly used confidence coefficients with corresponding critical values $z_{\alpha/2}$.

Table 10.1 Commonly Used Critical Values $z_{\alpha/2}$

Level of Confidence $(1-\alpha)100\%$	Critical Value $z_{\alpha/2}$
90%	1.645
95%	1.96
99%	2.576

PROBLEM   A bank accountant wants to estimate the average amount in checking accounts at one of the bank's branches. A random sample of 100 accounts at the targeted branch yielded a mean ($\bar{x}$) of $548.40. Assume σ is known to be $120.00. Construct a 95% confidence interval for μ, the average amount in any checking account at the targeted branch.

SOLUTION $\bar{x} \pm z_{\alpha/2} \dfrac{\sigma}{\sqrt{n}} = 548.40 \pm 1.96 \dfrac{120}{\sqrt{100}} = (524.88, 571.92)$

Thus, the accountant can be 95% confident that the average amount in checking accounts at the targeted branch is between $524.88 and $571.92.

PROBLEM   A university recruiter wants to estimate the mean SAT math score of students who have enrolled in the recruiter's university in the past five years. A random sample of 25 students who have enrolled in the recruiter's university in the past five years yielded a mean ($\bar{x}$) SAT math score of 650. Assume that the population of interest is normally distributed with $\sigma = 100$. Construct a 90% confidence interval for μ, the average SAT math score of students at the recruiter's university.

SOLUTION $\bar{x} \pm z_{\alpha/2} \dfrac{\sigma}{\sqrt{n}} = 650 \pm 1.645 \dfrac{100}{\sqrt{25}} = (617.1, 682.9)$

Thus, the recruiter can be 90% confident that the mean SAT math score of students at the recruiter's university is between 617 and 683 (rounded to a whole number).

Seldom in practical situations is the population standard deviation σ known. When the population standard deviation σ is unknown, theoretically, you should use the t distribution (which will be discussed in the next section) when determining E, rather than the normal distribution. However, when $n \geq 30$, you can use the sample standard deviation s as an estimate for σ. Thus, a large-sample $(1 - \alpha)100\%$ confidence interval for μ when σ is unknown is given by

$$\bar{x} \pm z_{\alpha/2} \frac{s}{\sqrt{n}} = (\bar{x} - E, \bar{x} + E)$$

PROBLEM   A consumer agency wants to find a 99% confidence interval about the true average (mean) price of regular gasoline sold at service stations throughout the United States. A random sample of 40 service stations yielded an average (mean) of $2.59 per gallon, with a standard deviation of $0.06. Calculate the interval.

SOLUTION $\bar{x} \pm z_{\alpha/2} \dfrac{s}{\sqrt{n}} = 2.59 \pm 2.576 \dfrac{0.06}{\sqrt{40}} = (2.566, 2.614)$

Thus, the consumer agency can be 99% confident that the true average (mean) price of regular gasoline sold at service stations throughout the United States is between $2.57 and $2.61 per gallon (rounded to the nearest cent).

For 1–5, a random sample of n measurements was selected from a population with unknown mean μ and standard deviation σ. Construct a 95% confidence interval for μ from the information given. Round to two decimal places when needed.

1. $n = 36$, $\bar{x} = 45$, $s = 4.2$

2. $n = 50$, $\bar{x} = 1620$, $s = 215$

3. $n = 200$, $\bar{x} = 105$, $s = 24$

4. $n = 100$, $\bar{x} = 7.8$, $s = 0.5$

5. $n = 75$, $\bar{x} = 412$, $s = 16$

6. A random sample of size $n = 50$ obtained from a population with unknown mean yielded $\bar{x} = 25$. Assume the standard deviation $\sigma = 8$. Construct a 95% confidence interval for μ.

7. A random sample of size $n = 9$ obtained from a normally distributed population with unknown mean μ yielded $\bar{x} = 26.7$. Assume the standard deviation $\sigma = 6$. Construct a 90% confidence interval for μ.

8. A random sample of size $n = 100$ obtained from a population with unknown mean μ and standard deviation σ yielded $\bar{x} = 301$ and $s = 37$. Construct a 90% confidence interval for μ.

9. A random sample of size $n = 36$ obtained from a population with unknown mean μ and standard deviation σ yielded $\bar{x} = 58$ and $s = 15$. Construct a 99% confidence interval for μ.

10. A random sample of size $n = 225$ obtained from a population with unknown mean μ and standard deviation σ yielded $\bar{x} = 123$ and $s = 25$. Construct a 90% confidence interval for μ.

11. A health science center researcher wants to estimate the average amount of fat grams in the signature sandwich of a local deli. A random sample of 40 signature sandwiches yielded $\bar{x} = 17$ fat grams and $s = 2.5$ fat grams. Construct a 95% confidence for the average amount of fat grams in the signature sandwich of the local deli.

12. The fundraising officer for a charity organization wants to estimate the average donation from contributors to the charity. A random sample of 100 donations yielded $\bar{x} = \$234.85$ and $s = \$95.23$. Construct a 90% confidence for the average donation from all contributors to the charity.

13. A manufacturer of car batteries needs to estimate the average life of its batteries. A random sample of 80 batteries had $\bar{x} = 39$ months and $s = 8$ months. Calculate a 95% confidence interval for the average life of the manufacturer's batteries.

14. A study of 500 randomly selected adults in the United States yielded an average of 2400 calories consumed per day, with a standard deviation of 930 calories. Calculate a 95% confidence for the true mean caloric intake of all adults in the United States.

15. A realtor needs to know the average price of a house in a metropolitan area. A random sample of 50 house prices in the metropolitan area yielded $\bar{x} = \$120,000$ and $s = \$47,000$. Give a 95% confidence interval for the average price of a house in the metropolitan area.

Small-sample confidence interval estimate of μ

As discussed in the previous section, when you have a small sample ($n < 30$) from a normally distributed population, you can use the normal distribution when estimating μ with a confidence interval, *provided the population standard deviation σ is known.* However, when you have a small sample ($n < 30$) from a normally distributed population for which σ is *unknown*, instead of using the standard normal distribution, you must use the t distribution when constructing confidence intervals for μ.

Like the normal distribution, the t distribution is symmetric and bell-shaped with mean equal to 0; however, for small sample sizes, it has greater variance than the normal distribution. The actual difference in variance is determined by the **degrees of freedom** parameter, *df*, of the t distribution. For any integer value of $df = 1, 2, 3$, and so on, you have a corresponding t distribution. As the degrees of freedom increases, the variance of the t distribution approaches 1, which is the same as the variance of the normal distribution. Thus, as *df* increases, the t distribution approaches the normal distribution. When you construct a confidence interval for a population mean μ, the degrees of freedom for the appropriate t distribution is the sample size minus one ($df = n - 1$).

To reiterate, the conditions when the t distribution, rather than the normal distribution, should be used are (1) the sample size is small (less than 30); (2) σ is unknown; and (3) the sampled population is normally distributed. Thus, a $(1 - \alpha)100\%$ confidence interval for μ when σ is unknown and sampling is done from a normal population is given by

$$\bar{x} \pm t_{\alpha/2} \frac{s}{\sqrt{n}} = (\bar{x} - E, \bar{x} + E)$$

where

> $\bar{x}$ = the mean of the sample
> s = the standard deviation of the population
> n = the sample size
> $t_{\alpha/2}$ = the critical value = the t value that cuts off a right-tail area of $\frac{\alpha}{2}$ for a t distribution
> with $(n - 1)$ degrees of freedom
> $t_{\alpha/2} \dfrac{s}{\sqrt{n}} = E$, the margin of error

Table C in the Appendix displays $t_{\alpha/2}$ critical values for degrees of freedom 1 to 32, and then shows values for selected degrees of freedom beyond 32. The last row in Table C, which is marked $df = \infty$, corresponds to the standard normal distribution. Because there are infinitely many t distributions (one for each $df = 1, 2, 3, \ldots$), tables for t distributions show only certain points on the t distribution. The entries in the table under "Area in One Tail" give $t_{\alpha/2}$ critical values that correspond to right-tail areas of **.100, .050, .025, .010,** and **.005** (from left to right across the top of Table C). Table 10.2 shows the confidence levels associated with the column headings given in Table C under "Area in One Tail."

Table 10.2 Confidence Levels for "Area in One Tail" $t_{\alpha/2}$ Column Headings in Table C

Level of Confidence $(1 - \alpha)100\%$	Column Heading $t_{\alpha/2}$
80%	$t_{.100}$
90%	$t_{.050}$
95%	$t_{.025}$
98%	$t_{.010}$
99%	$t_{.005}$

Notice that in Table 10.2 if you subtract 2 times the subscript on $t_{\alpha/2}$ from 1 and then multiply by 100%, you obtain the level of confidence for $t_{\alpha/2}$. For instance, for $t_{.100}$, you have $(1-2(.100))100\% = (1-.200)100\% = (.80)100\% = 80\%$.

Part of Table C is reproduced in Table 10.3.

Table 10.3 Critical Values of t for Selected Values of n and $t_{\alpha/2}$

			Area in One Tail		
	$t_{.100}$	$t_{.050}$	$t_{.025}$	$t_{.010}$	$t_{.005}$
			Area in Two Tails		
d.f.	$t_{.200}$	$t_{.100}$	$t_{.050}$	$t_{.020}$	$t_{.010}$
1	3.073	6.314	12.706	31.821	63.657
2	1.886	2.920	4.303	6.965	9.925
3	1.638	2.353	3.128	4.541	5.841
4	1.533	2.132	2.776	3.747	4.604
5	1.476	2.015	2.571	3.365	4.032
6	1.440	1.943	2.447	3.143	3.707
7	1.415	1.895	2.365	2.998	3.499
8	1.397	1.860	2.308	2.896	3.355
9	1.383	1.833	2.262	2.821	3.250
10	1.372	1.812	2.228	2.764	3.169

To use Table C, first read down the column labeled *d.f.* to locate $df = n - 1$. Now read across that row to the $t_{\alpha/2}$ column corresponding to the desired level of confidence. For example, to find the critical value $t_{\alpha/2}$ for $n = 10$ and a 95% level of confidence, you read down the *d.f.* column to the row for 9 *df*, and then you read across to the $t_{.025}$ (95% level of confidence) column under "Area in One Tail" to obtain the critical value 2.262.

PROBLEM   A random sample of size $n = 10$ obtained from a normally distributed population with unknown mean μ and standard deviation σ yielded $\bar{x} = 26.7$ and $s = 5.8$. Construct a 95% confidence interval for μ.

SOLUTION $\bar{x} \pm t_{\alpha/2} \dfrac{s}{\sqrt{n}} = 26.7 \pm 2.262 \dfrac{5.8}{\sqrt{10}} = (22.55, 30.85)$

Thus, you can be 95% confident that μ lies between 22.6 and 30.9 (rounded to tenths).

Note that for small samples, whether σ is known or unknown, you can construct confidence intervals for μ using basic statistical methods *only* if you can reasonably assume that the sampled population is normally distributed.

For 1–3, suppose you have obtained a random sample of n = 15 measurements from a normally distributed population. Compare $t_{\alpha/2}$ with $z_{\alpha/2}$ if you were to form a confidence interval at the indicated level of confidence.

1. 90% confidence interval

2. 95% confidence interval

3. 99% confidence interval

For 4–10, a random sample of n measurements obtained from a normally distributed population yielded $\bar{x} = 450$ and s = 60. Construct a confidence interval for μ at the indicated level of confidence.

4. 80% confidence interval, n = 16

5. 90% confidence interval, n = 9

6. 90% confidence interval, n = 25

7. 95% confidence interval, n = 4

8. 95% confidence interval, n = 25

9. 98% confidence interval, n = 25

10. 99% confidence interval, n = 25

11. Suppose that scores on a standardized exam are normally distributed. To estimate the average score on the exam for all test takers, a researcher obtains a random sample of 25 scores. The sample yielded $\bar{x} = 480$ and s = 75. Give a 95% confidence interval for the average score on the exam for all test takers.

12. A local deli chain advertises a "heart healthy" sandwich on the menu. Suppose that the amount of fat grams in a "heart healthy" sandwich is a normal random variable. To estimate the average amount of fat grams in "heart healthy" sandwiches, a nutritionist selects a random sample of four "heart healthy" sandwiches. The sample yielded $\bar{x} = 11$ grams and s = 1.8 grams. Construct a 90% confidence interval for the average amount of fat grams in a "heart healthy" sandwich.

13. A plumbing company has found that the length of time, in minutes, for installing a bathtub is normally distributed. The owner of the company hires a statistician to estimate the average length of time for installing a bathtub by his company. The statistician randomly selects a sample of 10 bathtub installations. The sample yielded $\bar{x} = 150$ minutes and s = 30 minutes. Construct a 95% confidence interval for the average length of time for installing a bathtub by the company.

14. The weights of newborn baby girls born at a local hospital are normally distributed. A hospital administrator conducts a study to estimate the mean weight of all newborn baby girls born at the local hospital. A random sample of size n = 20 had a mean weight of 95 ounces and a standard deviation of 8 ounces. Calculate a 99% confidence interval for the mean weight of all newborn baby girls born at the local hospital.

15. The lifetime for a certain brand of incandescent light bulbs is normally distributed. A random sample of five of these light bulbs had a mean lifetime of 520 hours and standard deviation of 50 hours. Give a 95% confidence interval for the mean lifetime of all incandescent light bulbs of this brand.

Large-sample confidence interval estimate of p

An **attribute** is a characteristic that a person or thing either does or does not possess. Attributes are measured as the **proportion** of the population with the characteristic in question. For example, a person might have the characteristic of agreeing that the president is handling domestic affairs well, a person might have the characteristic of being a smoker, or a battery might have the characteristic of being defective, and so on.

A $(1 - \alpha)100\%$ confidence interval for p, the proportion (or percentage) in the population with a certain characteristic is given by

$$\hat{p} \pm z_{\alpha/2} \sqrt{\frac{\hat{p}\hat{q}}{n}} = (\hat{p} - E, \hat{p} + E)$$

where

$\hat{p}$ = the **proportion in a random sample** with the characteristic of interest

$\hat{q} = 1 - \hat{p}$

$z_{\alpha/2}$ = the critical value corresponding to a $(1 - \alpha)100\%$ confidence interval

Note: This is the same $z_{\alpha/2}$ as seen in the section "Large-sample confidence interval estimate of μ."

$z_{\alpha/2} \sqrt{\frac{\hat{p}\hat{q}}{n}} = E$, the margin of error

Note: The above formula requires that the sample size be sufficiently large. A general rule of thumb is that both $n\hat{p}$ and $n(1 - \hat{p})$ are greater than or equal to 5. You can usually verify that this requirement is met by doing a quick rough mental calculation.

PROBLEM   In a random survey of 1000 U.S. citizens, 57.5 percent of the respondents agree that the President is handling domestic affairs well.
(a) Construct a 95% confidence interval for the proportion of all U.S. citizens who agree the President is handling domestic affairs well. Express your results as percents (to the nearest tenth of a percent).
(b) Give the margin of error E for the 95% confidence interval.

SOLUTION   (a) $\hat{p} \pm z_{\alpha/2} \sqrt{\frac{\hat{p}\hat{q}}{n}} = 0.575 \pm 1.96 \sqrt{\frac{(0.575)(0.425)}{1000}} = (0.544, 0.606)$

Thus, with 95% confidence the percent of all U.S. citizens who agree the President is handling domestic affairs well is between 54.4% and 60.6%.

(b) $E = z_{\alpha/2} \sqrt{\frac{\hat{p}\hat{q}}{n}} = 1.96 \sqrt{\frac{(0.575)(0.425)}{1000}} = 0.0306 \approx 3\%$ margin of error

PROBLEM   In a random survey of 1000 U.S. college students, 220 identified themselves as smokers. Construct a 90% confidence interval for the proportion of all U.S. college students who would identify themselves as smokers.

SOLUTION $\hat{p} = \frac{220}{1000} = 0.22$

$\hat{p} \pm z_{\alpha/2} \sqrt{\frac{\hat{p}\hat{q}}{n}} = 0.22 \pm 1.645 \sqrt{\frac{(0.22)(0.78)}{1000}} = (0.199, 0.242)$

Thus, with 90% confidence the proportion of all U.S. college students who would identify themselves as smokers lies between 0.199 and 0.242 (rounded to three decimal places).

For 1–5, for the given value of $\hat{p}$, determine whether the stated sample size n is large enough (both $n\hat{p}$ and $n(1-\hat{p})$ are greater than or equal to 5) to use the methods of this section to construct a confidence interval for p.

1. $n = 200, \hat{p} = 0.2$

2. $n = 20, \hat{p} = 0.2$

3. $n = 100, \hat{p} = 0.03$

4. $n = 15, \hat{p} = 0.6$

5. $n = 150, \hat{p} = 0.01$

For 6–10, use the sample data and confidence level to construct the confidence interval estimate of the population proportion p.

6. $n = 200, \hat{p} = 0.2, 90\%$

7. $n = 100, \hat{p} = 0.45, 99\%$

8. $n = 1500, \hat{p} = 0.03, 95\%$

9. $n = 15, \hat{p} = 0.6, 90\%$

10. $n = 1000, \hat{p} = 0.82, 95\%$

11. A random check of 500 batteries manufactured by a company found 15 defective batteries.
    (a) Construct a 95% confidence interval for the proportion of all batteries manufactured by the company that are defective.
    (b) Give the margin of error E for the 95% confidence interval.

12. Assume a study revealed that from a sample of 80 working women in a metropolitan area, 12 were over the age of 60.
    (a) Construct a 99% confidence interval for the true proportion of working women over the age of 60 in the metropolitan area.
    (b) Give the margin of error E for the 99% confidence interval.

13. A radio station advertising manager needs to know the proportion of radio listeners in the area who listen to the manager's radio station. Suppose that a random sample of 100 radio listeners in the area revealed that 34 listen to the manager's station.
    (a) Construct a 90% confidence interval for the proportion of radio listeners in the area who listen to the manager's radio station.
    (b) Give the margin of error E for the 90% confidence interval.

14. An interior designer needs to know the proportion of assisted living residents who prefer a blue hue on bedroom walls. A random survey of 300 assisted living residents revealed that 240 prefer a blue hue on bedroom walls.
    (a) Construct a 95% confidence interval for the proportion of all assisted living residents who prefer a blue hue on bedroom walls.
    (b) Give the margin of error E for the 95% confidence interval.

15. A market researcher wants to know the percent of households in a rural area that have no vehicle. In a random sample of 120 households, 6 households had no vehicle.
    (a) Construct a 90% confidence interval for the percent of households in the rural area that have no vehicle.
    (b) Give the margin of error E for the 90% confidence interval.

Sample size determination

An important question to ask yourself when you want to estimate a population parameter using a confidence interval is, "What size sample should I use?" Generally, larger samples will yield more accurate results than will smaller samples, so you should try to take as large a sample as you reasonably can. Nevertheless, limitations such as time and money constraints can make this goal unrealistic, so the question frequently becomes, "What is the minimum sample size that is needed?" This section presents ways to answer that question when you are estimating a population mean or a population proportion.

The minimum required sample size for a $(1 - \alpha)100\%$ confidence interval estimate of the population mean μ is given by

$$n = \left(\frac{z_{\alpha/2} \cdot \sigma}{E}\right)^2$$ (rounded *up* to the nearest whole number if the computed value is not

a whole number)

where

n = the minimum sample size

$z_{\alpha/2}$ = the critical value corresponding to a $(1 - \alpha)100\%$ level of confidence

E = the desired margin of error

Note: In practice, you will seldom know the true value of σ, so you will have to make an educated guess using prior information.

PROBLEM   A consumer agency wants to estimate the true average price per gallon of regular gasoline sold at service stations throughout the United States to within $0.025 with 99% confidence. From past data, an estimate of the population standard deviation is σ = $0.06. Find the minimum sample size required.

SOLUTION $$n = \left(\frac{z_{\alpha/2} \cdot \sigma}{E}\right)^2 = \left(\frac{2.576 \cdot 0.06}{0.025}\right)^2 = 38.222$$

Therefore, the minimum required sample size is 39.

The minimum required sample size for a $(1 - \alpha)100\%$ confidence interval estimate of the population proportion p is given by

$$n = \frac{z_{\alpha/2}^2 \cdot pq}{E^2}$$ (rounded *up* to the nearest whole number if the computed

value is not a whole number)

Note: To use the formula, you will need to make an educated guess of p, the population proportion. You can use any prior estimate of p. When no reliable prior estimate is available, use the value $p = 0.5$.

PROBLEM   A pollster wants to conduct a random survey to estimate the proportion of U.S. citizens who think that the President is doing his job well within a margin of error $E = 0.03$ ("3 percentage points") with 95 percent confidence. If a prior survey suggested that $p = 0.523$, find the minimum required sample size for the pollster's survey.

SOLUTION $n = \dfrac{z^2_{\alpha/2} \cdot pq}{E^2} = \dfrac{(1.96)^2(.523)(.477)}{(0.03)^2} = 1064.853$

Thus, the minimum required sample size is 1065.

PROBLEM   A national health organization wants to conduct a study to determine the proportion of U.S. college students who are smokers. The organization wants to know the population proportion p to within 0.02 with 90% confidence. If no prior information is available, find the minimum required sample size for this study.

SOLUTION $n = \dfrac{z^2_{\alpha/2} \cdot pq}{E^2} = \dfrac{(1.645)^2(.5)(.5)}{(0.02)^2} = 1691.266$

Thus, the minimum required sample size is 1692.

EXERCISE 10·5

For 1–5, find the sample size necessary to estimate the population mean μ to within the indicated margin of error E with 95% confidence, given that prior data suggest that σ is the given value.

1. $E = 2, \sigma = 10$

2. $E = 2, \sigma = 100$

3. $E = 0.2, \sigma = 100$

4. $E = 1.5, \sigma = 5$

5. $E = 0.15, \sigma = 5$

For 6–10, find the sample size necessary to estimate the population proportion p to within the indicated margin of error E with 95% confidence, given that prior data suggest that p has the given value.

6. $E = 0.02, p = 0.1$

7. $E = 0.02, p = 0.2$

8. $E = 0.02, p = 0.5$

9. $E = 0.02, p = 0.7$

10. $E = 0.02, p = 0.9$

11. A health professional wants to estimate the birth weights of infants. A previous study indicates that the standard deviation of infant birth weights is 7.6 ounces. What size sample is necessary if the health professional wants to estimate the true mean birth weights of infants to within 1.5 ounces with 99% confidence?

12. A pollster wants to conduct a random survey to estimate the proportion of U.S. citizens who favor a certain Presidential candidate within a margin of error $E = 0.04$ ("4 percentage points") with 95% confidence. If no prior information is available, find the minimum required sample size for the pollster's survey.

13. A manufacturer of car batteries needs to estimate the average life of its batteries. Prior data indicate that the standard deviation of the population of batteries is approximately eight months. What size sample is necessary if the manufacturer wants to estimate the true average life of its car batteries within two months with 90% confidence?

14. The fundraising officer for a charity organization wants to estimate the average donation from contributors to the charity. Prior data indicate that the standard deviation of charitable contributions to the organization is approximately $95. What size sample is necessary if the fundraising officer wants to estimate the true average donation from all contributors to the charity within $20 with 95% confidence?

15. A quality control inspector for a company that makes cell phones needs to estimate the proportion of defective cell phones produced by the company. The quality control inspector estimates that the proportion defective is about 0.1, corresponding to 10% defective. How many of the company's cell phones should be sampled and checked in order to estimate the proportion of defective cell phones to within 0.01 with 90% confidence?

Hypothesis testing

Hypothesis testing is a procedure for making a decision when you have competing hypotheses about a population parameter. In this chapter you are introduced to the concepts and techniques of hypothesis testing, a powerful tool of statistical inference that is used extensively in the real world. Statistical tests of hypotheses using z and t distributions are presented.

Formulating hypotheses

A **hypothesis** is an assertion about one or more population parameters. In this chapter your hypotheses will be concerned with only one population parameter: the population mean μ or the population proportion p. The hypothesis testing you will be conducting will have two hypotheses: H_0, called the **null hypothesis**, and H_a, called the **alternative hypothesis**.

In a test of hypothesis, you actually test only H_0. H_0 is called the null hypothesis because, in most situations, it is the hypothesis you hope to nullify. Nevertheless, it is the hypothesis you must hold true until you have sufficient evidence to conclude otherwise. The alternative hypothesis, H_a, is the hypothesis that you (normally) favor. In order to reach a decision, you collect sample data, analyze the data using a well-defined statistical process, and then draw a conclusion about whether to reject or fail to reject H_0. If the decision is to reject H_0, you can accept H_a. If you fail to reject H_0, your sample did not provide sufficient evidence to support H_a.

Formulating the null and alternative hypotheses is a challenging part of a test of a hypothesis. One very important guideline is that *no information from the sample* is used in the hypotheses statements. Another helpful guideline is that the *null hypothesis always contains equality*: $=$, $\leq$, or $\geq$.

You begin by identifying in the problem an assertion about the population parameter and then translating the assertion into symbolism. Next, you write the negation of this first assertion. Finally, you specify H_0 as the assertion containing equality and H_a as the remaining assertion. If H_a contains a "$\neq$" symbol, the hypothesis test is called a **two-tailed test**; if H_a contains a "$>$" symbol, the hypothesis test is called a **right-tailed test**; and if H_a contains a "$<$" symbol, the hypothesis test is called a **left-tailed test**.

PROBLEM   Suppose that an airline company claims that the average weight of checked baggage is less than 15 pounds. To support the claim, the airline company conducts a random sample of 150 passengers and finds that the average weight of checked baggage is 14.2 pounds, with a standard deviation of 6.5 pounds. Do these data indicate that the average weight of checked baggage is less than 15 pounds? State the null and alternative hypotheses for this problem, and then state whether the test of hypothesis will be a two-tailed test, a right-tailed test, or a left-tailed test.

SOLUTION The first sentence contains an assertion about the population parameter: "the average weight of checked baggage is less than 15 pounds." In symbols, you write "the average weight of checked baggage is less than 15 pounds" as $\mu < 15$. You write the negation of this assertion as $\mu \geq 15$. Therefore, because H_0 always contains equality, your statements of hypotheses are the following:

$H_0: \mu \geq 15$

$H_a: \mu < 15$

Since H_a contains a "<" symbol, the hypothesis test will be a left-tailed test.

Caution: The second sentence, "To support the claim, the airline company conducts a random sample of 150 passengers and finds that the average weight of checked baggage is 14.2 pounds, with a standard deviation of 6.5 pounds," contains information about the sample, so you cannot use any values from that sentence when formulating the hypotheses.

PROBLEM The lifetime for a certain brand of incandescent light bulbs is normally distributed. A consumer group conducts a random sample of 25 incandescent light bulbs of this certain brand and finds a sample mean lifetime of 520 hours and standard deviation of 50 hours. Prior to taking the sample, the consumer group conjectured that the mean lifetime of all incandescent light bulbs of this brand is no more than 500 hours. State the null and alternative hypotheses for this problem, and then state whether the test of hypothesis will be a two-tailed test, a right-tailed test, or a left-tailed test.

SOLUTION The third sentence contains an assertion about the population parameter: "the mean lifetime of all incandescent light bulbs of this brand is no more than 500 hours." In symbols, you write "the mean lifetime of all incandescent light bulbs of this brand is no more than 500 hours" as $\mu \leq 500$. You write the negation of this statement as $\mu > 500$. Therefore, because H_0 always contains equality, your statements of hypotheses are the following:

$H_0: \mu \leq 500$

$H_a: \mu > 500$

Since H_a contains a ">" symbol, the hypothesis test will be a right-tailed test.

Caution: The second sentence, "A consumer group conducts a random sample of 25 incandescent light bulbs of this certain brand and finds a sample mean lifetime of 520 hours and standard deviation of 50 hours," contains information about the sample, so you cannot use any values from that sentence when formulating the hypotheses.

PROBLEM Suppose that a campaign manager claims that the percent of registered voters who prefer his candidate is 60 percent. A pollster conducts a random survey of 500 registered voters to test the campaign manager's claim and finds that 58 percent of the sample of registered voters preferred the campaign manager's candidate. State the null and alternative hypotheses for this problem, and then state whether the test of hypothesis will be a two-tailed test, a right-tailed test, or a left-tailed test.

SOLUTION   The first sentence contains an assertion about the population parameter: "the percent of registered voters who prefer his candidate is 60 percent." In symbols, you write "the percent of registered voters who prefer his candidate is 60 percent" as $p = 0.60$. You write the negation of this assertion as $p \neq 0.60$. Therefore, because H_0 always contains equality, your statements of hypotheses are the following:

$H_0: p = 0.60$

$H_a: p \neq 0.60$

Since H_a contains a "$\neq$" symbol, the hypothesis test will be a two-tailed test.

Caution: The second sentence, "A pollster conducts a random survey of 500 registered voters to test the campaign manager's claim and finds that 58 percent of the sample of registered voters preferred the campaign manager's candidate," contains information about the sample, so you cannot use any values from that sentence when formulating the hypotheses.

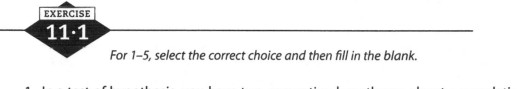

EXERCISE
11·1

For 1–5, select the correct choice and then fill in the blank.

1. In a test of hypothesis, you have two competing hypotheses about a population _____ (parameter, statistic).

2. In a test of hypothesis, you actually test only the _____ (alternative, null) hypothesis.

3. A very important guideline for formulating the hypotheses for a test of hypothesis is that no information from the _____ (population, sample) is used in the hypotheses statements.

4. A helpful guideline for formulating the hypotheses for a test of hypothesis is that the null hypothesis *always* contains _____ (equality, inequality).

5. If H_a contains a "$\neq$" symbol, the hypothesis test is called a _____ (two-tailed, right-tailed, left-tailed) test of hypothesis.

For 6–15, (a) state the null and alternative hypotheses and (b) state whether the test of hypothesis will be a two-tailed test, a right-tailed test, or a left-tailed test.

6. The fundraising officer for a charity organization claims the average donation from contributors to the charity is $250.00. To test the claim, a random sample of 100 donations is obtained. The sample yielded $\bar{x} = \$234.85$ and $s = \$95.23$.

7. A manufacturer of car batteries claims the average life of its batteries is at least 45 months. A random sample of 80 batteries had $\bar{x} = 39$ months and $s = 8$ months. Do these data dispute the manufacturer's claim?

8. A study of 500 randomly selected adults in the United States yielded an average of 2400 calories consumed per day, with a standard deviation of 930 calories. Prior to the study, the claim was made that the true mean caloric intake of all adults in the United States is no more than 2300 calories per day. Test the claim.

9. A local deli chain advertises that its "heart healthy" sandwich has only 10 fat grams. Suppose that the amount of fat grams in a "heart healthy" sandwich is a normal random variable. To test the deli chain's claim, a nutritionist selects a random sample of four "heart healthy" sandwiches. The sample yielded $\bar{x} = 11$ grams and $s = 1.8$ grams.

10. A realtor's newsletter lists the average price of a house in a metropolitan area as $100,000. A random sample of 50 house prices in the metropolitan area yielded $\bar{x} = \$120,000$ and $s = \$47,000$. Do these data dispute the listing in the realtor's newsletter?

11. The weights of newborn baby girls born at a local hospital are normally distributed. A hospital administrator speculates that the mean weight of newborn baby girls born at the hospital is greater than 90 ounces. A random sample of size $n = 20$ had a mean weight of 95 ounces and a standard deviation of 8 ounces. Do these data indicate that the mean weight of all newborn baby girls born at the local hospital is greater than 90 ounces?

12. A random check of 500 batteries manufactured by a company found 15 defective batteries. Quality control guidelines established by the manufacturer require that the proportion of all batteries manufactured by the company that are defective must be less than 0.05. With regard to quality control guidelines, will the manufacturer be satisfied with the results of a test of hypothesis based on the sample data?

13. Assume a study revealed that from a sample of 80 working women in a metropolitan area, 30 were over the age of 60. Do these data dispute a claim made prior to the study that the true proportion of working women over the age of 60 in the metropolitan area is no more than 0.18?

14. A radio station advertising manager wants to test the hypothesis that the percent of radio listeners in the area who listen to the manager's radio station is at least 40 percent. Suppose that a random sample of 100 radio listeners in the area revealed that 34 listen to the manager's station.

15. An interior designer believes that the proportion of assisted living residents who would prefer a blue hue on bedroom walls is greater than 0.75. A random survey of 300 assisted living residents revealed that 240 prefer a blue hue on bedroom walls. Do these data support the interior designer's belief?

Type I and Type II errors

The point of a hypothesis test is to make the correct decision about H_0. Unfortunately, hypothesis testing is not a simple matter of being right or wrong. A test of hypothesis is based on probability, so there is always a chance that an error has been made. In fact, you have two ways of making an error. You will make a **Type I error** if you reject H_0 and accept H_a when in fact H_0 is the correct choice. You will make a **Type II error** if you accept H_0 when in fact H_0 is the wrong choice, and, thus, H_a is the correct choice.

PROBLEM   Suppose that unknown to you, the reality of the following hypotheses are as shown:

H_0: $\mu \geq 15$ False
H_a: $\mu < 15$ True

You decide to accept H_0. Have you made an error? If so, what type of error did you make?

SOLUTION   Yes, you made the error of accepting H_0 when it is false. This error is called a Type II error.

PROBLEM   Suppose that unknown to you, the reality of the following hypotheses are as shown:

H_0: $\mu \leq 500$ False
H_a: $\mu > 500$ True

You decide to reject H_0 and accept H_a. Have you made an error? If so, what type of error did you make?

SOLUTION   No error was made. You decided to reject H_0 when it is false.

PROBLEM   Suppose that unknown to you, the reality of the following hypotheses are as shown:

H_0: $p = 0.60$ True

H_a: $p \neq 0.60$ False

You decide to reject H_0 and accept H_a. Have you made an error? If so, what type of error did you make?

SOLUTION   Yes, you made the error of rejecting H_0 when it is true. This error is called a Type I error.

The hypothesis test is designed to have a specified Type I error probability denoted α (alpha), which is called the **level of significance** of the test. When you begin your test of hypothesis (before you collect your sample data), you set the level of significance α to a small number: usually .05 or .01. The probability of making a Type II error is denoted β (beta). The probability of making a Type I error and the probability of making a Type II error are inversely related for a fixed sample size: Usually, as α is increased, β is decreased, and conversely. Therefore, α cannot be arbitrarily small, since β likely will then become large.

As you can see, the process of hypothesis testing allows you to control the risk of a Type I error because you set the value for α. However, (ordinarily) you do not have the same control over the risk of a Type II error, which is accepting a false null hypothesis. For this reason, it is best to avoid making Type II errors. Rather than "accepting" H_0 when the sample data fail to provide sufficient evidence to overturn H_0, you should simply "fail to reject" H_0. Thus, the test of hypothesis will be inconclusive.

EXERCISE
11·2

For 1–5, select the correct choice and then fill in the blank.

1. The point of a hypothesis test is to make the correct decision about _____ (H_0, H_a).

2. The mistake of rejecting H_0 and accepting H_a when in fact H_0 is the correct choice is called a _____ (Type I, Type II) error.

3. The mistake of accepting H_0 when in fact H_a is the correct choice is called a _____ (Type I, Type II) error.

4. The probability of making a Type I error is denoted _____ (α, β).

5. The probability of making a Type II error is denoted _____ (α, β).

In 6–10, respond to the questions posed.

6. Suppose that unknown to you, the reality of the following hypotheses are as shown:

H_0: $\mu \geq 20$ False

H_a: $\mu < 20$ True

You decide to accept H_0. Have you made an error? If so, what type of error did you make?

7. Suppose that unknown to you, the reality of the following hypotheses are as shown:

H_0: $\mu \leq 30$ False

H_a: $\mu > 30$ True

You decide to reject H_0 and accept H_a. Have you made an error? If so, what type of error did you make?

8. Suppose that unknown to you, the reality of the following hypotheses are as shown:

$H_0: p = 0.75$ True

$H_a: p \neq 0.75$ False

You decide to reject H_0 and accept H_a. Have you made an error? If so, what type of error did you make?

9. Suppose that unknown to you, the reality of the following hypotheses are as shown:

$H_0: p \leq 0.10$ False

$H_a: p > 0.10$ True

You decide to accept H_0. Have you made an error? If so, what type of error did you make?

10. Suppose that unknown to you, the reality of the following hypotheses are as shown:

$H_0: p \leq 0.10$ False

$H_a: p > 0.10$ True

Your decision is to fail to reject H_0 and consider the test inconclusive. Have you made an error? If so, what type of error did you make?

Steps for a test of hypothesis

In a manner parallel to that used in forming confidence intervals, hypothesis testing uses statistical theory about sampling distributions to formulate the hypothesis testing procedure. For hypothesis tests regarding the population mean μ, you use the z distribution when the sample size is large ($n \geq 30$), and you use the t distribution when the sample size is small ($n < 30$) *provided that the sampled population is normally distributed*. For hypothesis tests regarding the population proportion p, you used the z distribution, provided the sample size is sufficiently large (both np and $n(1 - p)$ are greater than 5).

The steps for a test of hypothesis are the following:

1. **State the hypotheses:** H_0 and H_a.

2. **Select the significance level:** α.

3. **State the decision rule:** a rule that specifies the conditions under which H_0 should be rejected. The decision rule is based on **critical points**, which are determined by α, the level of significance, and the sampling distribution of the statistic that is relevant to the test. One or more critical point defines a **rejection region**, the range of values for the test statistic for which you will reject the null hypothesis.

4. **Compute the test statistic (*T.S.*):** a statistic computed from the sample data. The value of the test statistic is used to determine whether to reject or fail to reject H_0.

5. **Make a decision:** the decision to reject H_0 and accept H_a or the decision to fail to reject H_0.

6. **State a conclusion:** an interpretation of the decision in the context of the problem.

The steps for a test of hypothesis will be further clarified and illustrated in the subsequent sections of this chapter.

Select the correct choice and then fill in the blank.

1. For hypothesis tests regarding the population mean μ, you use the _____ (z, t) distribution when the sample size is large.

2. For hypothesis tests regarding the population mean μ, you use the _____ (z, t) distribution when the sample size is small, *provided the sampled population is normally distributed.*

3. For hypothesis tests regarding the population proportion p, you use the _____ (z, t) distribution, provided the sample size is sufficiently large.

4. The decision rule for a test of hypothesis is a rule that specifies the conditions under which _____ (H_0, H_a) should be rejected.

5. The test statistic is a statistic computed from the _____ (population, sample) data.

Large-sample hypothesis test for μ

The steps for a large-sample ($n \geq 30$) hypothesis test for μ are the following:

1. **State the hypotheses:**

Two-Tailed Test	Right-Tailed Test	Left-Tailed Test
$H_0: \mu = \mu_0$ $H_a: \mu \neq \mu_0$	$H_0: \mu \leq \mu_0$ $H_a: \mu > \mu_0$	$H_0: \mu \geq \mu_0$ $H_a: \mu < \mu_0$

Note: μ_0 is the null-hypothesized value for the population parameter μ.

2. **Select the significance level:** α (commonly $\alpha = .05$ or $.01$).

3. **State the decision rule:**

Two-Tailed Test	Right-Tailed Test	Left-Tailed Test
Reject H_0 if either $z < -z_{\alpha/2}$ or $z > z_{\alpha/2}$, where $z_{\alpha/2}$ is the z value that cuts off a right-tail area of $\alpha/2$ under the standard normal curve. for $\alpha = .05$, $z_{\alpha/2} = 1.96$; for $\alpha = .01$, $z_{\alpha/2} = 2.576$. For other values of α, $z_{\alpha/2}$ is the $\left(1 - \alpha/2\right)$th percentile* for the standard normal distribution.	Reject H_0 if $z > z_\alpha$, where z_α is the z value that cuts off a right-tail area of α under the standard normal curve. For $\alpha = .05$, $z_\alpha = 1.645$; for $\alpha = .01$, $z_\alpha = 2.33$. For other values of α, z_α is the z value that is the $(1 - \alpha)$th percentile for the standard normal distribution.	Reject H_0 if $z < -z_\alpha$, where z_α is the z value that cuts off a right-tail area of α under the standard normal curve. For $\alpha = .05$, $z_\alpha = 1.645$; for $\alpha = .01$, $z_\alpha = 2.33$. For other values of α, z_α is the z value that is the $(1 - \alpha)$th percentile for the standard normal distribution.

*Note: See the section "Percentiles for the Standard Normal Distribution" in Chapter 9 for a discussion of percentiles.

4. **Compute the test statistic:** $T.S. = z = \dfrac{\bar{x} - \mu_0}{\dfrac{\sigma}{\sqrt{n}}}$

where

μ_0 = the null-hypothesized value for the population parameter μ

$\bar{x}$ = the mean of the sample

σ = the standard deviation of the population (if σ is unknown, use the sample standard deviation s as an estimate for σ provided $n \geq 30$)

n = the sample size

5. **Make a decision:** Reject H_0 and accept H_a or fail to reject H_0.

6. **State a conclusion:** Interpret the decision in the context of the problem.

PROBLEM   Suppose that an airline company claims that the average weight of checked baggage is less than 15 pounds. To support the claim, the airline company conducts a random sample of 150 passengers and finds that the average weight of checked baggage is 14.2 pounds, with a standard deviation of 6.5 pounds. Do these data support the airline company's claim at the $\alpha = .05$ level of significance? Use $s = 6.5$ as an estimate for Σ since $n \geq 30$.

SOLUTION   1. **State the hypotheses:**

H_0: $\mu \geq 15$

H_a: $\mu < 15$ (the airline company's claim)

(left-tailed test)

2. **Select the significance level:** $\alpha = .05$

3. **State the decision rule:** Reject H_0 if $z < -1.645$

4. **Compute the test statistic (T.S.):** $T.S. = z = \dfrac{\bar{x} - \mu_0}{\dfrac{\sigma}{\sqrt{n}}} = \dfrac{14.2 - 15}{\dfrac{6.5}{\sqrt{150}}} = -1.51$

5. **Make a decision:** Since $T.S. = -1.51 \not< -1.645$, then fail to reject H_0.

6. **State a conclusion:** The sample data failed to provide sufficient evidence at the $\alpha = .05$ level of significance to overturn the null hypothesis. Therefore, at the $\alpha = .05$ level of significance, these data do not support the airline company's claim that the average weight of checked baggage is less than 15 pounds.

PROBLEM   A consumer agency claims the true average price of regular gasoline sold at service stations throughout the United States equals $2.62 per gallon. A random sample of 40 service stations yielded an average of $2.59 per gallon, with a standard deviation of $0.06. Test the consumer agency's claim at the $\alpha = .05$ level of significance. Use $s = 0.06$ as an estimate for Σ since $n \geq 30$.

SOLUTION   1. **State the hypotheses:**

H_0: $\mu = 2.62$ (the consumer agency's claim)

H_a: $\mu \neq 2.62$

(two-tailed test)

2. **Select the significance level:** $\alpha = .05$

3. **State the decision rule:** Reject H_0 if either $z < -1.96$ or $z > 1.96$

4. **Compute the test statistic (T.S.):** $T.S. = z = \dfrac{\bar{x} - \mu_0}{\dfrac{\sigma}{\sqrt{n}}} = \dfrac{2.59 - 2.62}{\dfrac{0.06}{\sqrt{40}}} = -3.16$

5. **Make a decision:** Since $T.S. = -3.16 < -1.96$, reject H_0 and accept H_a.
6. **State a conclusion:** The sample data provide sufficient evidence at the $= .05$ level of significance to overturn the null hypothesis. Thus, the data indicate that the true average price of regular gasoline sold at service stations throughout the United States is not $2.62 per gallon.

You can also state the decision rule (Step 5 above) in terms of the **observed significance level**, called the **p-value**, of the test. Under the assumption that the null hypothesis is true, the **p-value** is the probability of observing a value of the test statistic as extreme or more extreme than the observed test statistic that you computed from the sample. In terms of the distribution associated with the test of hypothesis, the p-value is computed as follows:

1. For a right-tailed test, the p-value is the area to the right of the test statistic.

2. For a left-tailed test, the p-value is the area to the left of the test statistic.

3. For a two-tailed test, the p-value is two times the area to the right of a positive test statistic or to the left of a negative test statistic.

When you use the p-value (instead of the test statistic) in the decision rule, the rule becomes: If the p-value is less than α (the level of significance), reject H_0 and accept H_a; otherwise, fail to reject H_0.

PROBLEM   Calculate the p-value for the first example, and then answer the following questions: (a) Is the p-value less than α? (b) Based on your answer to (a), what decision should you make: reject H_0 and accept H_a or fail to reject H_0? (c) Does your answer to (b) confirm your decision in the first example?

SOLUTION   The distribution for the test statistic in the first example is the z-distribution. The hypothesis test in the first example is a left-tailed test. For a left-tailed test, the p-value is the area of the distribution to the left of the test statistic. The computed test statistic from the first example is $T.S. = -1.51$. Using the techniques in Chapter 9, in the section "Finding Probabilities for the Standard Normal Distribution," you obtain:

p-value $= P(Z \leq -1.51) = 0.0655$ (shown in Figure 11.1)

(a) No, $0.0655 \not< 0.05$ (b) Decision: Fail to reject H_0 (c) Yes.

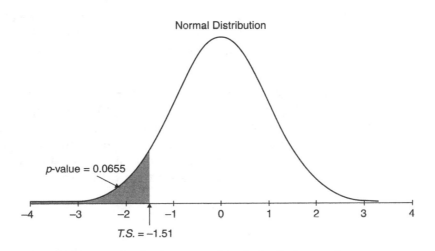

Figure 11.1 p-value for the test statistic in the first example.

1. The claim is made that the mean of a certain population is 22. To test the claim, a random sample of size $n = 50$ is obtained from the population. The sample yielded $\bar{x} = 25$. Assume the standard deviation $\sigma = 8$. Perform the test of hypothesis at the $\alpha = .05$ level of significance.

2. A random sample of size $n = 40$ obtained from a normally distributed population with unknown mean μ yielded $\bar{x} = 26.7$ and standard deviation $s = 6$. Prior to obtaining the sample, the mean was conjectured to be at least 28. Perform a test of hypothesis to test the conjecture at the $\alpha = .01$ level of significance.

3. The claim is made that the mean of a certain population is greater than 300. A random sample of size $n = 100$ obtained from the population yielded $\bar{x} = 301$ and $s = 37$. Do these data support the claim at the $\alpha = .05$ level of significance?

4. A random sample of size $n = 36$ obtained from a population with unknown mean μ and standard deviation σ yielded $\bar{x} = 58$ and $s = 15$. Prior to obtaining the sample, the mean was conjectured to be no more than 50. Perform a test of hypothesis at the $\alpha = .01$ level of significance to test the conjecture.

5. The claim is made that the mean of a population exceeds 120. A random sample of size $n = 225$ obtained from the population yielded $\bar{x} = 123$ and $s = 25$. Do these data support the claim at the $\alpha = .05$ level of significance?

6. The fundraising officer for a charity organization claims the average donation from contributors to the charity is $250.00. To test the claim, a random sample of 100 donations is obtained. The sample yielded $\bar{x} = \$234.85$ and $s = \$95.23$. Perform the test of hypothesis at the $\alpha = .05$ level of significance. What is the p-value?

7. A manufacturer of car batteries claims the average life of its batteries is at least 45 months. A random sample of 80 batteries had $\bar{x} = 39$ months and $s = 8$ months. Do these data dispute the manufacturer's claim at the $\alpha = .05$ level of significance? What is the p-value?

8. A study of 500 randomly selected adults in the United States yielded an average of 2400 calories consumed per day, with a standard deviation of 930 calories. Test the claim, which was made prior to the study, that the true mean caloric intake of all adults in the United States is no more than 2300 calories per day, use $\alpha = .05$. What is the p-value?

9. A realtor's newsletter lists the average price of a house in a metropolitan area as $100,000. A random sample of 50 house prices in the metropolitan area yielded $\bar{x} = \$120,000$ and $s = \$47,000$. At the $\alpha = .01$ level of significance, do these data dispute the listing in the realtor's newsletter? What is the p-value?

10. The weights of newborn baby boys born at a local hospital are normally distributed, with a known standard deviation of 9.5 ounces. A hospital administrator is concerned that the weights of newborn baby boys at the hospital might be less than 110 ounces. The administrator determines that a random sample of size $n = 35$ had a mean weight of 105 ounces. At the $\alpha = .01$ level of significance, do these data indicate that the mean weight of all newborn baby boys born at the local hospital is less than 110 ounces? What is the p-value?

For 11–15, suppose the given p-value is the p-value for a hypothesis test. At the $\alpha = 0.05$ level of significance, state the decision for the hypothesis test: reject H_0 or fail to reject H_0.

11. p-value = 0.0009

12. p-value = 0.1118

13. p-value = 0.0499

14. p-value = 0.0501

15. p-value = 0.02

Small-sample hypothesis test for μ

The steps for a small-sample ($n < 30$) hypothesis test for μ are the following:

1. **State the hypotheses:**

Two-Tailed Test	Right-Tailed Test	Left-Tailed Test
$H_0: \mu = \mu_0$	$H_0: \mu \le \mu_0$	$H_0: \mu \ge \mu_0$
$H_a: \mu \ne \mu_0$	$H_a: \mu > \mu_0$	$H_a: \mu < \mu_0$

Note: μ_0 is the null-hypothesized value for the population parameter μ.

2. **Select the significance level:** α (commonly $\alpha = .05$ or $.01$).

3. **State the decision rule:**

Two-Tailed Test	Right-Tailed Test	Left-Tailed Test
Reject H_0 if either $t < -t_{\alpha/2}$ or $t > t_{\alpha/2}$, where $t_{\alpha/2}$ is the t value that cuts off a right-tail area of $\alpha/2$ for a t distribution with $(n-1)$ degrees of freedom. For $\alpha = .05$, look under $t_{.025}$ in Table C (in the Appendix) under "Area in One Tail"; for $\alpha = .01$, look under $t_{.005}$ in Table C under "Area in One Tail." For other values of α, look under $t_{\alpha/2}$ in Table C under "Area in One Tail."	Reject H_0 if $t > t_\alpha$, where t_α is the t value that cuts off a right-tail area of α for a t distribution with $(n-1)$ degrees of freedom. For $\alpha = .05$, look under $t_{.050}$ in Table C under "Area in One Tail"; for $\alpha = .01$, look under $t_{.010}$ in Table C under "Area in One Tail." For other values of α, look under t_α in Table C under "Area in One Tail."	Reject H_0 if $t < -t_\alpha$, where t_α is the t value that cuts off a right-tail area of α for a t distribution with $(n-1)$ degrees of freedom. For $\alpha = .05$, look under $t_{.050}$ in Table C under "Area in One Tail"; for $\alpha = .01$, look under $t_{.010}$ in Table C under "Area in One Tail." For other values of α, look under t_α in Table C under "Area in One Tail."

4. **Compute the test statistic:** $T.S. = t = \dfrac{\bar{x} - \mu_0}{\dfrac{s}{\sqrt{n}}}$

where

μ_0 = the null-hypothesized value for the population parameter μ
$\bar{x}$ = the mean of the sample
s = the standard deviation of the sample
n = the sample size
Note: For $n < 30$, you must be able to reasonably assume that the sampled population is normally distributed.

5. **Make a decision:** Reject H_0 and accept H_a or fail to reject H_0.

6. **State a conclusion:** Interpret the decision in the context of the problem.

PROBLEM   The lifetime for a certain brand of incandescent light bulbs is normally distributed. A consumer group conducts a random sample of 25 incandescent light bulbs of this certain brand and finds a sample mean lifetime of 520 hours and standard deviation of 50 hours. Prior to taking the sample, the consumer group conjectured that the mean lifetime of all incandescent light bulbs of this brand is no more than 500 hours. Use the sample data to test the consumer group's conjecture at $\alpha = .10$.

SOLUTION   1. **State the hypotheses:**
$H_0: \mu \leq 500$ (the consumer group's conjecture)
$H_a: \mu > 500$
(right-tailed test)

2. **Select the significance level:** $\alpha = .10$

3. **State the decision rule:** Reject H_0 if $t > 1.318$. **Note:** Since $\alpha = .10$, look under $t_{.100}$ in Table C under "Area in One Tail" for the t value corresponding to $25 - 1 = 24$ $d.f.$

4. **Compute the test statistic (T.S.):** $T.S. = t = \dfrac{\bar{x} - \mu_0}{\dfrac{s}{\sqrt{n}}} = \dfrac{520 - 500}{\dfrac{50}{\sqrt{25}}} = 2.00$

5. **Make a decision:** Since $T.S. = 2.00 > 1.318$, reject H_0 and accept H_a.

6. **State a conclusion:** The sample data provide sufficient evidence at the $\alpha = .10$ level of significance to overturn the null hypothesis. Therefore, at the $\alpha = .10$ level of significance, the consumer group's conjecture (the null hypothesis) that the mean lifetime of all incandescent light bulbs of this brand is no more than 500 hours is rejected, and the alternative hypothesis that the mean lifetime of all incandescent light bulbs of this brand exceeds 500 hours is accepted.

EXERCISE

11·5

1. The claim is made that the mean of a certain normally distributed population is 22. To test the claim, a random sample of size $n = 16$ is obtained from the population. The sample yielded $\bar{x} = 25$ and a standard deviation $s = 8$. Perform the test of hypothesis at the $\alpha = .05$ level of significance.

2. A random sample of size $n = 25$ obtained from a normally distributed population with unknown mean μ yielded $\bar{x} = 26.7$ and standard deviation $s = 6$. Prior to obtaining the sample, the mean was conjectured to be at least 28. Perform a test of hypothesis to test the conjecture at the $\alpha = .05$ level of significance.

3. The claim is made that the mean of a certain normally distributed population is greater than 300. A random sample of size $n = 15$ obtained from the population yielded $\bar{x} = 301$ and $s = 37$. Do these data support the claim at the $\alpha = .10$ level of significance?

4. A random sample of size $n = 4$ obtained from a normally distributed population with unknown mean μ and standard deviation σ yielded $\bar{x} = 58$ and $s = 15$. Prior to obtaining the sample, the mean was conjectured to be no more than 50. Perform a test of hypothesis to test the conjecture at the $\alpha = .01$ level of significance.

5. The claim is made that the mean of a normally distributed population exceeds 120. A random sample of size $n = 20$ obtained from the population yielded $\bar{x} = 123$ and $s = 25$. Do these data support the claim at the $\alpha = .05$ level of significance?

6. Suppose that scores on a standardized exam are normally distributed. A test company claims that the average score on the exam for all test takers is 500. To test the claim, a researcher obtains a random sample of 25 scores. The sample yielded $\bar{x} = 480$ and $s = 75$. Perform the test of hypothesis at the $\alpha = .05$ level of significance.

7. A local deli chain advertises that its "heart healthy" sandwich has 10 fat grams. To test the claim, a nutritionist selects a random sample of four "heart healthy" sandwiches. The sample yielded $\bar{x} = 11$ grams and $s = 1.8$ grams. Suppose that the amount of fat grams in a "heart healthy" sandwich is a normal random variable. Perform the test of hypothesis at the $\alpha = .05$ level of significance.

8. A plumbing company has found that the average length of time, in minutes, for installing a bathtub is normally distributed. The plumbing company advertises that a bathtub installation takes no more than two hours. The owner of the company hires a statistician to test the company's claim. The statistician randomly selects a sample of 10 bathtub installations. The sample yielded $\bar{x} = 150$ minutes and $s = 30$ minutes. Perform the test of hypothesis at the $\alpha = .10$ level of significance.

9. The weights of newborn baby girls born at a local hospital are normally distributed. A hospital administrator conducts a study to determine whether the mean weight of all newborn baby girls born at the local hospital is less than 100 ounces. A random sample of size $n = 20$ had a mean weight of 95 ounces and a standard deviation of 8 ounces. Perform the test of hypothesis at the $\alpha = .01$ level of significance.

10. The lifetime for a certain brand of incandescent light bulbs is normally distributed. A consumer group complains that the mean lifetime of this brand of incandescent light bulbs is no more than 500 hours. A random sample of five of these light bulbs had a mean lifetime of 520 hours and standard deviation of 50 hours. Perform the test of hypothesis at the $\alpha = .10$ level of significance.

Large-sample hypothesis test for p

The steps for a large-sample hypothesis test for p are the following:

1. **State the hypotheses:**

Two-Tailed Test	Right-Tailed Test	Left-Tailed Test
$H_0: p = p_0$	$H_0: p \leq p_0$	$H_0: p \geq p_0$
$H_a: p \neq p_0$	$H_a: p > p_0$	$H_a: p < p_0$

Note: p_0 is the null-hypothesized value for the population parameter p. To check whether the sample size is sufficiently large for the methods of this section, verify that both np_0 and $n(1-p_0)$ are greater than or equal to 5.

2. **Select the significance level:** α (commonly $\alpha = .05$ or .01).

3. **State the decision rule:**

Two-Tailed Test	Right-Tailed Test	Left-Tailed Test
Reject H_0 if either $z < -z_{\alpha/2}$ or $z > z_{\alpha/2}$, where $z_{\alpha/2}$ is the z value that cuts off a right-tail area of $\frac{\alpha}{2}$ under the standard normal curve. For $\alpha = .05$, $z_{\alpha/2} = 1.96$; for $\alpha = .01$, $z_{\alpha/2} = 2.576$. For other values of α, $z_{\alpha/2}$ is the $\left(1 - \frac{\alpha}{2}\right)$th percentile for the standard normal distribution.	Reject H_0 if $z > z_\alpha$, where z_α is the z value that cuts off a right-tail area of α under the standard normal curve. For $\alpha = .05$, $z_\alpha = 1.645$; for $\alpha = .01$, $z_\alpha = 2.33$. For other values of α, z_α is the z value that is the $(1-\alpha)$th percentile for the standard normal distribution.	Reject H_0 if $z < -z_\alpha$, where z_α is the z value that cuts off a right-tail area of α under the standard normal curve. For $\alpha = .05$, $z_\alpha = 1.645$; for $\alpha = .01$, $z_\alpha = 2.33$. For other values of α, z_α is the z value that is the $(1-\alpha)$th percentile for the standard normal distribution.

4. **Compute the test statistic:** $T.S. = z = \dfrac{\hat{p} - p_0}{\sqrt{\dfrac{p_0(1 - p_0)}{n}}}$

where

p_0 = the null-hypothesized value for the population parameter p

$\hat{p}$ = the proportion in the sample with the characteristic of interest

n = the sample size

5. **Make a decision:** Reject H_0 and accept H_a or fail to reject H_0.

6. **State a conclusion:** Interpret the decision in the context of the problem.

PROBLEM   Suppose that a campaign manager claims that the percent of registered voters who prefer his candidate is 60 percent. A pollster conducts a random survey of 500 registered voters to test the campaign manager's claim and finds that 58 percent of the sample of registered voters preferred the campaign manager's candidate. Perform the test of hypothesis at the $\alpha = .10$ level of significance.

SOLUTION   1. **State the hypotheses:**
   H_0: $p = 0.60$ (the campaign manager's claim)
   H_a: $p \neq 0.60$
   (two-tailed test)
2. **Select the significance level:** $\alpha = .10$
3. **State the decision rule:** Reject H_0 if either $z < -1.645$ or $z > 1.645$

4. **Compute the test statistic (T.S.):** $T.S. = z = \dfrac{\hat{p} - p_0}{\sqrt{\dfrac{p_0(1 - p_0)}{n}}} = \dfrac{0.58 - 0.60}{\sqrt{\dfrac{0.60(0.40)}{500}}} = -0.913$

5. **Make a decision:** Since $T.S. = -0.913 \not< -1.645$, fail to reject H_0.
6. **State a conclusion:** The sample data do not provide sufficient evidence at the $\alpha = .10$ level of significance to refute the campaign manager's claim (the null hypothesis) that the percent of registered voters who prefer his candidate is 60 percent.

PROBLEM   In a random survey of 1000 U.S. college students, 220 identified themselves as smokers. Prior to the survey, a health scientist conjectured that the prevalence of smoking in college students would exceed the national percentage of 19.8 percent for smokers of all age groups. Do the data from the survey support the health scientist's conjecture? Use $\alpha = .05$.

SOLUTION $\hat{p} = \dfrac{220}{1000} = 0.22$

1. **State the hypotheses:**
   $H_0: p \leq 0.198$
   $H_a: p > 0.198$ (the health scientist's conjecture)
   (right-tailed test)
2. **Select the significance level:** $\alpha = .05$
3. **State the decision rule:** Reject H_0 if $z > 1.645$
4. **Compute the test statistic (T.S.):** $T.S. = z = \dfrac{\hat{p} - p_0}{\sqrt{\dfrac{p_0(1 - p_0)}{n}}} = \dfrac{0.22 - 0.198}{\sqrt{\dfrac{0.198(0.802)}{1000}}} = 1.746$
5. **Make a decision:** Since $T.S. = 1.746 > 1.645$, reject H_0 and accept H_a.
6. **State a conclusion:** The sample data provide sufficient evidence at the $\alpha = .05$ level of significance to overturn the null hypothesis. Thus, there is sufficient evidence at the $\alpha = .05$ level of significance to indicate that the prevalence of smoking in college students exceeds the national percentage of 19.8 percent for smokers of all age groups.

EXERCISE

11·6

For 1–5, determine whether the stated sample size n is large enough, for the given value of p_0, to use the methods of this section to perform a test of hypothesis for p.

1. $n = 500$, $p_0 = 0.05$

2. $n = 80$, $p_0 = 0.18$

3. $n = 100$, $p_0 = 0.40$

4. $n = 300$, $p_0 = 0.75$

5. $n = 120$, $p_0 = 0.01$

For 6–10, perform the appropriate test of hypothesis.

6. A random check of 500 batteries manufactured by a company found 15 defective batteries. Quality control guidelines established by the manufacturer require that the proportion of all batteries manufactured by the company that are defective must be less than 0.05. With regard to quality control guidelines, will the manufacturer be satisfied with the results of a test of hypothesis based on the sample data? Use $\alpha = .01$.

7. Assume a study revealed that from a sample of 80 working women in a metropolitan area, 30 were over the age of 60. Do these data dispute a claim made prior to the study that the true proportion of working women over the age of 60 in the metropolitan area is no more than 0.18? Use $\alpha = .05$.

8. A radio station advertising manager wants to test the hypothesis that the percent of radio listeners in the area who listen to the manager's radio station is at least 40 percent. Suppose that a random sample of 100 radio listeners in the area revealed that 34 listen to the manager's station. Perform the test of hypothesis at the $\alpha = .05$ level of significance.

9. An interior designer believes that the proportion of assisted living residents who would prefer a blue hue on bedroom walls is greater than 0.75. A random survey of 300 assisted living residents revealed that 240 prefer a blue hue on bedroom walls. Do these data support the interior designer's belief at the $\alpha = .05$ level of significance?

10. A market researcher predicts that the percent of households in a particular rural area that have no vehicle is at least 10 percent. In a random sample of 120 households, 6 households had no vehicle. Test the market researcher's prediction at the $\alpha = .10$ level of significance.

Hypothesis comparing two means, independent samples

This section and the next one present techniques for using the information in two samples to make comparisons between the means, μ_1 and μ_2, of the two populations, population 1 and population 2, from which the two samples are drawn. This section will focus on comparisons of μ_1 and μ_2 based on independent samples drawn from their respective populations. Two samples are considered independent if they are drawn from different populations and the data from one sample is not connected to the data from the other sample in any way. The steps used in a test of hypothesis comparing μ_1 and μ_2 are similar to the corresponding steps for a test of hypothesis based on a single sample from one population. There are two main differences: the hypotheses and the test statistic.

When you are formulating the hypotheses for comparing two population means μ_1 and μ_2, you are interested in the difference $\mu_1 - \mu_2$. In a given problem, one of the following sets of hypotheses will occur:

Two-Tailed Test	Right-Tailed Test	Left-Tailed Test
$H_0: \mu_1 - \mu_2 = 0$	$H_0: \mu_1 - \mu_2 \leq 0$	$H_0: \mu_1 - \mu_2 \geq 0$
$H_a: \mu_1 - \mu_2 \neq 0$	$H_a: \mu_1 - \mu_2 > 0$	$H_a: \mu_1 - \mu_2 < 0$

Notice that these hypotheses can be written in the following equivalent forms:

Two-Tailed Test	Right-Tailed Test	Left-Tailed Test
$H_0: \mu_1 = \mu_2$ (no difference)	$H_0: \mu_1 \leq \mu_2$	$H_0: \mu_1 \geq \mu_2$
$H_a: \mu_1 \neq \mu_2$	$H_a: \mu_1 > \mu_2$	$H_a: \mu_1 < \mu_2$

The most commonly used test statistic for the comparison of two population means, μ_1 and μ_2, using independent random samples from the two populations when: (1) the sample size is at least 30 or the sample is drawn from a population that is approximately normally distributed for each sample and (2) the variance of the two sampled populations are equal follows the t distribution, and is given by:

$$t = \frac{(\bar{x}_1 - \bar{x}_2) - (\mu_1 - \mu_2)}{\sqrt{s_p^2 \left(\frac{1}{n_1} + \frac{1}{n_2} \right)}}$$

with degrees of freedom $= df = n_1 + n_2 - 2$

where

$$s_p^2 = \frac{(n_1 - 1)s_1^2 + (n_2 - 1)s_2^2}{n_1 + n_2 - 2}$$ (called the **pooled variance**)

n_1 = the size of the sample drawn from population 1
n_2 = the size of the sample drawn from population 2
$\bar{x}_1$ = the mean of the sample drawn from population 1
$\bar{x}_2$ = the mean of the sample drawn from population 2
s_1 = the standard deviation of the sample drawn from population 1
s_2 = the standard deviation of the sample drawn from population 2

Note: The value of $\mu_1 - \mu_2$ in the test statistic typically is set to zero.

PROBLEM   A researcher conducts a study to investigate whether the average time (in hours) spent by teenage boys playing video games per week is greater than the average time (in hours) spent by teenage girls playing video games per week. Independent random samples are obtained with the following results:

Sample 1 (Teenage Boys)	Sample 2 (Teenage Girls)
$n_1 = 25$	$n_2 = 22$
$\bar{x}_1 = 9.25$ hours	$\bar{x}_2 = 5.5$ hours
$s_1 = 2.75$ hours	$s_2 = 3.5$ hours

Perform the test of hypothesis assuming that the population variances are equal and that two populations from which the samples are drawn are normally distributed. Use a significance level of $\alpha = .05$.

SOLUTION   1. **State the hypotheses:** Let μ_1 be the true average time (in hours) spent by teenage boys playing video games per week and μ_2 be the true average time (in hours) spent by teenage girls playing video games per week. The first sentence of the problem contains the following statement comparing the population means: "the average time (in hours) spent by teenage boys playing video games per week is greater than the average time (in hours) spent by teenage girls playing video games per week." Symbolically, this statement is $\mu_1 > \mu_2$. Its negation is $\mu_1 \leq \mu_2$. Thus, the hypotheses are:
H_0: $\mu_1 \leq \mu_2$ (or $\mu_1 - \mu_2 \leq 0$)
H_a: $\mu_1 > \mu_2$ (or $\mu_1 - \mu_2 > 0$)
(right-tailed test)

2. **Select the significance level:** $\alpha = .05$

3. **State the decision rule:**
$df = n_1 + n_2 - 2 = 25 + 22 - 2 = 45$
Reject H_0 if $t > 1.679$

4. **Compute the test statistic (T.S.):**

$$s_p^2 = \frac{(n_1 - 1)s_1^2 + (n_2 - 1)s_2^2}{n_1 + n_2 - 2} = \frac{(24)(2.75)^2 + (21)(3.5)^2}{45} = 9.75$$

$$T.S. = t = \frac{(\bar{x}_1 - \bar{x}_2) - (\mu_1 - \mu_2)}{\sqrt{s_p^2 \left(\frac{1}{n_1} + \frac{1}{n_2}\right)}} = \frac{(9.25 - 5.5) - (0)}{\sqrt{9.75 \left(\frac{1}{25} + \frac{1}{22}\right)}} = 4.108$$

5. **Make a decision:** Since $T.S. = 4.108 > 1.679$, reject H_0 and accept H_a.
6. **State a conclusion:** The sample data provide sufficient evidence at the $\alpha = .05$ level of significance to overturn the null hypothesis. Therefore, at the $\alpha = .05$ level of significance, the data provide sufficient evidence to conclude that the true average time (in hours) spent by teenage boys playing video games per week is greater than the true average time (in hours) spent by teenage girls playing video games per week.

EXERCISE
11·7

1. In order to compare the means, μ_1 and μ_2, of two populations, independent random samples of sizes $n_1 = 77$ and $n_2 = 125$ are obtained from each population with the following results:

Sample 1	Sample 2
$\bar{x}_1 = 435$	$\bar{x}_2 = 440$
$s_1 = 15$	$s_2 = 20$

Test the null hypothesis of no difference between μ_1 and μ_2. Assume that the population variances are equal and that two populations from which the samples are drawn are normally distributed. Use a significance level of $\alpha = .01$

2. In order to compare the means, μ_1 and μ_2, of two populations, independent random samples of sizes $n_1 = 38$ and $n_2 = 29$ are obtained from each population with the following results:

Sample 1	Sample 2
$\bar{x}_1 = 8.4$	$\bar{x}_2 = 7.8$
$s_1 = 0.9$	$s_2 = 2.6$

Test the hypothesis that μ_1 is no more than μ_2. Assume that the population variances are equal and that two populations from which the samples are drawn are normally distributed. Use a significance level of $\alpha = .10$.

3. A graduate recruiter for a university believes that the average Graduate Record Examinations (GRE) quantitative score of students who applied in the past five years is less than the average GRE quantitative score of students who applied more than five years ago.

Using university records, independent random samples are obtained with the following results:

Sample 1 (Recent Applicants)	Sample 2 (Prior Applicants)
$n_1 = 38$	$n_2 = 44$
$\bar{x}_1 = 650$	$\bar{x}_2 = 670$
$s_1 = 25$	$s_2 = 30$

Perform the test of hypothesis assuming that the population variances are equal and that two populations from which the samples are drawn are normally distributed. Use a significance level of $\alpha = .05$.

4. A retail store executive wants to know whether the store's Internet sales exceed its mail-order sales. A random sample of 15 Internet sales yielded a mean sale amount of $86.40, with a standard deviation of $18.75. A random sample of 10 mail-order sales yielded a mean sale amount of $75.20, with a standard deviation of $14.25. Do these data indicate that the true mean Internet sale amount exceeds the true mean mail-order sale amount? Perform the test of hypothesis assuming that the population variances are equal and that two populations from which the samples are drawn are normally distributed. Use a significance level of $\alpha = .01$.

5. A consumer group conducts a study to compare the average miles per gallon (mpg) achieved in an actual road test of two popular car brands. A random sample of five cars from Brand 1 were road-tested and yielded $\bar{x}_1 = 29.5$ mpg and $s_1 = 7.4$ mpg. A random sample of eight cars from Brand 2 were road-tested and yielded $\bar{x}_2 = 31.6$ and $s_2 = 8.4$ mpg. Test the null hypothesis of no difference between μ_1, the true average miles per gallon for Brand 1, and μ_2, the true average miles per gallon for Brand 2. Assume that the population variances are equal and that two populations from which the samples are drawn are normally distributed. Use a significance level of $\alpha = .05$.

Hypothesis comparing two means, paired data

This section deals with hypothesis testing using data from two populations that are paired in some way. The data for the hypothesis test come from two samples drawn from the two populations, but they are **dependent** (not independent) samples, called matched pairs. In **matched pairs**, each data value, called an **experimental unit**, in one sample is matched with a corresponding data value in the other sample. Data might be paired as a result of coming from the same experimental unit, as in certain "before and after" studies, or the data might be paired as a result of matching two experimental units with similar traits to form matched pairs. An important advantage of pairing the data is that it reduces the effects of extraneous factors, such as differences among the experimental units in terms of innate characteristics.

You are interested in differences between the two paired populations; therefore, the parameter of interest is μ_D, the mean of the differences between the values in each matched pair. The corresponding sample statistic is $\bar{x}_D$, the mean of the differences between the values in each matched pair in the dependent samples. Provided the population of differences has a normal distribution, the sampling distribution for $\bar{x}_D$ has a t-distribution with $n_D - 1$ degrees of freedom, where n_D = number of matched pairs.

The hypotheses take one of the following forms:

Two-Tailed Test	Right-Tailed Test	Left-Tailed Test
$H_0: \mu_D = 0 \ (\mu_1 - \mu_2 = 0)$	$H_0: \mu_D \leq 0 \ (\mu_1 - \mu_2 \leq 0)$	$H_0: \mu_D \geq 0 \ (\mu_1 - \mu_2 \geq 0)$
$H_a: \mu_D \neq 0 \ (\mu_1 - \mu_2 \neq 0)$	$H_a: \mu_D > 0 \ (\mu_1 - \mu_2 > 0)$	$H_a: \mu_D < 0 \ (\mu_1 - \mu_2 < 0)$

where
  μ_D = the mean of the population of all paired differences
  μ_1 = the mean of population 1
  μ_2 = the mean of population 2

The test statistic is given by

$$t = \frac{\bar{x}_D - 0}{\dfrac{s_D}{\sqrt{n_D}}}$$

with degrees of freedom = $df = n_D - 1$

where

n_D = number of matched pairs

$\bar{x}_D$ = sample mean difference between n_D matched pairs

s_D = sample standard deviation of n_D differences of matched pairs

PROBLEM   A researcher conducts a study to determine whether there is a significant age difference in married couples. Data collected by the researcher from six married couples are shown in the following chart. Test the null hypothesis that the true mean difference between the ages of married couples is zero. Assume the population of differences is normally distributed. Use $\alpha = .05$.

Husband's Age (in years)	65	48	33	65	44	24
Wife's Age (in years)	57	49	29	65	41	23
Difference (in years)	8	-1	4	0	3	1

SOLUTION   1. **State the hypotheses:**
$H_0: \mu_D = 0$
$H_a: \mu_D \neq 0$
(two-tailed test)

2. **Select the significance level:** $\alpha = .05$

3. **State the decision rule:**
$df = 5$
Reject H_0 if either $t < -2.571$ or $t > 2.571$

4. **Compute the test statistic (T.S.):**
$n_D = 6$

$$\bar{x}_D = \frac{8 - 1 + 4 + 0 + 3 + 1}{6} = \frac{15}{6} = 2.5$$

$$s_D = \sqrt{\frac{(8-2.5)^2 + (-1-2.5)^2 + (4-2.5)^2 + (0-2.5)^2 + (3-2.5)^2 + (1-2.5)^2}{5}} = 3.271$$

Note: Remember that when computing the standard deviation of a sample, you divide by one less than the sample size; in this case, $n_D - 1$.

$$T.S. = t = \frac{\bar{x}_D - 0}{\dfrac{s_D}{\sqrt{n_D}}} = \frac{2.5 - 0}{\dfrac{3.271}{\sqrt{6}}} = 1.872$$

5. **Make a decision:** Since $T.S. = 1.872 \not> 2.571$, fail to reject H_0.

6. **State a conclusion:** The sample data failed to provide sufficient evidence at the $\alpha = .05$ level of significance to overturn the null hypothesis. Therefore, at the $\alpha = .05$ level of significance, these data do not indicate that there is a significant age difference in married couples.

1. The data for a matched-pair medical study in which one of the pair received a treatment drug to reduce coughing (as measured by the number of times a person coughs in a four-hour period) and the other one of the pair received a placebo are shown in the following table.

	Pair 1	Pair 2	Pair 3	Pair 4	Pair 5
Placebo	110	105	125	122	111
Treatment	96	80	104	101	92
Difference	14	25	21	21	19

Assuming the population of differences is normally distributed, test the hypothesis of no difference. Use $\alpha = .01$.

2. A researcher conducted a study to determine the effectiveness of a reading intervention. The pre- and post-assessment data for eight students are shown in the following table.

Pre-Assessment Score	44	55	25	54	63	38	31	34
Post-Assessment Score	55	68	40	55	75	52	49	48

Assuming the population of differences is normally distributed, determine whether the intervention produces higher post-assessment scores. Use $\alpha = .05$.

3. A paired-difference experiment was performed to determine whether people who go on a low-fat diet for a month lose weight. The data for the experiment are shown in the following table.

Before Weight (in pounds)	165	148	210	154	198	145
After Weight (in pounds)	159	149	195	150	187	142
Difference (in pounds)	6	−1	15	4	11	3

Assuming the population of differences is normally distributed, do these data provide evidence that the low-fat one-month diet is effective? Use $\alpha = .10$.

4. The data shown in the following table are from a matched-pair study conducted to determine whether a new experimental drug is effective against panic attacks. In each matched pair, one patient was given the experimental drug and the other patient was given a placebo daily for one week. Patients were instructed to record the number of panic attacks they experienced in the one-week period.

Placebo	4	15	6	24	11	30	14
Experimental Drug	2	17	4	7	5	0	1
Difference	2	−2	2	17	6	30	13

Assuming the population of differences is normally distributed, determine whether the drug is effective against panic attacks. Use $\alpha = .05$.

5. A consumer group wants to test the performance of two types of gasoline fuel. Miles per gallon were calculated for five matched vehicles that were driven the same distance under the same conditions. The data are displayed in the following table.

	Pair 1	Pair 2	Pair 3	Pair 4	Pair 5
Gasoline 1	33.0	24.7	37.6	21.4	35.9
Gasoline 2	35.2	28.1	35.0	23.5	32.5
Difference	−2.2	−3.4	2.6	−2.1	3.4

Assuming the population of differences is normally distributed, test the hypothesis of no difference in performance between the two gasoline fuels. Use $\alpha = .05$.

Hypothesis comparing two proportions

This section deals with making inferences about two population proportions, p_1 and p_2, of two populations that have some characteristic in common. The data consist of two independent random samples drawn from two populations, population 1 and population 2. The concepts and procedures for hypothesis testing parallel those given for performing hypothesis tests comparing two means given two independent samples.

When you are formulating the hypotheses for comparing two population proportions, p_1 and p_2, you are interested in the difference $p_1 - p_2$. In a given problem, one of the following sets of hypotheses will occur:

Two-Tailed Test	Right-Tailed Test	Left-Tailed Test
$H_0: p_1 - p_2 = 0$ $H_a: p_1 - p_2 \neq 0$	$H_0: p_1 - p_2 \leq 0$ $H_a: p_1 - p_2 > 0$	$H_0: p_1 - p_2 \geq 0$ $H_a: p_1 - p_2 < 0$

Notice that, as was the case with comparisons of two means, these hypotheses can be written in the following equivalent forms:

Two-Tailed Test	Right-Tailed Test	Left-Tailed Test
$H_0: p_1 = p_2$ (no difference) $H_a: p_1 \neq p_2$	$H_0: p_1 \leq p_2$ $H_a: p_1 > p_2$	$H_0: p_1 \geq p_2$ $H_a: p_1 < p_2$

When you have independent random samples and the sample sizes are sufficiently large (that is, the conditions $np \geq 5$ and $n(1-p) \geq 5$ are satisfied for both samples), the test statistic for comparing two population proportions, p_1 and p_2, follows a z distribution and is given by

$$z = \frac{\left(\dfrac{x_1}{n_1} - \dfrac{x_2}{n_2}\right) - (p_1 - p_2)}{\sqrt{\dfrac{x_1 + x_2}{n_1 + n_2}\left(1 - \dfrac{x_1 + x_2}{n_1 + n_2}\right)\left(\dfrac{1}{n_1} + \dfrac{1}{n_2}\right)}} = \frac{(\hat{p}_1 - \hat{p}_2) - (p_1 - p_2)}{\sqrt{\bar{p}(1 - \bar{p})\left(\dfrac{1}{n_1} + \dfrac{1}{n_2}\right)}}$$

where
n_1 = the size of sample 1, which is drawn from population 1
n_2 = the size of sample 2, which is drawn from population 2

x_1 = the number of people or things with the characteristic of interest in sample 1

x_2 = the number of people or things with the characteristic of interest in sample 2

$\hat{p}_1 = \dfrac{x_1}{n_1}$ = the proportion of sample 1 with the characteristic of interest

$\hat{p}_2 = \dfrac{x_2}{n_2}$ = the proportion of sample 2 with the characteristic of interest

$\bar{p} = \dfrac{x_1 + x_2}{n_1 + n_2}$ = the proportion of people or things with the characteristic of interest in

the two samples combined

Note: The value of $p_1 - p_2$ in the test statistic typically is set to zero.

PROBLEM A pollster is interested in whether there is a difference in female and male registered voters on their approval of the way the President is handling domestic affairs. The pollster conducted a random survey of 452 female registered voters and 348 male registered voters and found that 282 of the female registered voters and 191 of the male registered voters approved of the way the President is handling domestic affairs. Test the hypothesis of no difference at the $\alpha = .05$ level of significance.

SOLUTION
1. **State the hypotheses:** Let p_1 be the true proportion of all female registered voters who approve of the way the President is handling domestic affairs and p_2 be the true proportion of all male registered voters who approve of the way the President is handling domestic affairs. Thus, the hypotheses are

   H_0: $p_1 = p_2$ (no difference)

   H_a: $p_1 \neq p_2$ (two-tailed test)

2. **Select the significance level:** $\alpha = .05$

3. **State the decision rule:** Reject H_0 if either $z < -1.96$ or $z > 1.96$

4. **Compute the test statistic (T.S.):**

$$\hat{p}_1 = \frac{x_1}{n_1} = \frac{282}{452} = 0.6239$$

$$\hat{p}_2 = \frac{x_2}{n_2} = \frac{191}{348} = 0.5489$$

$$\bar{p} = \frac{x_1 + x_2}{n_1 + n_2} = \frac{473}{800} = 0.59125$$

$$z = \frac{\left(\dfrac{x_1}{n_1} - \dfrac{x_2}{n_2}\right) - (p_1 - p_2)}{\sqrt{\dfrac{x_1 + x_2}{n_1 + n_2}\left(1 - \dfrac{x_1 + x_2}{n_1 + n_2}\right)\left(\dfrac{1}{n_1} + \dfrac{1}{n_2}\right)}} = \frac{(\hat{p}_1 - \hat{p}_2) - (p_1 - p_2)}{\sqrt{\bar{p}(1 - \bar{p})\left(\dfrac{1}{n_1} + \dfrac{1}{n_2}\right)}}$$

$$= \frac{(0.6239 - 0.5489) - (0)}{\sqrt{(0.59125)(0.40875)\left(\dfrac{1}{452} + \dfrac{1}{348}\right)}} = 2.139$$

Note: To avoid round-off error, carry calculations to five decimal places, and then round off to three decimal places at the end of the computation.

5. **Make a decision:** Since $T.S. = 2.139 > 1.96$, reject H_0 and accept H_a.
6. **State a conclusion:** The sample data provide sufficient evidence at the $\alpha = .05$ level of significance to overturn the null hypothesis of no difference. Therefore, the conclusion is that the true proportion of all female registered voters who approve of the way the President is handling domestic affairs differs from the true proportion of all male registered voters who approve of the way the President is handling domestic affairs.

EXERCISE
11·9

1. In order to compare the proportions, p_1 and p_2, of adults age 25 years or older that have college degrees in two different populations, independent random samples, each containing 200 participants, are selected from each population, with the following results:

Sample 1	Sample 2
$n_1 = 200$	$n_2 = 200$
$x_1 = 62$	$x_2 = 44$
$\hat{p}_1 = 0.31$	$\hat{p}_2 = 0.22$

Conduct a test of hypothesis to determine whether the proportion p_1 of adults age 25 or older that have college degrees in population 1 is greater than the proportion p_2 of adults age 25 or older that have college degrees in population 2. Use $\alpha = .05$.

2. In order to compare the proportion p_1 of middle school girls who work a summer job before entering high school to the proportion p_2 of middle school boys who work a summer job before entering high school, independent random samples are selected from each population, with the following results:

Sample 1 (Middle School Girls)	Sample 2 (Middle School Boys)
$n_1 = 175$	$n_2 = 150$
$x_1 = 21$	$x_2 = 30$
$\hat{p}_1 = 0.12$	$\hat{p}_2 = 0.20$

Test the hypothesis at the $\alpha = .01$ level of significance that the proportion p_1 of middle school girls who work a summer job before entering high school is at least as great as the proportion p_2 of middle school boys who work a summer job before entering high school.

3. A health organization asserted that the prevalence of smoking among male adults 18 years or older in the United States exceeds the prevalence of smoking among female adults 18 years or older. In a random survey of 1000 U.S. adults 18 years or older, 129 of the 516 male respondents identified themselves as smokers, and 87 of the 484 female respondents identified themselves as smokers. Do the data from the survey support the health organization's assertion? Use $\alpha = .05$.

4. Interior designers maintain that blue is the universal favorite hue of most people. An interior designer believes that adults 25 to 39 years old are less strong in their preference for blue as a favorite hue compared to the preference for blue as a favorite hue of adults 40 to 59 years old. A random survey of 430 adults 25 to 39 years old showed that 292 chose blue as their favorite hue, and a random survey of 245 adults 40 to 59 years old showed that 180 chose blue as their favorite hue. Do these data support the interior designer's belief? Use $\alpha = .10$.

5. Random samples of size $n_1 = 40$ and $n_2 = 30$ were drawn from populations 1 and 2, respectively. The samples yielded $\hat{p}_1 = .1$ and $\hat{p}_2 = .5$. Prior to collecting the data, a pollster predicted no difference between p_1 and p_2. Is it appropriate to use the methods of this section to test the hypothesis of no difference? Explain.

Correlation analysis

Correlation analysis is the study of the relationship between two (or more) variables. This unit presents a discussion of correlation between two variables when the relationship is linear.

Correlation

The statistical **correlation** between two variables x and y is a measure of the degree of linear relationship between the two variables. Scatterplots can be helpful in determining the type of relationship, if any, that exists between the two variables. A **scatterplot** is a graph of ordered pairs of matched values from the two variables, plotted on a coordinate grid. As illustrated in Figure 12.1, the pattern of the plotted pairs can offer insight as to whether there is a linear relationship between the two variables and, if there is, whether that relationship is positive or negative.

The relationship can be numerically quantified using a **correlation coefficient**. The population correlation coefficient is denoted by the Greek letter ρ. The coefficient ρ can take on any value from -1, through 0, to 1. When $\rho = -1$, x and y have a perfect negative linear correlation, meaning that whenever one of the variables increases, the other variable decreases, and reciprocally. When $\rho = 0$, x and y have no linear relationship. When $\rho = 1$, x and y have a perfect positive linear correlation, meaning that whenever one of the variables increases or decreases, the other variable increases or decreases in the same direction. Nevertheless, the existence of a recognizable correlation between two variables does *not* imply a causative relationship between the variables. The correlation might be a reflection of outside variables that affect both variables under study.

Population correlation coefficients that are very close to either -1 or 1 indicate very strong linear relationships. The greater the absolute value of the correlation coefficient ρ, the stronger is the relationship. For example, a correlation that has a coefficient ρ of -0.92 indicates a rather strong negative linear relationship between two variables, whereas in comparison, a correlation that has a coefficient ρ of 0.75 indicates a weaker positive linear relationship between two variables. In terms of magnitude, a correlation that has a coefficient ρ that is near 0.10 or -0.10 is considered a weak linear correlation.

Positive Linear Relationship

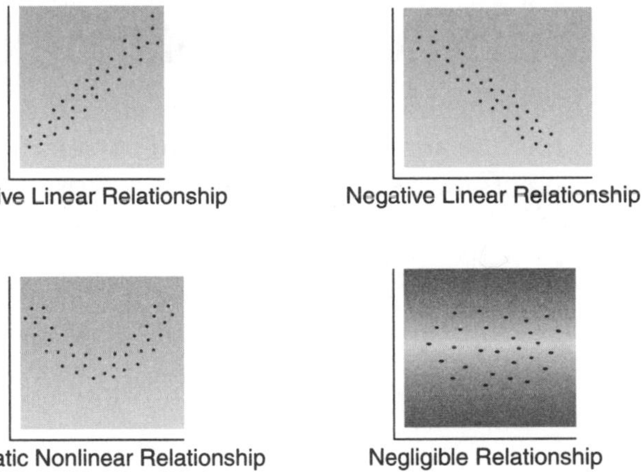

Negative Linear Relationship

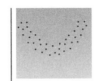
Quadratic Nonlinear Relationship

Negligible Relationship

Figure 12.1 Illustrations of possible relationships in plotted pairs

PROBLEM   Which population correlation coefficient indicates a stronger linear relationship, -0.90 or 0.50?

SOLUTION   The correlation coefficient -0.90 indicates a stronger linear relationship because $|-0.90| = 0.90$, which is greater than $|0.50| = 0.50$.

EXERCISE
12·1

Compare the strengths of the linear relationships indicated by the given population correlation coefficients by putting one of the following phrases in the blank: "is weaker than," "is stronger than," or "is the same strength as."

1. 0.40 _____ 0.75

2. −0.40 _____ −0.75

3. 0.40 _____ −0.75

4. −0.40 _____ .75

5. −1.00 _____ .99

6. 0.82 _____ 0.68

7. −0.54 _____ 0.54

8. 1.00 _____ −1.00

9. 0.49 _____ −.49

10. −1.00 _____ .0.00

Pearson product-moment correlation coefficient r

As with other population parameters, usually ρ is unknown. The corresponding sample statistic that is an estimate of ρ is the **Pearson product-moment correlation coefficient r**. It is computed for a sample of n measurements on x and y as follows:

$$r = \frac{n\sum xy - \left(\sum x\right)\left(\sum y\right)}{\sqrt{n\sum x^2 - \left(\sum x\right)^2}\sqrt{n\sum y^2 - \left(\sum y\right)^2}}$$

where

$n =$ the number of x-y pairs in the data set

$\sum xy =$ the sum of the products of all the x-y pairs

$\sum x =$ the sum of the x values

$\sum y =$ the sum of the y values

$\sum x^2 =$ the sum of the squares of the x values

$\sum y^2 =$ the sum of the squares of the y values.

PROBLEM
A biologist is interested in the relationship between age (in years) and the maximum pulse rate (in beats per minute) for women. A sample of five women yielded the following five pairs of data:

Age (years) x	20	39	18	44	50
Pulse Rate y (beats per minute)	210	180	200	165	120

Calculate the correlation coefficient r for the sample. Round your answer to three decimal places.

SOLUTION
In this example, x is "Age" and y is "Pulse Rate."

To find n, count the number of pairs you have in your data set.

$n = 5$

To find $\sum xy$, multiply each x value by its corresponding y value, and then add the products you obtain.

$$\sum xy = 20 \cdot 210 + 39 \cdot 180 + 18 \cdot 200 + 44 \cdot 165 + 50 \cdot 120 = 28080$$

To find $\sum x$, add the x values.

$$\sum x = 20 + 39 + 18 + 44 + 50 = 171$$

To find $\sum y$, add the y values.

$$\sum y = 210 + 180 + 200 + 165 + 120 = 875$$

To find $\sum x^2$, square each x value, and then add the squares you obtain.

$$\sum x^2 = 20^2 + 39^2 + 18^2 + 44^2 + 50^2 = 6681$$

To find $\sum y^2$, square each y value, and then add the squares you obtain.

$$\sum y^2 = 210^2 + 180^2 + 200^2 + 165^2 + 120^2 = 158125$$

Now, plug into the formula and compute r.

$$r = \frac{n\sum xy - (\sum x)(\sum y)}{\sqrt{n\sum x^2 - (\sum x)^2}\sqrt{n\sum y^2 - (\sum y)^2}} = \frac{5(28080) - (171)(875)}{\sqrt{5(6681) - (171)^2}\sqrt{5(158125) - (875)^2}}$$

$$= -0.90415 \approx -0.904$$

For 1–4, calculate r for the pairs of sample observations. Round your answers to three decimal places.

1.

x	33	60	20	19	45
y	25	36	65	26	36

2.

x	90	101	120	136	41
y	81	95	75	52	136

3.

x	5	20	15	10	6
y	81	85	91	82	86

4.

x	2	16	4	10
y	12	3	15	22

5. The following data give the number of hours each of six students in a statistics class spent studying and the students corresponding grades on the midterm exam.

Hours Spent Studying x	1.50	2.75	3	4.5	5.75	6
Grade on Midterm y	54	73	70	82	91	89

Calculate the correlation coefficient r for these data. Round your answer to three decimal places.

APPENDIX TABLES
Table A: Binomial probabilities

		ρ								
n	x	0.1	0.2	0.3	0.4	0.5	0.6	0.7	0.8	0.9
1	0	0.900	0.800	0.700	0.600	0.500	0.400	0.300	0.200	0.100
	1	0.100	0.200	0.300	0.400	0.500	0.600	0.700	0.800	0.900
2	0	0.810	0.640	0.490	0.360	0.250	0.160	0.090	0.040	0.010
	1	0.180	0.320	0.420	0.480	0.500	0.480	0.420	0.320	0.180
	2	0.010	0.040	0.090	0.160	0.250	0.360	0.490	0.640	0.810
3	0	0.729	0.512	0.343	0.216	0.125	0.064	0.027	0.008	0.001
	1	0.243	0.384	0.441	0.432	0.375	0.288	0.189	0.096	0.027
	2	0.027	0.096	0.189	0.288	0.375	0.432	0.441	0.384	0.243
	3	0.001	0.008	0.027	0.064	0.125	0.216	0.343	0.512	0.729
4	0	0.656	0.410	0.240	0.130	0.062	0.026	0.008	0.002	0.000
	1	0.292	0.410	0.412	0.346	0.250	0.154	0.076	0.026	0.004
	2	0.049	0.154	0.265	0.346	0.375	0.346	0.265	0.154	0.049
	3	0.004	0.026	0.076	0.154	0.250	0.346	0.412	0.410	0.292
	4	0.000	0.002	0.008	0.026	0.062	0.130	0.240	0.410	0.656
5	0	0.590	0.328	0.168	0.078	0.031	0.010	0.002	0.000	0.000
	1	0.328	0.410	0.360	0.259	0.156	0.077	0.028	0.006	0.000
	2	0.073	0.205	0.309	0.346	0.312	0.230	0.132	0.051	0.008
	3	0.008	0.051	0.132	0.230	0.312	0.346	0.309	0.205	0.073
	4	0.000	0.006	0.028	0.077	0.156	0.259	0.360	0.410	0.328
	5	0.000	0.000	0.002	0.010	0.031	0.078	0.168	0.328	0.590
6	0	0.531	0.262	0.118	0.047	0.016	0.004	0.001	0.000	0.000
	1	0.354	0.393	0.303	0.187	0.094	0.037	0.010	0.002	0.000
	2	0.098	0.246	0.324	0.311	0.234	0.138	0.060	0.015	0.001
	3	0.015	0.082	0.185	0.276	0.312	0.276	0.185	0.082	0.015
	4	0.001	0.015	0.060	0.138	0.234	0.311	0.324	0.246	0.098
	5	0.000	0.002	0.010	0.037	0.094	0.187	0.303	0.393	0.354
	6	0.000	0.000	0.001	0.004	0.016	0.047	0.118	0.262	0.531
7	0	0.478	0.210	0.082	0.028	0.008	0.002	0.000	0.000	0.000
	1	0.372	0.367	0.247	0.131	0.055	0.017	0.004	0.000	0.000
	2	0.124	0.275	0.318	0.261	0.164	0.077	0.025	0.004	0.000

(Continued)

n	x	0.1	0.2	0.3	0.4	0.5	0.6	0.7	0.8	0.9
	3	0.023	0.115	0.227	0.290	0.273	0.194	0.097	0.029	0.003
	4	0.003	0.029	0.097	0.194	0.273	0.290	0.227	0.115	0.023
	5	0.000	0.004	0.025	0.077	0.164	0.261	0.318	0.275	0.124
	6	0.000	0.000	0.004	0.017	0.055	0.131	0.247	0.367	0.372
	7	0.000	0.000	0.000	0.002	0.008	0.028	0.082	0.210	0.478
8	0	0.430	0.168	0.058	0.017	0.004	0.001	0.000	0.000	0.000
	1	0.383	0.336	0.198	0.090	0.031	0.008	0.001	0.000	0.000
	2	0.149	0.294	0.296	0.209	0.109	0.041	0.010	0.001	0.000
	3	0.033	0.147	0.254	0.279	0.219	0.124	0.047	0.009	0.000
	4	0.005	0.046	0.136	0.232	0.273	0.232	0.136	0.046	0.005
	5	0.000	0.009	0.047	0.124	0.219	0.279	0.254	0.147	0.033
	6	0.000	0.001	0.010	0.041	0.109	0.209	0.296	0.294	0.149
	7	0.000	0.000	0.001	0.008	0.031	0.090	0.198	0.336	0.383
	8	0.000	0.000	0.000	0.001	0.004	0.017	0.058	0.168	0.430
9	0	0.387	0.134	0.040	0.010	0.002	0.000	0.000	0.000	0.000
	1	0.387	0.302	0.156	0.060	0.018	0.004	0.000	0.000	0.000
	2	0.172	0.302	0.267	0.161	0.070	0.021	0.004	0.000	0.000
	3	0.045	0.176	0.267	0.251	0.164	0.074	0.021	0.003	0.000
	4	0.007	0.066	0.172	0.251	0.246	0.167	0.074	0.017	0.001
	5	0.001	0.017	0.074	0.167	0.246	0.251	0.172	0.066	0.007
	6	0.000	0.003	0.021	0.074	0.164	0.251	0.267	0.176	0.045
	7	0.000	0.000	0.004	0.021	0.070	0.161	0.267	0.302	0.172
	8	0.000	0.000	0.000	0.004	0.018	0.060	0.156	0.302	0.387
	9	0.000	0.000	0.000	0.000	0.002	0.010	0.040	0.134	0.387
10	0	0.349	0.107	0.028	0.006	0.001	0.000	0.000	0.000	0.000
	1	0.387	0.268	0.121	0.040	0.010	0.002	0.000	0.000	0.000
	2	0.194	0.302	0.233	0.121	0.044	0.011	0.001	0.000	0.000
	3	0.057	0.201	0.267	0.215	0.117	0.042	0.009	0.001	0.000
	4	0.011	0.088	0.200	0.251	0.205	0.111	0.037	0.006	0.000
	5	0.001	0.026	0.103	0.201	0.246	0.201	0.103	0.026	0.001
	6	0.000	0.006	0.037	0.111	0.205	0.251	0.200	0.088	0.011
	7	0.000	0.001	0.009	0.042	0.117	0.215	0.267	0.201	0.057
	8	0.000	0.000	0.001	0.011	0.044	0.121	0.233	0.302	0.194
	9	0.000	0.000	0.000	0.002	0.010	0.040	0.121	0.268	0.387
	10	0.000	0.000	0.000	0.000	0.001	0.006	0.028	0.107	0.349
11	0	0.314	0.086	0.020	0.004	0.000	0.000	0.000	0.000	0.000
	1	0.384	0.236	0.093	0.027	0.005	0.001	0.000	0.000	0.000
	2	0.213	0.295	0.200	0.089	0.027	0.005	0.001	0.000	0.000

n	x	0.1	0.2	0.3	0.4	0.5	0.6	0.7	0.8	0.9
						ρ				
	3	0.071	0.221	0.257	0.177	0.081	0.023	0.004	0.000	0.000
	4	0.016	0.111	0.220	0.236	0.161	0.070	0.017	0.002	0.000
	5	0.002	0.039	0.132	0.221	0.226	0.147	0.057	0.010	0.000
	6	0.000	0.010	0.057	0.147	0.226	0.221	0.132	0.039	0.002
	7	0.000	0.002	0.017	0.070	0.161	0.236	0.220	0.111	0.016
	8	0.000	0.000	0.004	0.023	0.081	0.177	0.257	0.221	0.071
	9	0.000	0.000	0.001	0.005	0.027	0.089	0.200	0.295	0.213
	10	0.000	0.000	0.000	0.001	0.005	0.027	0.093	0.236	0.384
	11	0.000	0.000	0.000	0.000	0.000	0.004	0.020	0.086	0.314
12	0	0.282	0.069	0.014	0.002	0.000	0.000	0.000	0.000	0.000
	1	0.377	0.206	0.071	0.017	0.003	0.000	0.000	0.000	0.000
	2	0.230	0.283	0.168	0.064	0.016	0.002	0.000	0.000	0.000
	3	0.085	0.236	0.240	0.142	0.054	0.012	0.001	0.000	0.000
	4	0.021	0.133	0.231	0.213	0.121	0.042	0.008	0.001	0.000
	5	0.004	0.053	0.158	0.227	0.193	0.101	0.029	0.003	0.000
	6	0.000	0.016	0.079	0.177	0.226	0.177	0.079	0.016	0.000
	7	0.000	0.003	0.029	0.101	0.193	0.227	0.158	0.053	0.004
	8	0.000	0.001	0.008	0.042	0.121	0.213	0.231	0.133	0.021
	9	0.000	0.000	0.001	0.012	0.054	0.142	0.240	0.236	0.085
	10	0.000	0.000	0.000	0.002	0.016	0.064	0.168	0.283	0.230
	11	0.000	0.000	0.000	0.000	0.003	0.017	0.071	0.206	0.377
	12	0.000	0.000	0.000	0.000	0.000	0.002	0.014	0.069	0.282
13	0	0.254	0.055	0.001	0.001	0.000	0.000	0.000	0.000	0.000
	1	0.367	0.179	0.054	0.011	0.002	0.000	0.000	0.000	0.000
	2	0.245	0.268	0.139	0.045	0.010	0.001	0.000	0.000	0.000
	3	0.100	0.246	0.218	0.111	0.035	0.006	0.001	0.000	0.000
	4	0.028	0.154	0.234	0.184	0.087	0.024	0.003	0.000	0.000
	5	0.006	0.069	0.180	0.221	0.157	0.066	0.014	0.001	0.000
	6	0.001	0.023	0.103	0.197	0.209	0.131	0.044	0.006	0.000
	7	0.000	0.006	0.044	0.131	0.209	0.197	0.103	0.023	0.001
	8	0.000	0.001	0.014	0.066	0.157	0.221	0.180	0.069	0.006
	9	0.000	0.000	0.003	0.024	0.087	0.184	0.234	0.154	0.028
	10	0.000	0.000	0.001	0.006	0.035	0.111	0.218	0.246	0.100
	11	0.000	0.000	0.000	0.001	0.010	0.045	0.139	0.268	0.245
	12	0.000	0.000	0.000	0.000	0.002	0.011	0.054	0.179	0.367
	13	0.000	0.000	0.000	0.000	0.000	0.001	0.010	0.055	0.254
14	0	0.229	0.044	0.007	0.001	0.000	0.000	0.000	0.000	0.000
	1	0.356	0.154	0.041	0.007	0.001	0.000	0.000	0.000	0.000
	2	0.257	0.250	0.113	0.032	0.006	0.001	0.000	0.000	0.000

(Continued)

n	x	0.1	0.2	0.3	0.4	0.5	0.6	0.7	0.8	0.9
					ρ					
	3	0.114	0.250	0.194	0.085	0.022	0.003	0.000	0.000	0.000
	4	0.035	0.172	0.229	0.155	0.061	0.014	0.001	0.000	0.000
	5	0.008	0.086	0.196	0.207	0.122	0.041	0.007	0.000	0.000
	6	0.001	0.032	0.126	0.207	0.183	0.092	0.023	0.002	0.000
	7	0.000	0.009	0.062	0.157	0.209	0.157	0.062	0.009	0.000
	8	0.000	0.002	0.023	0.092	0.183	0.207	0.126	0.032	0.001
	9	0.000	0.000	0.007	0.041	0.122	0.207	0.196	0.086	0.008
	10	0.000	0.000	0.001	0.014	0.061	0.155	0.229	0.172	0.035
	11	0.000	0.000	0.000	0.003	0.022	0.085	0.194	0.250	0.114
	12	0.000	0.000	0.000	0.001	0.006	0.032	0.113	0.250	0.257
	13	0.000	0.000	0.000	0.000	0.001	0.007	0.041	0.154	0.356
	14	0.000	0.000	0.000	0.000	0.000	0.001	0.007	0.044	0.229
15	0	0.206	0.035	0.005	0.000	0.000	0.000	0.000	0.000	0.000
	1	0.343	0.132	0.031	0.005	0.000	0.000	0.000	0.000	0.000
	2	0.267	0.231	0.092	0.022	0.003	0.000	0.000	0.000	0.000
	3	0.129	0.250	0.170	0.063	0.014	0.002	0.000	0.000	0.000
	4	0.043	0.188	0.219	0.127	0.042	0.007	0.001	0.000	0.000
	5	0.010	0.103	0.206	0.186	0.092	0.024	0.003	0.000	0.000
	6	0.002	0.043	0.147	0.207	0.153	0.061	0.012	0.001	0.000
	7	0.000	0.014	0.081	0.177	0.196	0.118	0.035	0.003	0.000
	8	0.000	0.003	0.035	0.118	0.196	0.177	0.081	0.014	0.000
	9	0.000	0.001	0.017	0.061	0.153	0.207	0.147	0.043	0.002
	10	0.000	0.000	0.003	0.024	0.092	0.186	0.206	0.103	0.010
	11	0.000	0.000	0.001	0.007	0.042	0.127	0.219	0.188	0.043
	12	0.000	0.000	0.000	0.002	0.014	0.063	0.170	0.250	0.129
	13	0.000	0.000	0.000	0.000	0.003	0.022	0.092	0.231	0.267
	14	0.000	0.000	0.000	0.000	0.000	0.005	0.031	0.132	0.343
	15	0.000	0.000	0.000	0.000	0.000	0.000	0.005	0.035	0.206
16	0	0.185	0.028	0.003	0.000	0.000	0.000	0.000	0.000	0.000
	1	0.329	0.113	0.023	0.003	0.000	0.000	0.000	0.000	0.000
	2	0.275	0.211	0.073	0.015	0.002	0.000	0.000	0.000	0.000
	3	0.142	0.246	0.146	0.047	0.009	0.001	0.000	0.000	0.000
	4	0.051	0.200	0.204	0.101	0.028	0.004	0.000	0.000	0.000
	5	0.014	0.120	0.210	0.162	0.067	0.014	0.001	0.000	0.000
	6	0.003	0.055	0.165	0.198	0.122	0.039	0.006	0.000	0.000
	7	0.000	0.020	0.101	0.189	0.175	0.084	0.019	0.001	0.000
	8	0.000	0.006	0.049	0.142	0.196	0.142	0.049	0.006	0.000
	9	0.000	0.001	0.019	0.084	0.175	0.189	0.101	0.020	0.000
	10	0.000	0.000	0.006	0.039	0.122	0.198	0.165	0.055	0.003

					ρ					
n	x	0.1	0.2	0.3	0.4	0.5	0.6	0.7	0.8	0.9
	11	0.000	0.000	0.001	0.014	0.067	0.162	0.210	0.120	0.014
	12	0.000	0.000	0.000	0.004	0.028	0.101	0.204	0.200	0.051
	13	0.000	0.000	0.000	0.001	0.009	0.047	0.146	0.246	0.142
	14	0.000	0.000	0.000	0.000	0.002	0.015	0.073	0.211	0.275
	15	0.000	0.000	0.000	0.000	0.000	0.003	0.023	0.113	0.329
	16	0.000	0.000	0.000	0.000	0.000	0.000	0.003	0.028	0.185
17	0	0.167	0.023	0.002	0.000	0.000	0.000	0.000	0.000	0.000
	1	0.315	0.096	0.017	0.002	0.000	0.000	0.000	0.000	0.000
	2	0.280	0.191	0.058	0.010	0.001	0.000	0.000	0.000	0.000
	3	0.156	0.239	0.125	0.034	0.005	0.000	0.000	0.000	0.000
	4	0.060	0.209	0.187	0.080	0.018	0.002	0.000	0.000	0.000
	5	0.017	0.136	0.208	0.138	0.047	0.008	0.001	0.000	0.000
	6	0.004	0.068	0.178	0.184	0.094	0.024	0.003	0.000	0.000
	7	0.001	0.027	0.120	0.193	0.148	0.057	0.009	0.000	0.000
	8	0.000	0.008	0.064	0.161	0.185	0.107	0.028	0.002	0.000
	9	0.000	0.002	0.028	0.107	0.185	0.161	0.064	0.008	0.000
	10	0.000	0.000	0.009	0.057	0.148	0.193	0.120	0.027	0.001
	11	0.000	0.000	0.003	0.024	0.094	0.184	0.178	0.068	0.004
	12	0.000	0.000	0.001	0.008	0.047	0.138	0.208	0.136	0.017
	13	0.000	0.000	0.000	0.002	0.018	0.080	0.187	0.209	0.060
	14	0.000	0.000	0.000	0.000	0.005	0.034	0.125	0.239	0.156
	15	0.000	0.000	0.000	0.000	0.001	0.010	0.058	0.191	0.280
	16	0.000	0.000	0.000	0.000	0.000	0.002	0.017	0.096	0.315
	17	0.000	0.000	0.000	0.000	0.000	0.000	0.002	0.023	0.167
18	0	0.150	0.018	0.002	0.000	0.000	0.000	0.000	0.000	0.000
	1	0.300	0.081	0.013	0.001	0.000	0.000	0.000	0.000	0.000
	2	0.284	0.172	0.046	0.007	0.001	0.000	0.000	0.000	0.000
	3	0.168	0.230	0.105	0.025	0.003	0.000	0.000	0.000	0.000
	4	0.070	0.215	0.168	0.061	0.012	0.001	0.000	0.000	0.000
	5	0.022	0.151	0.202	0.115	0.033	0.004	0.000	0.000	0.000
	6	0.005	0.082	0.187	0.166	0.071	0.015	0.001	0.000	0.000
	7	0.001	0.035	0.138	0.189	0.121	0.037	0.005	0.000	0.000
	8	0.000	0.012	0.081	0.173	0.167	0.077	0.015	0.001	0.000
	9	0.000	0.003	0.039	0.128	0.185	0.128	0.039	0.003	0.000
	10	0.000	0.001	0.015	0.077	0.167	0.173	0.081	0.012	0.000
	11	0.000	0.000	0.005	0.037	0.121	0.189	0.138	0.035	0.001
	12	0.000	0.000	0.001	0.015	0.071	0.166	0.187	0.082	0.005
	13	0.000	0.000	0.000	0.004	0.033	0.115	0.202	0.151	0.022

(Continued)

		p								
n	*x*	**0.1**	**0.2**	**0.3**	**0.4**	**0.5**	**0.6**	**0.7**	**0.8**	**0.9**
	14	0.000	0.000	0.000	0.001	0.012	0.061	0.168	0.215	0.070
	15	0.000	0.000	0.000	0.000	0.003	0.025	0.105	0.230	0.168
	16	0.000	0.000	0.000	0.000	0.001	0.007	0.046	0.172	0.284
	17	0.000	0.000	0.000	0.000	0.000	0.001	0.013	0.081	0.300
	18	0.000	0.000	0.000	0.000	0.000	0.000	0.002	0.018	0.150
19	0	0.135	0.014	0.001	0.000	0.000	0.000	0.000	0.000	0.000
	1	0.285	0.068	0.009	0.001	0.000	0.000	0.000	0.000	0.000
	2	0.285	0.154	0.036	0.005	0.000	0.000	0.000	0.000	0.000
	3	0.180	0.218	0.087	0.017	0.002	0.000	0.000	0.000	0.000
	4	0.080	0.218	0.149	0.047	0.007	0.001	0.000	0.000	0.000
	5	0.027	0.164	0.192	0.093	0.022	0.002	0.000	0.000	0.000
	6	0.007	0.095	0.192	0.145	0.052	0.008	0.001	0.000	0.000
	7	0.001	0.044	0.153	0.180	0.096	0.024	0.002	0.000	0.000
	8	0.000	0.017	0.098	0.180	0.144	0.053	0.008	0.000	0.000
	9	0.000	0.005	0.051	0.146	0.176	0.098	0.022	0.001	0.000
	10	0.000	0.001	0.022	0.098	0.176	0.146	0.051	0.005	0.000
	11	0.000	0.000	0.008	0.053	0.144	0.180	0.098	0.017	0.000
	12	0.000	0.000	0.002	0.024	0.096	0.180	0.153	0.044	0.001
	13	0.000	0.000	0.001	0.008	0.052	0.145	0.192	0.095	0.007
	14	0.000	0.000	0.000	0.002	0.022	0.093	0.192	0.164	0.027
	15	0.000	0.000	0.000	0.001	0.007	0.047	0.149	0.218	0.080
	16	0.000	0.000	0.000	0.000	0.002	0.017	0.087	0.218	0.180
	17	0.000	0.000	0.000	0.000	0.000	0.005	0.036	0.154	0.285
	18	0.000	0.000	0.000	0.000	0.000	0.001	0.009	0.068	0.285
	19	0.000	0.000	0.000	0.000	0.000	0.000	0.001	0.014	0.135
20	0	0.122	0.012	0.001	0.000	0.000	0.000	0.000	0.000	0.000
	1	0.270	0.058	0.007	0.000	0.000	0.000	0.000	0.000	0.000
	2	0.285	0.137	0.028	0.003	0.000	0.000	0.000	0.000	0.000
	3	0.190	0.205	0.072	0.012	0.001	0.000	0.000	0.000	0.000
	4	0.090	0.218	0.130	0.035	0.005	0.000	0.000	0.000	0.000
	5	0.032	0.175	0.179	0.075	0.015	0.001	0.000	0.000	0.000
	6	0.009	0.109	0.192	0.124	0.037	0.005	0.000	0.000	0.000
	7	0.002	0.055	0.164	0.166	0.074	0.015	0.001	0.000	0.000
	8	0.000	0.022	0.114	0.180	0.120	0.035	0.004	0.000	0.000
	9	0.000	0.007	0.065	0.160	0.160	0.071	0.012	0.000	0.000
	10	0.000	0.002	0.031	0.117	0.176	0.117	0.031	0.002	0.000
	11	0.000	0.000	0.012	0.071	0.160	0.160	0.065	0.007	0.000
	12	0.000	0.000	0.004	0.035	0.120	0.180	0.114	0.022	0.000

n	x	0.1	0.2	0.3	0.4	0.5	0.6	0.7	0.8	0.9
						ρ				
	13	0.000	0.000	0.001	0.015	0.074	0.166	0.164	0.055	0.002
	14	0.000	0.000	0.000	0.005	0.037	0.124	0.192	0.109	0.009
	15	0.000	0.000	0.000	0.001	0.015	0.075	0.179	0.175	0.032
	16	0.000	0.000	0.000	0.000	0.005	0.035	0.130	0.218	0.090
	17	0.000	0.000	0.000	0.000	0.001	0.012	0.072	0.205	0.190
	18	0.000	0.000	0.000	0.000	0.000	0.003	0.028	0.137	0.285
	19	0.000	0.000	0.000	0.000	0.000	0.000	0.007	0.058	0.270
	20	0.000	0.000	0.000	0.000	0.000	0.000	0.001	0.012	0.122

Table B: Cumulative standard normal distribution

Table B1 Standard normal distribution −∞ to z

Numerical entries represent the probability that a standard normal random variable is between −∞ and z, where $z = (x − \mu)/\sigma$.

z	0.09	0.08	0.07	0.06	0.05	0.04	0.03	0.02	0.01	0.00
−3.4	0.0002	0.0003	0.0003	0.0003	0.0003	0.0003	0.0003	0.0003	0.0003	0.0003
−3.3	0.0003	0.0004	0.0004	0.0004	0.0004	0.0004	0.0004	0.0005	0.0005	0.0005
−3.2	0.0005	0.0005	0.0005	0.0006	0.0006	0.0006	0.0006	0.0006	0.0007	0.0007
−3.1	0.0007	0.0007	0.0008	0.0008	0.0008	0.0008	0.0009	0.0009	0.0009	0.0010
−3.0	0.0010	0.0010	0.0011	0.0011	0.0011	0.0012	0.0012	0.0013	0.0013	0.0013
−2.9	0.0014	0.0014	0.0015	0.0015	0.0016	0.0016	0.0017	0.0018	0.0018	0.0019
−2.8	0.0019	0.0020	0.0021	0.0021	0.0022	0.0023	0.0023	0.0024	0.0025	0.0026
−2.7	0.0026	0.0027	0.0028	0.0029	0.0030	0.0031	0.0032	0.0033	0.0034	0.0035
−2.6	0.0036	0.0037	0.0038	0.0039	0.0040	0.0041	0.0043	0.0044	0.0045	0.0047
−2.5	0.0048	0.0049	0.0051	0.0052	0.0054	0.0055	0.0057	0.0059	0.0060	0.0062
−2.4	0.0064	0.0066	0.0068	0.0069	0.0071	0.0073	0.0075	0.0078	0.0080	0.0082
−2.3	0.0084	0.0087	0.0089	0.0091	0.0094	0.0096	0.0099	0.0102	0.0104	0.0107
−2.2	0.0110	0.0113	0.0116	0.0119	0.0122	0.0125	0.0129	0.0132	0.0136	0.0139
−2.1	0.0143	0.0146	0.0150	0.0154	0.0158	0.0162	0.0166	0.0170	0.0174	0.0179
−2.0	0.0183	0.0188	0.0192	0.0197	0.0202	0.0207	0.0212	0.0217	0.0222	0.0228
−1.9	0.0233	0.0239	0.0244	0.0250	0.0256	0.0262	0.0268	0.0274	0.0281	0.0287
−1.8	0.0294	0.0301	0.0307	0.0314	0.0322	0.0329	0.0336	0.0344	0.0351	0.0359
−1.7	0.0367	0.0375	0.0384	0.0392	0.0401	0.0409	0.0418	0.0427	0.0436	0.0446
−1.6	0.0455	0.0465	0.0475	0.0485	0.0495	0.0505	0.0516	0.0526	0.0537	0.0548
−1.5	0.0559	0.0571	0.0582	0.0594	0.0606	0.0618	0.0630	0.0643	0.0655	0.0668
−1.4	0.0681	0.0694	0.0708	0.0721	0.0735	0.0749	0.0764	0.0778	0.0793	0.0808
−1.3	0.0823	0.0838	0.0853	0.0869	0.0885	0.0901	0.0918	0.0934	0.0951	0.0968
−1.2	0.0985	0.1003	0.1020	0.1038	0.1056	0.1075	0.1093	0.1112	0.1131	0.1151

(Continued)

z	0.09	0.08	0.07	0.06	0.05	0.04	0.03	0.02	0.01	0.00
−1.1	0.1170	0.1190	0.1210	0.1230	0.1251	0.1271	0.1292	0.1314	0.1335	0.1357
−1.0	0.1379	0.1401	0.1423	0.1446	0.1469	0.1492	0.1515	0.1539	0.1562	0.1587
−0.9	0.1611	0.1635	0.1660	0.1685	0.1711	0.1736	0.1762	0.1788	0.1814	0.1841
−0.8	0.1867	0.1894	0.1922	0.1949	0.1977	0.2005	0.2033	0.2061	0.2090	0.2119
−0.7	0.2148	0.2177	0.2206	0.2236	0.2266	0.2296	0.2327	0.2358	0.2389	0.2420
−0.6	0.2451	0.2483	0.2514	0.2546	0.2578	0.2611	0.2643	0.2676	0.2709	0.2743
−0.5	0.2776	0.2810	0.2843	0.2877	0.2912	0.2946	0.2981	0.3015	0.3050	0.3085
−0.4	0.3121	0.3156	0.3192	0.3228	0.3264	0.3300	0.3336	0.3372	0.3409	0.3446
−0.3	0.3483	0.3520	0.3557	0.3594	0.3632	0.3669	0.3707	0.3745	0.3783	0.3821
−0.2	0.3859	0.3897	0.3936	0.3974	0.4013	0.4052	0.4090	0.4129	0.4168	0.4207
−0.1	0.4247	0.4286	0.4325	0.4364	0.4404	0.4443	0.4483	0.4522	0.4562	0.4602
0.0	0.4641	0.4681	0.4721	0.4761	0.4801	0.4840	0.4880	0.4920	0.4960	0.5000

Table B2 Standard normal distribution −∞ to z

Numerical entries represent the probability that a standard normal random variable is between −∞ and z, where $z = (x − \mu)/\sigma$.

Area

z	0.00	0.01	0.02	0.03	0.04	0.05	0.06	0.07	0.08	0.09
0.0	0.5000	0.5040	0.5080	0.5120	0.5160	0.5199	0.5239	0.5279	0.5319	0.5359
0.1	0.5398	0.5438	0.5478	0.5517	0.5557	0.5596	0.5636	0.5675	0.5714	0.5753
0.2	0.5793	0.5832	0.5871	0.5910	0.5948	0.5987	0.6026	0.6064	0.6103	0.6141
0.3	0.6179	0.6217	0.6255	0.6293	0.6331	0.6368	0.6406	0.6443	0.6480	0.6517
0.4	0.6554	0.6591	0.6628	0.6664	0.6700	0.6736	0.6772	0.6808	0.6844	0.6879
0.5	0.6915	0.6950	0.6985	0.7019	0.7054	0.7088	0.7123	0.7157	0.7190	0.7224
0.6	0.7257	0.7291	0.7324	0.7357	0.7389	0.7422	0.7454	0.7486	0.7517	0.7549
0.7	0.7580	0.7611	0.7642	0.7673	0.7704	0.7734	0.7764	0.7794	0.7823	0.7852
0.8	0.7881	0.7910	0.7939	0.7967	0.7995	0.8023	0.8051	0.8078	0.8106	0.8133
0.9	0.8159	0.8186	0.8212	0.8238	0.8264	0.8289	0.8315	0.8340	0.8365	0.8389
1.0	0.8413	0.8438	0.8461	0.8485	0.8508	0.8531	0.8554	0.8577	0.8599	0.8621
1.1	0.8643	0.8665	0.8686	0.8708	0.8729	0.8749	0.8770	0.8790	0.8810	0.8830
1.2	0.8849	0.8869	0.8888	0.8907	0.8925	0.8944	0.8962	0.8980	0.8997	0.9015
1.3	0.9032	0.9049	0.9066	0.9082	0.9099	0.9115	0.9131	0.9147	0.9162	0.9177
1.4	0.9192	0.9207	0.9222	0.9236	0.9251	0.9265	0.9279	0.9292	0.9306	0.9319
1.5	0.9332	0.9345	0.9357	0.9370	0.9382	0.9394	0.9406	0.9418	0.9429	0.9441
1.6	0.9452	0.9463	0.9474	0.9484	0.9495	0.9505	0.9515	0.9525	0.9535	0.9545
1.7	0.9554	0.9564	0.9573	0.9582	0.9591	0.9599	0.9608	0.9616	0.9625	0.9633
1.8	0.9641	0.9649	0.9656	0.9664	0.9671	0.9678	0.9686	0.9693	0.9699	0.9706
1.9	0.9713	0.9719	0.9726	0.9732	0.9738	0.9744	0.9750	0.9756	0.9761	0.9767
2.0	0.9772	0.9778	0.9783	0.9788	0.9793	0.9798	0.9803	0.9808	0.9812	0.9817
2.1	0.9821	0.9826	0.9830	0.9834	0.9838	0.9842	0.9846	0.9850	0.9854	0.9857
2.2	0.9861	0.9864	0.9868	0.9871	0.9875	0.9878	0.9881	0.9884	0.9887	0.9890
2.3	0.9893	0.9896	0.9898	0.9901	0.9904	0.9906	0.9909	0.9911	0.9913	0.9916
2.4	0.9918	0.9920	0.9922	0.9925	0.9927	0.9929	0.9931	0.9932	0.9934	0.9936
2.5	0.9938	0.9940	0.9941	0.9943	0.9945	0.9946	0.9948	0.9949	0.9951	0.9952
2.6	0.9953	0.9955	0.9956	0.9957	0.9959	0.9960	0.9961	0.9962	0.9963	0.9964
2.7	0.9965	0.9966	0.9967	0.9968	0.9969	0.9970	0.9971	0.9972	0.9973	0.9974
2.8	0.9974	0.9975	0.9976	0.9977	0.9977	0.9978	0.9979	0.9979	0.9980	0.9981
2.9	0.9981	0.9982	0.9982	0.9983	0.9984	0.9984	0.9985	0.9985	0.9986	0.9986
3.0	0.9987	0.9987	0.9987	0.9988	0.9988	0.9989	0.9989	0.9989	0.9990	0.9990
3.1	0.9990	0.9991	0.9991	0.9991	0.9992	0.9992	0.9992	0.9992	0.9993	0.9993
3.2	0.9993	0.9993	0.9994	0.9994	0.9994	0.9994	0.9994	0.9995	0.9995	0.9995
3.3	0.9995	0.9995	0.9995	0.9996	0.9996	0.9996	0.9996	0.9996	0.9996	0.9997
3.4	0.9997	09997	0.9997	0.9997	0.9997	0.9997	0.9997	0.9997	0.9997	0.9998

Table C: Critical values of t

	Area in One Tail				
	$t_{.100}$	$t_{.050}$	$t_{.025}$	$t_{.010}$	$t_{.005}$
	Area in Two Tails				
d.f.	$t_{.200}$	$t_{.100}$	$t_{.050}$	$t_{.020}$	$t_{.010}$
1	3.078	6.314	12.706	31.821	63.657
2	1.886	2.920	4.303	6.965	9.925
3	1.638	2.353	3.182	4.541	5.841
4	1.533	2.132	2.776	3.747	4.604
5	1.476	2.015	2.571	3.365	4.032
6	1.440	1.943	2.447	3.143	3.707
7	1.415	1.895	2.365	2.998	3.499
8	1.397	1.860	2.306	2.896	3.355
9	1.383	1.833	2.262	2.821	3.250
10	1.372	1.812	2.228	2.764	3.169
11	1.363	1.796	2.201	2.718	3.106
12	1.356	1.782	2.179	2.681	3.055
13	1.350	1.771	2.160	2.650	3.012
14	1.345	1.761	2.145	2.624	2.977
15	1.341	1.753	2.131	2.602	2.947
16	1.337	1.746	2.120	2.583	2.921
17	1.333	1.740	2.110	2.567	2.898
18	1.330	1.734	2.101	2.552	2.878
19	1.328	1.729	2.093	2.539	2.861
20	1.325	1.725	2.086	2.528	2.845
21	1.323	1.721	2.080	2.518	2.831
22	1.321	1.717	2.074	2.508	2.819
23	1.319	1.714	2.069	2.500	2.807
24	1.318	1.711	2.064	2.492	2.797
25	1.316	1.708	2.060	2.485	2.787
26	1.315	1.706	2.056	2.479	2.779
27	1.314	1.703	2.052	2.473	2.771
28	1.313	1.701	2.048	2.467	2.763

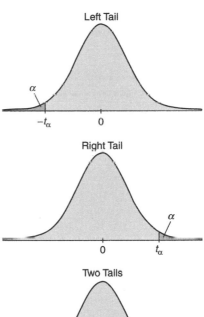

(Continued)

d.f.	Area in One Tail				
	$t_{.100}$	$t_{.050}$	$t_{.025}$	$t_{.010}$	$t_{.005}$
	Area in Two Tails				
	$t_{.200}$	$t_{.100}$	$t_{.050}$	$t_{.020}$	$t_{.010}$
29	1.311	1.699	2.045	2.462	2.756
30	1.310	1.697	2.042	2.457	2.750
31	1.309	1.696	2.040	2.453	2.744
32	1.309	1.694	2.037	2.449	2.738
34	1.307	1.691	2.032	2.441	2.728
36	1.306	1.688	2.028	2.434	2.719
38	1.304	1.686	2.024	2.429	2.712
40	1.303	1.684	2.021	2.423	2.704
45	1.301	1.679	2.014	2.412	2.690
50	1.299	1.676	2.009	2.403	2.678
55	1.297	1.673	2.004	2.396	2.668
60	1.296	1.671	2.000	2.390	2.660
65	1.295	1.669	1.997	2.385	2.654
70	1.294	1.667	1.994	2.381	2.648
75	1.293	1.665	1.992	2.377	2.643
80	1.292	1.664	1.990	2.374	2.639
90	1.291	1.662	1.987	2.368	2.632
100	1.290	1.660	1.984	2.364	2.656
120	1.289	1.658	1.980	2.358	2.617
200	1.286	1.653	1.972	2.345	2.601
300	1.284	1.650	1.968	2.339	2.592
400	1.284	1.649	1.966	2.336	2.588
500	1.283	1.648	1.965	2.334	2.586
750	1.283	1.647	1.963	2.331	2.582
1000	1.282	1.646	1.962	2.330	2.581
2000	1.282	1.646	1.961	2.328	2.578
∞	1.282	1.645	1.960	2.326	2.576

Answer key

I DESCRIPTIVE STATISTICS

1 Classification of data

1·1
1. qualitative
2. quantitative
3. quantitative
4. quantitative
5. quantitative
6. qualitative
7. quantitative
8. qualitative
9. qualitative
10. qualitative

1·2
1. continuous
2. continuous
3. continuous
4. discrete
5. discrete
6. continuous
7. continuous
8. discrete
9. discrete
10. continuous

1·3
1. ordinal
2. ratio
3. ratio
4. interval
5. ratio
6. interval
7. ratio
8. nominal
9. ordinal
10. nominal

2 Organizing quantitative data

2·1
1. 123
2. 169
3. 2
4. 1
5. 147
6. 3
7. none
8. 14
9. 4
10. none

2·2
1. 1
2. 19
3. 7
4. 65–69
5. 6
6. 65–69
7. none
8. 24%
9. 20%
10. 76%

3 Measures of central tendency

3·1
1. 25.6
2. 8.5
3. 5.225
4. 3
5. 256
6. 50
7. 50
8. 50
9. −50
10. 77

3·2
1. 30
2. 7.5
3. 5.25
4. 3
5. 300
6. 50
7. 50
8. 50
9. −50
10. 4

3·3
1. no mode
2. 4, unimodal
3. 4.7, 5.6, bimodal
4. 3, unimodal
5. no mode
6. 0, 100, bimodal
7. 50, unimodal
8. 50, unimodal
9. −50, unimodal
10. 4, 10, bimodal

123

4 Measures of variability

4·1

1. $50 - 0 = 50$
2. $25 - (-4) = 29$
3. $7.3 - 2.5 = 4.8$
4. $16 - (-10) = 26$
5. $500 - 0 = 500$
6. $100 - 0 = 100$
7. $50 - 50 = 0$
8. $70 - 30 = 40$
9. $-30 - (-70) = 40$
10. $10 - 1 = 9$

4·2

1. (a) mean $= \bar{x} = 25.6$

   $$\text{variance} = s^2 = \frac{\sum (x_i - \bar{x})^2}{n-1}$$

   $$= \frac{(15 - 25.6)^2 + (33 - 25.6)^2 + (30 - 25.6)^2 + (50 - 25.6)^2 + (0 - 25.6)^2}{4} = 359.3$$

   (b) standard deviation $= s = \sqrt{s^2} = \sqrt{359.3} = 18.955$

2. (a) mean $= \bar{x} = 8.5$

   $$\text{variance} = s^2 = \frac{\sum (x_i - \bar{x})^2}{n-1}$$

   $$= \frac{(-4 - 8.5)^2 + (25 - 8.5)^2 + (-4 - 8.5)^2 + (11 - 8.5)^2 + (19 - 8.5)^2 + (4 - 8.5)^2}{5} = 144.3$$

   (b) standard deviation $= s = \sqrt{s^2} = \sqrt{144.3} = 12.0125$

3. (a) mean $= \bar{x} = 5.225$

   $$\text{variance} = s^2 = \frac{\sum (x_i - \bar{x})^2}{n-1}$$

   $$= \frac{(4.7 - 5.225)^2 + (5.6 - 5.225)^2 + (2.5 - 5.225)^2 + (4.9 - 5.225)^2 +}{7}$$

   $$\frac{+(7.3 - 5.225)^2 + (4.7 - 5.225)^2 + (5.6 - 5.225)^2 + (6.5 - 5.225)^2}{7} = 2.0421$$

   (b) standard deviation $= s = \sqrt{s^2} = \sqrt{2.0421} = 1.429$

4. (a) mean $= \bar{x} = 3$

   $$\text{variance} = s^2 = \frac{\sum (x_i - \bar{x})^2}{n-1}$$

   $$= \frac{(-10 - 3)^2 + (0 - 3)^2 + (3 - 3)^2 + (3 - 3)^2 + (6 - 3)^2 + (16 - 3)^2}{5} = 71.2$$

   (b) standard deviation $= s = \sqrt{s^2} = \sqrt{71.2} = 8.438$

5. (a) mean $= \bar{x} = 256$

   $$\text{variance} = s^2 = \frac{\sum (x_i - \bar{x})^2}{n-1}$$

   $$= \frac{(150 - 256)^2 + (330 - 256)^2 + (300 - 256)^2 + (500 - 256)^2 + (0 - 256)^2}{4} = 35930$$

   (b) standard deviation $= s = \sqrt{s^2} = \sqrt{35930} = 189.552$

6. (a) mean $= \bar{x} = 50$

   $$\text{variance} = s^2 = \frac{\sum (x_i - \bar{x})^2}{n-1}$$

   $$= \frac{(0 - 50)^2 + (0 - 50)^2 + (0 - 50)^2 + (100 - 50)^2 + (100 - 50)^2 + (100 - 50)^2}{5} = 3000$$

   (b) standard deviation $= s = \sqrt{s^2} = \sqrt{3000} = 54.7723$

7. (a) mean $= \bar{x} = 50$

variance $= s^2 = \dfrac{\sum(x_i - \bar{x})^2}{n-1}$

$= \dfrac{(50-50)^2 + (50-50)^2 + (50-50)^2 + (50-50)^2 + (50-50)^2 + (50-50)^2 + (50-50)^2}{6} = 0$

(b) standard deviation $= s = \sqrt{s^2} = \sqrt{0} = 0$

8. (a) mean $= \bar{x} = 50$

variance $= s^2 = \dfrac{\sum(x_i - \bar{x})^2}{n-1}$

$= \dfrac{(30-50)^2 + (40-50)^2 + (50-50)^2 + (50-50)^2 + (60-50)^2 + (70-50)^2}{5} = 200$

(b) standard deviation $= s = \sqrt{s^2} = \sqrt{200} = 14.1421$

9. (a) mean $= \bar{x} = -50$

variance $= s^2 = \dfrac{\sum(x_i - \bar{x})^2}{n-1}$

$= \dfrac{(-30-(-50))^2 + (-40-(-50))^2 + (-50-(-50))^2 + (-50-(-50))^2 + (-60-(-50))^2 + (-70-(-50))^2}{5} = 200$

(b) standard deviation $= s = \sqrt{s^2} = \sqrt{200} = 14.1421$

10. (a) mean $= \bar{x} = 5.5$

variance $= s^2 = \dfrac{\sum(x_i - \bar{x})^2}{n-1}$

$= \dfrac{(1-5.5)^2 + (1-5.5)^2 + (4-5.5)^2 + (4-5.5)^2 + (4-5.5)^2 + (10-5.5)^2 + (10-5.5)^2 + (10-5.5)^2}{7}$

$= 15.429$

(b) standard deviation $= s = \sqrt{s^2} = \sqrt{15.429} = 3.928$

5   Interquartile range and the five-number summary

5·1
1. 25%
2. 450
3. 25%
4. 24
5. 192

5·2
1. range = Max − Min = 88 − 11 = 77
2. 25%
3. $IQR = Q_3 - Q_1 = 81.5 - 51 = 30.5$
4. 5
5. range = Max − Min = 9.3 − 6.7 = 2.6

II   FUNDAMENTALS OF CLASSICAL PROBABILITY

6   Counting techniques

6·1
1. $8 \cdot 5 \cdot 7 = 280$ different meals
2. $10 \cdot 10 \cdot 10 \cdot 10 \cdot 10 = 100{,}000$ different possible codes
3. $30 \cdot 29 \cdot 28 = 24{,}360$ different ways
4. $26 \cdot 26 \cdot 10 \cdot 10 \cdot 10 \cdot 10 \cdot 10 \cdot 10 = 676{,}000{,}000$ different ID numbers
5. $26 \cdot 26 \cdot 26 \cdot 10 \cdot 10 \cdot 10 = 17{,}576{,}000$ different car license plates

6. $10 \cdot 10 \cdot 10 \cdot 10 = 10,000$ possible telephone numbers
7. $15 \cdot 15 \cdot 15 = 3375$ possible three-letter codes
8. $2 \cdot 2 \cdot 2 = 8$ possible three-letter codes
9. $3 \cdot 2 \cdot 1 = 6$ different ways
10. $5 \cdot 4 \cdot 3 \cdot 2 \cdot 1 = 120$ different ways

6·2
1. 1
2. 120
3. 120
4. 42
5. 100
6. 6720
7. 420
8. 1
9. 30
10. 100
11. $_5P_5 = \dfrac{5!}{0!} = 120$ different ways
12. $_{10}P_8 = \dfrac{10!}{2!} = 1,814,400$ different arrangements
13. $\dfrac{10!}{3!3!2!} = 50,400$ possible arrangements
14. $_{25}P_3 = \dfrac{25!}{22!} = 25 \cdot 24 \cdot 23 = 13,800$ different ways
15. $10 \cdot 9 \cdot 8 \cdot 7 \cdot 6 \cdot 5 = 151,200$ different passwords

6·3
1. 1
2. 10
3. 15
4. 10
5. 1287
6. 1
7. 10
8. 1287
9. 1140
10. 100
11. $_{20}C_3 = 1140$ different ways
12. $_{52}C_5 = 2,598,960$ possible 5-card hands
13. $_{12}C_3 = 220$ different ways
14. $_{15}C_7 = 6435$ different ways
15. $_8C_5 \cdot {}_{10}C_4 \cdot {}_6C_3 = 235,200$ different ways

7 Basic probability concepts

7·1
1. $S = \{H1, H2, H3, H4, H5, H6, T1, T2, T3, T4, T5, T6\}$
2. $S = \{HH, HT, TH, TT\}$
3. From the Fundamental Counting Principle, you know there are $6 \cdot 6 = 36$ possible outcomes. When listing the outcomes, you need to distinguish between the two dice. You can do this with an ordered pair (x, y), where x is the number of dots on the up face of the first die and y is the number of dots on the up face of the second die. Thus, $S = \{(1,1), (1,2), (1,3), (1,4), (1,5), (1,6), (2,1), (2,2), (2,3), (2,4), (2,5), (2,6), (3,1), (3,2), (3,3), (3,4), (3,5), (3,6), (4,1), (4,2), (4,3), (4,4), (4,5), (4,6), (5,1), (5,2), (5,3), (5,4), (5,5), (5,6), (6,1), (6,2), (6,3), (6,4), (6,5), (6,6)\}$.
4. $52 \cdot 52 = 2704$
5. The total number of marbles available is 17. The number of ways you can select 4 marbles from 17 marbles is $_{17}C_4 = 2380$. **Note:** In this sample space, you count all of these outcomes as separate, even though some might look the same.

7·2

1. $\dfrac{3}{6} = \dfrac{1}{2}$

2. $\dfrac{3}{6} = \dfrac{1}{2}$

3. $\dfrac{1}{2}$

4. $S = \{HH, HT, TH, TT\}$. Thus, $P(\text{at least one head}) = \dfrac{3}{4}$.

5. $S = \{(1,1), (1,2), (1,3), (1,4), (1,5), \mathbf{(1,6)}, (2,1), (2,2), (2,3), (2,4), \mathbf{(2,5)}, (2,6), (3,1), (3,2), (3,3), \mathbf{(3,4)}, (3,5), (3,6), (4,1), (4,2), \mathbf{(4,3)}, (4,4), (4,5), (4,6), (5,1), \mathbf{(5,2)}, (5,3), (5,4), (5,5), (5,6), \mathbf{(6,1)}, (6,2), (6,3), (6,4), (6,5), (6,6)\}$.

   Thus, $P(\text{sum is 7}) = \dfrac{6}{36} = \dfrac{1}{6}$.

6. $\dfrac{12}{52} = \dfrac{3}{13}$

7. $\dfrac{13}{52} = \dfrac{1}{4}$

8. $\dfrac{10}{23}$

9. $\dfrac{1}{4}$

10. $\dfrac{3}{30} = \dfrac{1}{10}$

7·3

1. $P(\bar{E}) = \dfrac{5}{8}$

2. $P(\bar{E}) = \dfrac{95}{100}$

3. $P(\bar{E}) = 70\%$

4. $P(\bar{E}) = 0.75$

5. $P(\bar{E}) = \dfrac{1}{2}$

6. $P(E) = \dfrac{1}{2}$, so $P(\bar{E}) = \dfrac{1}{2}$

7. $P(E) = \dfrac{1}{2}$, so $P(\bar{E}) = \dfrac{1}{2}$

8. $P(E) = \dfrac{1}{2}$, so $P(\bar{E}) = \dfrac{1}{2}$

9. $P(E) = \dfrac{3}{4}$, so $P(\bar{E}) = \dfrac{1}{4}$

10. $P(E) = \dfrac{1}{6}$, so $P(\bar{E}) = \dfrac{5}{6}$

11. $P(E) = \dfrac{12}{52} = \dfrac{3}{13}$, so $P(\bar{E}) = \dfrac{10}{13}$

12. $P(E) = \dfrac{13}{52} = \dfrac{1}{4}$, so $P(\bar{E}) = \dfrac{3}{4}$

13. $P(E) = \dfrac{10}{23}$, so $P(\bar{E}) = \dfrac{13}{23}$

14. $P(E) = \dfrac{1}{4}$, so $P(\bar{E}) = \dfrac{3}{4}$

15. $P(E) = \dfrac{3}{30} = \dfrac{1}{10}$, so $P(\bar{E}) = \dfrac{9}{10}$

7·4

1. not mutually exclusive
2. mutually exclusive
3. mutually exclusive
4. not mutually exclusive
5. not mutually exclusive

6. $P(A \text{ or } B) = P(A) + P(B) - P(A \text{ and } B) = .5 + .3 - .06 = .74$

7. $P(A \text{ or } B) = P(A) + P(B) - P(A \text{ and } B) = .4 + .1 - .05 = .45$

8. $P(A \text{ or } B) = P(A) + P(B) - P(A \text{ and } B) = .65 + .22 - .08 = .79$

9. $P(A \text{ or } B) = P(A) + P(B) - P(A \text{ and } B) = \dfrac{4}{52} + \dfrac{13}{52} - \dfrac{1}{52} = \dfrac{16}{52} = \dfrac{4}{13}$

10. $P(A \text{ or } B) = P(A) + P(B) - P(A \text{ and } B) = \dfrac{3}{8} + \dfrac{5}{8} - 0 = 1$

11. $P(\text{odd or less than 3}) = P(\text{odd}) + P(\text{less than 3}) - P(\text{odd and less than 3}) = \dfrac{3}{6} + \dfrac{2}{6} - \dfrac{1}{6} = \dfrac{4}{6} = \dfrac{2}{3}$

12. There are 4 aces, 12 spades that are not aces, and 12 diamonds that are not aces in the deck. Thus, $P \text{ (ace or either a spade or a diamond)} = \dfrac{4+12+12}{52} = \dfrac{28}{52} = \dfrac{7}{13}$

13. $S = \{HHH, HHT, HTH, HTT, THH, THT, TTH, TTT\}$, so P(probability that at least two heads are observed or the number of heads observed is an odd number) $= \dfrac{7}{8}$

14. $S = \{HHH, HHT, HTH, HTT, THH, THT, TTH, TTT\}$, so P (all heads or all tails) $= \dfrac{2}{8} = \dfrac{1}{4}$

15. $P \text{ (red or green)} = \dfrac{10+6}{23} = \dfrac{16}{23}$

7·5

1. Since $P(A \text{ and } B) = \dfrac{1}{4}$, which is the same as $P(A)\,P(B) = \dfrac{1}{2} \cdot \dfrac{1}{2} = \dfrac{1}{4}$, the events A and B are independent.

2. Since $P(A \text{ and } B) = .32$, which is not the same as $P(A)\,P(B) = (.35)(.63) = .2205$, the events A and B are dependent.

3. Since $P(A \text{ and } B) = \dfrac{3}{22}$, which is not the same as $P(A)\,P(B) = \dfrac{1}{2} \cdot \dfrac{21}{55} = \dfrac{21}{110}$, the events A and B are dependent.

4. Since $P(A) = .7 = P(A|B) = .7$, the events A and B are independent.

5. Since $P(A) = .7 \neq P(A|B) = .9$, the events A and B are dependent.

6. $\dfrac{1}{2} \cdot \dfrac{2}{6} = \dfrac{1}{6}$

7. $\dfrac{4}{52} \cdot \dfrac{12}{51} = \dfrac{4}{221}$

8. $\dfrac{1}{2} \cdot \dfrac{1}{2} \cdot \dfrac{1}{2} = \dfrac{1}{8}$

9. $\dfrac{12}{52} \cdot \dfrac{8}{52} = \dfrac{6}{169}$

10. $\dfrac{6}{14} = \dfrac{3}{7}$

 THE BINOMIAL AND NORMAL DISTRIBUTIONS

8 The binomial distribution

8·1

1. The binomial distribution is an appropriate model for the probability distribution of this experiment.
2. The binomial distribution is not an appropriate model for the probability distribution of this experiment because p, the probability of success (card is a diamond), changes from trial to trial since the selections are made without replacement.
3. The binomial distribution is an appropriate model for the probability distribution of this experiment.
4. The binomial distribution is an appropriate model for the probability distribution of this experiment.
5. The binomial distribution is an appropriate model for the probability distribution of this experiment.

8·2

1. a. Yes, the binomial distribution is an appropriate model for the probability distribution of the given process because (1) there are n identical trials: 15 random inspections; (2) each trial (inspection) results in only two outcomes: defective or not defective, where the outcome defective will denote "success;" (3) p, the probability of success (defective) on a single trial (inspection) is 10 percent and is the same from trial to trial; (4) the trials (inspections) are independent since the outcome of one inspection does not affect the outcome of any other; and (5) the random variable of interest is the number of successes (defectives) in the 15 trials (inspections).

   b. $n = 15$ and $p = 0.10$

   c. $\mu = np = 15(0.10) = 1.5$, $\sigma^2 = np(1-p) = 15(.10)(.90) = 1.35$, $\sigma = \sqrt{np(1-p)} = \sqrt{15(.10)(.90)} \approx 1.16$

2. $\mu = np = 8(0.2) = 1.6$, $\sigma^2 = np(1-p) = 8(.2)(.8) = 1.28$, $\sigma = \sqrt{np(1-p)} = \sqrt{8(.2)(.8)} \approx 1.13$

3. $\mu = np = 15(0.9) = 13.5$, $\sigma^2 = np(1-p) = 15(.9)(.1) = 1.35$, $\sigma = \sqrt{np(1-p)} = \sqrt{15(.9)(.1)} \approx 1.16$

4. $\mu = np = 3(0.25) = 0.75$, $\sigma^2 = np(1-p) = 3(.25)(.75) = 0.5625$, $\sigma = \sqrt{np(1-p)} = \sqrt{3(.25)(.75)} = 0.75$

5. $\mu = np = 100(0.5) = 50$, $\sigma^2 = np(1-p) = 100(.5)(.5) = 25$, $\sigma = \sqrt{np(1-p)} = \sqrt{100(.5)(.5)} = 5$

6. $\mu = np = 20(0.15) = 3$, $\sigma^2 = np(1-p) = 20(.15)(.85) = 2.55$, $\sigma = \sqrt{np(1-p)} = \sqrt{3(.15)(.85)} \approx 1.60$

7. $\mu = np = 150(0.9) = 135$, $\sigma^2 = np(1-p) = 150(.9)(.1) = 13.5$, $\sigma = \sqrt{np(1-p)} = \sqrt{150(.9)(.1)} \approx 3.67$

8. $\mu = np = 300(0.25) = 75$, $\sigma^2 = np(1-p) = 300(.25)(.75) = 56.25$, $\sigma = \sqrt{np(1-p)} = \sqrt{300(.25)(.75)} = 7.5$

9. $\mu = np = 475(0.55) = 261.25$, $\sigma^2 = np(1-p) = 475(.55)(.45) = 117.5625$,

   $\sigma = \sqrt{np(1-p)} = \sqrt{475(.55)(.45)} \approx 10.84$

10. $\mu = np = 800(0.7) = 560$, $\sigma^2 = np(1-p) = 800(.7)(.3) = 168$, $\sigma = \sqrt{np(1-p)} = \sqrt{800(.7)(.3)} \approx 12.96$

8·3

1. When $n = 5$ and $p = \dfrac{1}{6}$, $P(X = 3) = \dfrac{5!}{3!(5-3)!}\left(\dfrac{1}{6}\right)^3\left(\dfrac{5}{6}\right)^{5-3} \approx 0.03215$

2. When $n = 3$ and $p = \dfrac{1}{2} = .5$, $P(X < 2) = P(X = 0) + P(X = 1) = \dfrac{3!}{0!3!}(.5)^0(.5)^3 + \dfrac{3!}{1!2!}(.5)^1(.5)^2 = 0.5$

3. When $n = 10$ and $p = .4$, $P(X = 8) = \dfrac{10!}{8!2!}(.4)^8(.6)^2 - 0.010616832$

4. When $n = 5$ and $p = .1$, $P(X = 2) = \dfrac{5!}{2!3!}(.1)^2(.9)^3 = 0.0729$

5. When $n = 5$ and $p = \dfrac{1}{4} = .25$, $P(X = 5) = \dfrac{5!}{5!0!}(.25)^5(.75)^0 = 0.0009765625$

6. When $n = 5$ and $p = .2$, $P(X < 1) = \dfrac{5!}{0!5!}(.2)^0(.8)^5 = 0.32768$

7. When $n = 5$ and $p = .2$, $P(X \leq 1) = \dfrac{5!}{0!5!}(.2)^0(.8)^5 + \dfrac{5!}{1!4!}(.2)^1(.8)^4 = 0.73728$

8. When $n = 10$ and $p = .5$, $P(X > 8) = \dfrac{10!}{9!1!}(.5)^9(.5)^1 + \dfrac{10!}{10!0!}(.5)^{10}(.5)^0 = 0.0107421875$

9. When $n = 10$ and $p = .5$, $P(X < 1) = \dfrac{10!}{0!10!}(.5)^0(.5)^{10} = 0.0009765625$

10. When $n = 3$ and $p = .7$, $P(X = 2) = \dfrac{3!}{2!1!}(.7)^2(.3)^1 = 0.441$

11. When $n = 3$ and $p = .7$, $P(X < 2) = \dfrac{3!}{0!3!}(.7)^0(.3)^3 + \dfrac{3!}{1!2!}(.7)^1(.3)^2 = 0.216$

12. When $n = 3$ and $p = .7$, $P(X \leq 2) = \dfrac{3!}{0!3!}(.7)^0(.3)^3 + \dfrac{3!}{1!2!}(.7)^1(.3)^2 + \dfrac{3!}{2!1!}(.7)^2(.3)^1 = 0.657$

13. When $n = 3$ and $p = .7$, $P(X = 3) = \dfrac{3!}{3!0!}(.7)^3(.3)^0 = 0.343$

14. When $n = 3$ and $p = .7$, $P(X \geq 2) - \dfrac{3!}{2!1!}(.7)^2(.3)^1 + \dfrac{3!}{3!0!}(.7)^3(.3)^0 = 0.784$

15. When $n = 6$ and $p = .4$, $P(X = 5) = \dfrac{6!}{5!1!}(.4)^5(.6)^1 = 0.036864$

8·4

1. When $n = 5$ and $p = \dfrac{3}{6} = .5$, $P(X = 4) = 0.156$

2. When $n = 3$ and $p = .5$, $P(X \le 2) = P(X = 0) + P(X = 1) + P(X = 2) = 0.125 + 0.375 + 0.375 = 0.875$

3. When $n = 10$ and $p = .4$, $P(X = 8) = 0.011$

4. When $n = 20$ and $p = .1$, $P(X < 2) = P(X = 0) + P(X = 1) = 0.122 + 0.270 = 0.392$

5. When $n = 10$ and $p = \dfrac{1}{5} = .2$, $P(X \ge 7) = P(X = 7) + P(X = 8) + P(X = 9) + P(X = 10) = 0.001$
   $+ 0.000 + 0.000 + 0.000 \approx 0.001$

6. When $n = 15$ and $p = .2$, $P(X < 1) = P(X = 0) = 0.035$

7. When $n = 10$ and $p = .9$, $P(X \ge 8) = P(X = 8) + P(X = 9) + P(X = 10) = 0.194 + 0.387 + 0.349 = 0.930$

8. When $n = 10$ and $p = .5$, $P(X > 8) = P(X = 9) + P(X = 10) = 0.010 + 0.001 = 0.011$

9. When $n = 12$ and $p = .2$, $P(X \le 3) = P(X = 0) + P(X = 1) + P(X = 2) + P(X = 3) = 0.069 + 0.206$
   $+ 0.283 + 0.236 = 0.794$

10. When $n = 19$ and $p = .8$, $P(X = 17) = 0.154$

11. When $n = 11$ and $p = .4$, $P(X \le 2) = P(X = 0) + P(X = 1) + P(X = 2) = 0.004 + 0.027 + 0.089 = 0.120$

12. When $n = 9$ and $p = .7$, $P(X \ge 6) = P(X = 6) + P(X = 7) + P(X = 8) + P(X = 9) = 0.267 + 0.267 + 0.156$
    $+ 0.040 = 0.730$

13. When $n = 20$ and $p = .9$, $P(X > 18) = P(X = 19) + P(X = 20) = 0.270 + 0.122 = 0.392$

14. When $n = 15$ and $p = .2$, $P(X \le 1) = P(X = 0) + P(X = 1) = 0.035 + 0.132 = 0.167$

15. When $n = 16$ and $p = .7$, $P(X \ge 15) = P(X = 15) + P(X = 16) = 0.023 + 0.003 = 0.026$

9   The normal distribution

9·1

1. About 68.26 percent of the values fall between 22 and 28, about 95.44 percent fall between 19 and 31, and about 99.74 percent fall between 16 and 34.

2. About 68.26 percent of the values fall between 250 and 350, about 95.44 percent fall between 200 and 400, and about 99.74 percent fall between 150 and 450.

3. About 68.26 percent of the values fall between 70 and 80, about 95.44 percent fall between 65 and 85, and about 99.74 percent fall between 60 and 90.

4. About 68.26 percent of the values fall between 4.3 and 4.7, about 95.44 percent fall between 4.1 and 4.9, and about 99.74 percent fall between 3.9 and 5.1.

5. About 68.26 percent of the values fall between −1 and 1, about 95.44 percent fall between −2 and 2, and about 99.74 percent fall between −3 and 3.

6. $P(\mu - 1\sigma < X < \mu + 1\sigma) = P(75 - 1 \cdot 5 < X < 75 + 1 \cdot 5) = P(70 < X < 80) = 0.6826$

7. $P(\mu - 2\sigma < X < \mu + 2\sigma) = P(75 - 2 \cdot 5 < X < 75 + 2 \cdot 5) = P(65 < X < 85) = 0.9544$

8. Since the total area under the normal curve is 1, the probability that X assumes a value more than one standard deviation from its mean $= 1 - 0.6826 = 0.3174$.

9. Since the total area under the normal curve is 1, the probability that X assumes a value more than two standard deviations from its mean $= 1 - 0.9544 = 0.0456$.

10. Since the total area under the normal curve is 1, the probability that X assumes a value more than three standard deviations from its mean $= 1 - 0.9974 = 0.0026$.

11. $P(260 < X < 340) = P(300 - 2 \cdot 20 < X < 300 + 2 \cdot 20) = P(\mu - 2\sigma < X < \mu + 2\sigma) = 0.9544$

12. $P(240 < X < 360) = P(300 - 3 \cdot 20 < X < 300 + 3 \cdot 20) = P(\mu - 3\sigma < X < \mu + 3\sigma) = 0.9974$

13. $1 - P(260 < X < 340) = 1 - 0.9544 = 0.0456$

14. $P(X < 300) = P(X < \mu) = 0.5$

15. $P(X > 300) = P(X > \mu) = 0.5$

16. $P(-1 < X < 1) = P(\mu - 1\sigma < X < \mu + 1\sigma) = 0.6826$

17. $P(-2 < X < 2) = P(\mu - 2\sigma < X < \mu + 2\sigma) = 0.9544$

18. $P(-3 < X < 3) = P(\mu - 3\sigma < X < \mu + 3\sigma) = 0.9974$

19. $P(X \le 0) = 0.5$

20. $P(X \ge 0) = 0.5$

9·2

1. The point $z = -2$ is 2 standard deviations below the mean.

2. The point $z = -1.5$ is 1.5 standard deviations below the mean.

3. The point $z = 2.33$ is 2.33 standard deviations above the mean.

4. The point $z = -1.99$ is 1.99 standard deviations below the mean.

5. The point $z = 3.05$ is 3.05 standard deviations above the mean.

6. The point $z = -1.04$ is 1.04 standard deviations below the mean.

7. The point $z = -1.96$ is 1.96 standard deviations below the mean.

8. The point $z = 1.96$ is 1.96 standard deviations above the mean.
9. The point $z = 2$ is 2 standard deviations above the mean.
10. The point $z = -2.1$ is 2.1 standard deviations below the mean.
11. $P(-1 < Z < 1) = 0.6826$
12. $P(-2 < Z < 2) = 0.9544$
13. $P(-3 < Z < 3) = 0.9974$
14. $P(Z \leq 0) = 0.5$
15. $P(Z \geq 0) = 0.5$

9·3
1. $P(Z = 2.23) = 0$
2. $P(Z < 0.08) = 0.5319$
3. $P(Z < 2.33) = 0.9901$
4. $P(Z \leq -1.99) = 0.0233$
5. $P(Z \leq -0.05) = 0.4801$
6. $P(Z < -1.04) = 0.1492$
7. $P(Z < 2.8) = 0.9974$
8. $P(Z < -1.96) = 0.0250$
9. $P(Z < -3) = 0.0013$
10. $P(Z < 3) = 0.9987$
11. $P(Z \leq 0) = 0.5000$
12. $P(Z > 2.33) = 1.0000 - 0.9901 = 0.0099$
13. $P(Z \geq -1.99) = 1.0000 - 0.0233 = 0.9767$
14. $P(Z \geq 0) = 0.5000$
15. $P(0 < Z < 1.65) = P(Z < 1.65) - P(Z < 0) = 0.9505 - 0.5000 = 0.4505$
16. $P(-1 < Z < 1) = P(Z < 1) - P(Z < -1) = 0.8413 - 0.1587 = 0.6826$
17. $P(-2 < Z < 2) = P(Z < 2) - P(Z < -2) = 0.9772 - 0.0228 = 0.9544$
18. $P(-3 < Z < 3) = P(Z < 3) - P(Z < -3) = 0.9987 - 0.0013 = 0.9974$
19. $P(-2.28 < Z < -1.45) = P(Z < -1.45) - P(Z < -2.28) = 0.0735 - 0.0113 = 0.0622$
20. $P(1.28 < Z < 1.95) = P(Z < 1.95) - P(Z < 1.28) = 0.9744 - 0.8997 = 0.0747$

9·4
1. 0.62th percentile
2. 99.38th percentile
3. 6.81th percentile
4. $z = $ 94.95th percentile
5. $z = $ 95.05th percentile
6. $z = 1.28$
7. $z = -0.84$
8. $z = -1.08$
9. $z = 0.25$
10. $z = -1.88$
11. $z_0 = 1.16$
12. $z_0 = -2.24$
13. $z_0 = 2.49$
14. $z_0 = -1.96$
15. $z_0 = 1.18$

9·5
1. $P(X = 60) = 0$
2. $P(X \leq 60) = P\left(Z \leq \dfrac{60 - 60}{10} \right) = P(Z \leq 0) = 0.5000$
3. $P(50 \leq X \leq 70) = P\left(\dfrac{50 - 60}{10} \leq Z \leq \dfrac{70 - 60}{10} \right) = P(-1 \leq Z \leq 1) = 0.6826$
4. $P(40 \leq X \leq 80) = P\left(\dfrac{40 - 60}{10} \leq Z \leq \dfrac{80 - 60}{10} \right) = P(-2 \leq Z \leq 2) = 0.9544$
5. $P(30 \leq X \leq 90) = P\left(\dfrac{30 - 60}{10} \leq Z \leq \dfrac{90 - 60}{10} \right) = P(-3 \leq Z \leq 3) = 0.9974$
6. $P(X \leq 20) = P\left(Z \leq \dfrac{20 - 25}{5} \right) = P(Z \leq -1) = 0.1587$

7. $P(150 \le X \le 250) = P\left(\dfrac{150-300}{50} \le Z \le \dfrac{250-300}{50}\right) = P(-3 \le Z \le -1) = 0.1587 - 0.0013 = 0.1574$

8. $P(X \ge 40.5) = P\left(Z \ge \dfrac{40.5-30}{6}\right) = P(Z \ge 1.75) = 1 - 0.9599 = 0.0401$

9. $P(X \ge 100) = P\left(Z \ge \dfrac{100-120}{15}\right) = P(Z \ge -1.33) = 1 - 0.0918 = 0.9082$

10. $P(X \le 1900) = P\left(Z \le \dfrac{1900-1600}{200}\right) = P(Z \le 1.5) = 0.9332$

11. $P(X \ge 1900) = P\left(Z \ge \dfrac{1900-1600}{200}\right) = P(Z \ge 1.5) = 1 - 0.9332 = 0.0668$

12. $P(X > 130) = P\left(Z > \dfrac{130-100}{15}\right) = P(Z > 2) = 1 - 0.9772 = 0.0228$

13. $P(X \ge 750) = P\left(Z \ge \dfrac{750-500}{100}\right) = P(Z \ge 2.5) = 1 - 0.9938 = 0.0062$

14. $P(X \le 19) = P\left(Z \le \dfrac{19-16}{1.5}\right) = P(Z \le 2) = 0.9772$

15. $P(X \le 189) = P\left(Z \le \dfrac{189-160}{25}\right) = P(Z \le 1.16) = 0.8770$

16. $P(X \ge 105) = P\left(Z \ge \dfrac{105-100}{8}\right) = P(Z \ge 0.63) = 1 - 0.7357 = 0.2643$

17. $P(100 < X < 120) = P\left(\dfrac{100-118}{9.5} < Z < \dfrac{120-118}{9.5}\right) = P(-1.89 \le Z \le 0.21) = 0.5832 - 0.0294 = 0.5538 = 55.38\%$

18. $P(X \le 6) = P\left(Z \le \dfrac{6-5}{.5}\right) = P(Z \le 2) = 0.9772$

19. $P(X > 9.5) = P\left(Z > \dfrac{9.5-8}{1}\right) = P(Z > 1.5) = 1 - 0.9332 = 0.0668$

20. $P(X \ge 500) = P\left(Z \ge \dfrac{500-480}{40}\right) = P(Z \ge 0.5) = 1 - 0.6915 = 0.3085 = 30.85\%$

9·6

1. Step 1. Find z_0 such that $P(Z \le z_0) = 90\% = 0.9000$; $z_0 = 1.28$
   Step 2. $x_0 = \mu + z_0\sigma = 100 + (1.28)(15) = 119.2$

2. Step 1. Find z_0 such that $P(Z \le z_0) = 20\% = 0.2000$; $z_0 = -0.84$
   Step 2. $x_0 = \mu + z_0\sigma = 100 + (-0.84)(15) = 87.4$

3. Step 1. Find z_0 such that $P(Z \le z_0) = 14\% = 0.1400$; $z_0 = -1.08$
   Step 2. $x_0 = \mu + z_0\sigma = 100 + (-1.08)(15) = 83.8$

4. Step 1. Find z_0 such that $P(Z \le z_0) = 60\% = 0.6000$; $z_0 = 0.25$
   Step 2. $x_0 = \mu + z_0\sigma = 100 + (0.25)(15) = 103.75$

5. Step 1. Find z_0 such that $P(Z \le z_0) = 3\% = 0.0300$; $z_0 = -1.88$
   Step 2. $x_0 = \mu + z_0\sigma = 100 + (-1.88)(15) = 71.8$

6. Step 1. Find z_0 such that $P(Z \le z_0) = 0.8771$; $z_0 = 1.16$
   Step 2. $x_0 = \mu + z_0\sigma = 500 + (1.16)(100) = 616$

7. Step 1. Find z_0 such that $P(Z \le z_0) = 0.0124$; $z_0 = -2.24$
   Step 2. $x_0 = \mu + z_0\sigma = 500 + (-2.24)(100) = 276$

8. Step 1. Find z_0 such that $P(Z \le z_0) = 0.9936$; $z_0 = 2.49$
   Step 2. $x_0 = \mu + z_0\sigma = 500 + (2.49)(100) = 749$

9. Step 1. Find z_0 such that $P(Z \le z_0) = 0.025$; $z_0 = -1.96$
   Step 2. $x_0 = \mu + z_0\sigma = 500 + (-1.96)(100) = 304$

10. Step 1. Find z_0 such that $P(Z \le z_0) = 0.881$; $z_0 = 1.18$
    Step 2. $x_0 = \mu + z_0\sigma = 500 + (1.18)(100) = 618$

11. Step 1. Find z_0 such that $P(Z \le z_0) = 0.9000$; $z_0 = 1.28$
    Step 2. $x_0 = \mu + z_0\sigma = 500 + (1.28)(100) = 628$

12. Step 1. Find z_0 such that $P(Z \le z_0) = 0.5000$; $z_0 = 0$
    Step 2. $x_0 = \mu + z_0\sigma = 16 + (0)(1.5) = 16$ grams
13. Step 1. Find z_0 such that $P(Z \le z_0) = 0.8000$; $z_0 = 0.84$
    Step 2. $x_0 = \mu + z_0\sigma = 160 + (0.84)(25) = 181$ minutes
14. Step 1. Find z_0 such that $P(Z \le z_0) = 0.2500$; $z_0 = -0.67$
    Step 2. $x_0 = \mu + z_0\sigma = 100 + (-0.67)(8) = 94.64$ ounces
15. You need to find z_0 such that $P(Z \ge z_0) = 0.9505$, which is equivalent to finding z_0 such that
    $P(Z \le z_0) = 1 - 0.9505 = 0.0495$
    Step 1. Find z_0 such that $P(Z \le z_0) = 0.0495$; $z_0 = -1.65$
    Step 2. $x_0 = \mu + z_0\sigma = 480 + (-1.65)(40) = 414$ hours

IV BASIC INFERENTIAL STATISTICS

10 Estimation

10·1

1. The sampling distribution of $\bar{X}$ is approximately normal, with mean $\mu = 300$
   and standard deviation $\dfrac{\sigma}{\sqrt{n}} = \dfrac{50}{\sqrt{100}} = 5$

2. The sampling distribution of $\bar{X}$ is approximately normal, with mean $\mu = 60$
   and standard deviation $\dfrac{\sigma}{\sqrt{n}} = \dfrac{10}{\sqrt{35}} \approx 1.69$

3. The sampling distribution of $\bar{X}$ has a normal distribution, with mean $\mu = 25$
   and standard deviation $\dfrac{\sigma}{\sqrt{n}} = \dfrac{6}{\sqrt{9}} = 2$

4. The sampling distribution of $\bar{X}$ is approximately normal, with mean $\mu = 30$
   and standard deviation $\dfrac{\sigma}{\sqrt{n}} = \dfrac{12}{\sqrt{36}} = 2$

5. The sampling distribution of $\bar{X}$ is approximately normal, with mean $\mu = 120$
   and standard deviation $\dfrac{\sigma}{\sqrt{n}} = \dfrac{27}{\sqrt{225}} = 1.8$

6. $P(299 < \bar{X} < 301) = P\left(\dfrac{299-300}{50/\sqrt{100}} < Z < \dfrac{301-300}{50/\sqrt{100}} \right) = P(-0.2 < Z < 0.2) = 0.5793 - 0.4207 = 0.1586$

7. $P(\bar{X} \ge 58) = P\left(Z \ge \dfrac{58-60}{15/\sqrt{36}} \right) = P(Z \ge -0.8) = 1 - 0.2119 = 0.7881$

8. $P(\bar{X} > 26.7) = P\left(Z > \dfrac{26.7-25}{6/\sqrt{9}} \right) = P(Z > 0.85) = 1 - 0.8023 = 0.1977$

9. $P(\bar{X} \le 26.08) = P\left(Z \le \dfrac{26.08-30}{12/\sqrt{36}} \right) = P(Z \le -1.96) = 0.0250$

10. $P(122 < \bar{X} < 124) = P\left(\dfrac{122-120}{27/\sqrt{225}} < Z < \dfrac{124-120}{27/\sqrt{225}} \right) = P(1.11 < Z < 2.22) = 0.9868 - 0.8665 = 0.1203$

11. $P(\overline{X} \le 126) = P\left(Z \le \dfrac{126-120}{15\big/\sqrt{25}}\right) = P(Z \le 2) = 0.9772$

12. $P(1200 < \overline{X} < 1250) = P\left(\dfrac{1200-1200}{250\big/\sqrt{100}} < Z < \dfrac{1250-1200}{250\big/\sqrt{100}}\right) = P(0 < Z < 2) = 0.9772 - 0.5000 = 0.4772$

13. $P(\overline{X} \ge 92.5) = P\left(Z \ge \dfrac{92.5-100}{15\big/\sqrt{16}}\right) = P(Z \ge -2) = 1 - 0.0228 = 0.9772$

14. $P(500 < \overline{X} < 520) = P\left(\dfrac{500-500}{100\big/\sqrt{200}} < Z < \dfrac{520-500}{100\big/\sqrt{200}}\right) = P(0 < Z < 2.83) = 0.9977 - 0.5000 = 0.4977$

15. $P(\overline{X} \le 17) = P\left(Z \le \dfrac{17-16}{1.5\big/\sqrt{4}}\right) = P(Z \le 1.33) = 0.9082$

10·2

1. $\bar{x} \pm 1.96\dfrac{s}{\sqrt{n}} = 45 \pm 1.96\dfrac{4.2}{\sqrt{36}} = (43.63, 46.37)$

2. $\bar{x} \pm 1.96\dfrac{s}{\sqrt{n}} = 1620 \pm 1.96\dfrac{215}{\sqrt{50}} = (1560.41, 1679.59)$

3. $\bar{x} \pm 1.96\dfrac{s}{\sqrt{n}} = 105 \pm 1.96\dfrac{24}{\sqrt{200}} = (101.67, 108.33)$

4. $\bar{x} \pm 1.96\dfrac{s}{\sqrt{n}} = 7.8 \pm 1.96\dfrac{0.5}{\sqrt{100}} = (7.7, 7.9)$

5. $\bar{x} \pm 1.96\dfrac{s}{\sqrt{n}} = 412 \pm 1.96\dfrac{16}{\sqrt{75}} = (408.38, 415.62)$

6. $\bar{x} \pm z_{\alpha/2}\dfrac{\sigma}{\sqrt{n}} = 25 \pm 1.96\dfrac{8}{\sqrt{50}} = (22.78, 27.22)$

7. $\bar{x} \pm z_{\alpha/2}\dfrac{\sigma}{\sqrt{n}} = 26.7 \pm 1.645\dfrac{6}{\sqrt{9}} = (23.41, 29.99)$

8. $\bar{x} \pm z_{\alpha/2}\dfrac{s}{\sqrt{n}} = 301 \pm 1.645\dfrac{37}{\sqrt{100}} = (294.91, 307.09)$

9. $\bar{x} \pm z_{\alpha/2}\dfrac{s}{\sqrt{n}} = 58 \pm 2.576\dfrac{15}{\sqrt{36}} = (51.56, 64.44)$

10. $\bar{x} \pm z_{\alpha/2}\dfrac{s}{\sqrt{n}} = 123 \pm 1.645\dfrac{25}{\sqrt{225}} = (120.26, 125.74)$

11. $\bar{x} \pm z_{\alpha/2}\dfrac{s}{\sqrt{n}} = 17 \pm 1.96\dfrac{2.5}{\sqrt{40}} = (16.23, 17.77)$

Thus, the health science researcher can be 95% confident that the true average amount of fat grams in the signature sandwich of the local deli is between 16.2 and 17.8 fat grams (rounded to the nearest tenth).

12. $\bar{x} \pm z_{\alpha/2}\dfrac{s}{\sqrt{n}} = 234.85 \pm 1.645\dfrac{95.23}{\sqrt{100}} = (219.18, 250.52)$

Thus, the fundraising officer can be 90% confident that the true average donation from contributors to the charity is between $219.18 and $250.52.

13. $\bar{x} \pm z_{\alpha/2} \dfrac{s}{\sqrt{n}} = 39 \pm 1.96 \dfrac{8}{\sqrt{80}} = (37.25, 40.75)$

Thus, the manufacturer can be 95% confident that the true average life of its batteries is between 37.3 and 40.8 months (rounded to the nearest tenth).

14. $\bar{x} \pm z_{\alpha/2} \dfrac{s}{\sqrt{n}} = 2400 \pm 1.96 \dfrac{930}{\sqrt{500}} = (2318.48, 2481.52)$

Thus, with 95% confidence, the true mean caloric intake of all adults in the United States is between 2318.5 and 2481.5 calories (rounded to the nearest tenth).

15. $\bar{x} \pm z_{\alpha/2} \dfrac{s}{\sqrt{n}} = 120000 \pm 1.96 \dfrac{47000}{\sqrt{50}} = (106972.26, 133027.74)$

Thus, the realtor can be 95% confident that the true average price of a house in the metropolitan area is between \$106,972 and \$133,028 (rounded to the nearest dollar).

10·3

1. $t_{\alpha/2} = 1.761$ is greater than $z_{\alpha/2} = 1.645$

2. $t_{\alpha/2} = 2.145$ is greater than $z_{\alpha/2} = 1.96$

3. $t_{\alpha/2} = 2.977$ is greater than $z_{\alpha/2} = 2.576$

4. $\bar{x} \pm t_{\alpha/2} \dfrac{s}{\sqrt{n}} = 450 \pm 1.341 \dfrac{60}{\sqrt{16}} = (429.89, 470.12)$

5. $\bar{x} \pm t_{\alpha/2} \dfrac{s}{\sqrt{n}} = 450 \pm 1.860 \dfrac{60}{\sqrt{9}} = (412.8, 487.2)$

6. $\bar{x} \pm t_{\alpha/2} \dfrac{s}{\sqrt{n}} = 450 \pm 1.711 \dfrac{60}{\sqrt{25}} = (429.47, 470.53)$

7. $\bar{x} \pm t_{\alpha/2} \dfrac{s}{\sqrt{n}} = 450 \pm 3.182 \dfrac{60}{\sqrt{4}} = (354.54, 545.46)$

8. $\bar{x} + t_{\alpha/2} \dfrac{s}{\sqrt{n}} = 450 \pm 2.064 \dfrac{60}{\sqrt{25}} = (425.232, 474.768)$

9. $\bar{x} \pm t_{\alpha/2} \dfrac{s}{\sqrt{n}} = 450 \pm 2.492 \dfrac{60}{\sqrt{25}} = (420.096, 479.904)$

10. $\bar{x} \pm t_{\alpha/2} \dfrac{s}{\sqrt{n}} = 450 \pm 2.797 \dfrac{60}{\sqrt{25}} = (416.436, 483.564)$

11. $\bar{x} \pm t_{\alpha/2} \dfrac{s}{\sqrt{n}} = 480 \pm 2.064 \dfrac{75}{\sqrt{25}} = (449.04, 510.96)$

Thus, the researcher can be 95% confident that the true average score on the standardized exam for all test takers is between 449 and 511 (to the nearest whole number).

12. $\bar{x} \pm t_{\alpha/2} \dfrac{s}{\sqrt{n}} = 11 \pm 2.353 \dfrac{1.8}{\sqrt{4}} = (8.88, 13.12)$

Thus, the nutritionist can be 90% confident that the true average amount of fat grams in "heart healthy" sandwiches is between 8.9 and 13.1 fat grams (to the nearest tenth).

13. $\bar{x} \pm t_{\alpha/2} \dfrac{s}{\sqrt{n}} = 150 \pm 2.262 \dfrac{30}{\sqrt{10}} = (128.54, 171.46)$

Thus, the statistician can be 95% confident that the true average length of time for installing a bathtub by the company is between 128.5 and 171.5 minutes (to the nearest tenth).

14. $\bar{x} \pm t_{\alpha/2} \dfrac{s}{\sqrt{n}} = 95 \pm 2.861 \dfrac{8}{\sqrt{20}} = (89.88, 100.12)$

Thus, the hospital administrator can be 99% confident that the true mean weight of all newborn baby girls born at the administrator's hospital is between 89.9 and 100.1 ounces (to the nearest tenth).

15. $\bar{x} \pm t_{\alpha/2} \dfrac{s}{\sqrt{n}} = 520 \pm 2.776 \dfrac{50}{\sqrt{5}} = (457.93, 582.07)$

Thus, with 95% confidence, the true mean lifetime of all incandescent light bulbs of this brand is between 457.9 and 582.1 hours (to the nearest tenth).

10·4
1. Since $n\hat{p} = (200)(0.2) = 40$ and $n(1-\hat{p}) = (200)(0.8) = 160$, n is large enough.
2. Since $n\hat{p} = (20)(0.2) = 4$, n is too small.
3. Since $n\hat{p} = (100)(0.03) = 3$, n is too small.
4. Since $n\hat{p} = (15)(0.6) = 9$ and $n(1-\hat{p}) = (15)(0.4) = 6$, n is large enough.
5. Since $n\hat{p} = (150)(0.01) = 1.5$, n is too small

6. $\hat{p} \pm z_{\alpha/2}\sqrt{\dfrac{\hat{p}\hat{q}}{n}} = 0.2 \pm 1.645\sqrt{\dfrac{(0.2)(0.8)}{200}} = (0.1535, 0.2465)$

7. $\hat{p} \pm z_{\alpha/2}\sqrt{\dfrac{\hat{p}\hat{q}}{n}} = 0.45 \pm 2.576\sqrt{\dfrac{(0.45)(0.55)}{100}} = (0.3218, 0.5782)$

8. $\hat{p} \pm z_{\alpha/2}\sqrt{\dfrac{\hat{p}\hat{q}}{n}} = 0.03 \pm 1.96\sqrt{\dfrac{(0.03)(0.97)}{1500}} = (0.0214, 0.0386)$

9. $\hat{p} \pm z_{\alpha/2}\sqrt{\dfrac{\hat{p}\hat{q}}{n}} = 0.6 \pm 1.645\sqrt{\dfrac{(0.6)(0.4)}{15}} = (0.3919, 0.8081)$

10. $\hat{p} \pm z_{\alpha/2}\sqrt{\dfrac{\hat{p}\hat{q}}{n}} = 0.82 \pm 1.96\sqrt{\dfrac{(0.82)(0.18)}{1000}} = (0.7962, 0.8438)$

11. (a) $\hat{p} = \dfrac{15}{500} = 0.03$; $\hat{p} \pm z_{\alpha/2}\sqrt{\dfrac{\hat{p}\hat{q}}{n}} = 0.03 \pm 1.96\sqrt{\dfrac{(0.03)(0.97)}{500}} = (0.015, 0.045)$

   (b) $E = 1.96\sqrt{\dfrac{(0.03)(0.97)}{500}} = 0.015$

12. (a) $\hat{p} = \dfrac{12}{80} = 0.15$; $\hat{p} \pm z_{\alpha/2}\sqrt{\dfrac{\hat{p}\hat{q}}{n}} = 0.15 \pm 2.576\sqrt{\dfrac{(0.15)(0.85)}{80}} = (0.0472, 0.2528)$

   (b) $E = 2.576\sqrt{\dfrac{(0.15)(0.85)}{80}} = 0.1028$

13. (a) $\hat{p} = \dfrac{34}{100} = 0.34$; $\hat{p} \pm z_{\alpha/2}\sqrt{\dfrac{\hat{p}\hat{q}}{n}} = 0.34 \pm 1.645\sqrt{\dfrac{(0.34)(0.66)}{100}} = (0.2621, 0.4179)$

   (b) $E = 1.645\sqrt{\dfrac{(0.34)(0.66)}{100}} = 0.0779$

14. (a) $\hat{p} = \dfrac{240}{300} = 0.8$; $\hat{p} \pm z_{\alpha/2}\sqrt{\dfrac{\hat{p}\hat{q}}{n}} = 0.8 \pm 1.96\sqrt{\dfrac{(0.8)(0.2)}{300}} = (0.7547, 0.8453)$

   (b) $E = 1.96\sqrt{\dfrac{(0.8)(0.2)}{300}} = 0.0453$

15. (a) $\hat{p} = \dfrac{6}{120} = 0.05$; $\hat{p} \pm z_{\alpha/2}\sqrt{\dfrac{\hat{p}\hat{q}}{n}} = 0.05 \pm 1.645\sqrt{\dfrac{(0.05)(0.95)}{120}} = (0.0173, 0.0827)$

   (b) $E = 1.645\sqrt{\dfrac{(0.05)(0.95)}{120}} = 0.0327$

10·5
1. $n = \left(\dfrac{z_{\alpha/2} \cdot \sigma}{E}\right)^2 = \left(\dfrac{1.96 \cdot 10}{2}\right)^2 = 96.04$; thus, the minimum sample size is 97.

2. $n = \left(\dfrac{z_{\alpha/2} \cdot \sigma}{E}\right)^2 = \left(\dfrac{1.96 \cdot 100}{2}\right)^2 = 9604$; thus, the minimum sample size is 9604.

3. $n = \left(\dfrac{z_{\alpha/2} \cdot \sigma}{E}\right)^2 = \left(\dfrac{1.96 \cdot 100}{0.2}\right)^2 = 960400$; thus, the minimum sample size is 960,400.

4. $n = \left(\dfrac{z_{\alpha/2} \cdot \sigma}{E}\right)^2 = \left(\dfrac{1.96 \cdot 5}{1.5}\right)^2 = 42.7$; thus, the minimum sample size is 43.

5. $n = \left(\dfrac{z_{\alpha/2} \cdot \sigma}{E}\right)^2 = \left(\dfrac{1.96 \cdot 5}{.15}\right)^2 = 4268.4$; thus, the minimum sample size is 4269.

6. $n = \dfrac{z_{\alpha/2}^2 \cdot pq}{E^2} = \dfrac{(1.96)^2(.1)(.9)}{(0.02)^2} = 864.4$; thus, the minimum sample size is 865.

7. $n = \dfrac{z_{\alpha/2}^2 \cdot pq}{E^2} = \dfrac{(1.96)^2(.2)(.8)}{(0.02)^2} = 1536.6$; thus, the minimum sample size is 1537.

8. $n = \dfrac{z_{\alpha/2}^2 \cdot pq}{E^2} = \dfrac{(1.96)^2(.5)(.5)}{(0.02)^2} = 2401$; thus, the minimum sample size is 2401.

9. $n = \dfrac{z_{\alpha/2}^2 \cdot pq}{E^2} = \dfrac{(1.96)^2(.7)(.3)}{(0.02)^2} = 2016.8$; thus, the minimum sample size is 2017.

10. $n = \dfrac{z_{\alpha/2}^2 \cdot pq}{E^2} = \dfrac{(1.96)^2(.9)(.1)}{(0.02)^2} = 864.4$; thus, the minimum sample size is 865.

11. $n = \left(\dfrac{z_{\alpha/2} \cdot \sigma}{E}\right)^2 = \left(\dfrac{2.576 \cdot 7.6}{1.5}\right)^2 = 170.3$; thus, the minimum sample size is 171.

12. $n = \dfrac{z_{\alpha/2}^2 \cdot pq}{E^2} = \dfrac{(1.96)^2(.5)(.5)}{(0.04)^2} = 600.25$; thus, the minimum sample size is 601.

13. $n = \left(\dfrac{z_{\alpha/2} \cdot \sigma}{E}\right)^2 = \left(\dfrac{1.645 \cdot 8}{2}\right)^2 = 43.3$; thus, the minimum sample size is 44.

14. $n = \left(\dfrac{z_{\alpha/2} \cdot \sigma}{E}\right)^2 = \left(\dfrac{1.96 \cdot 95}{20}\right)^2 = 86.7$; thus, the minimum sample size is 87.

15. $n = \dfrac{z_{\alpha/2}^2 \cdot pq}{E^2} = \dfrac{(1.645)^2(.1)(.9)}{(0.01)^2} = 2435.4$; thus, the minimum sample size is 2436.

11 Hypothesis testing

11·1
1. parameter
2. null
3. sample
4. equality
5. two-tailed
6. H_0: $\mu = 250.00$; H_a: $\mu \neq 250.00$; two-tailed test
7. H_0: $\mu \geq 45$; H_a: $\mu < 45$; left-tailed test
8. H_0: $\mu \leq 2300$; H_a: $\mu > 2300$; right-tailed test
9. H_0: $\mu = 10$; H_a: $\mu \neq 10$; two-tailed test
10. H_0: $\mu = 100{,}000$; H_a: $\mu \neq 100{,}000$; two-tailed test
11. H_0: $\mu \leq 90$; H_a: $\mu > 90$; right-tailed test
12. H_0: $p \geq 0.05$; H_a: $p < 0.05$; left-tailed test
13. H_0: $p \leq 0.18$; H_a: $p > 0.18$; right-tailed test
14. H_0: $p \geq 0.40$; H_a: $p < 0.40$; left-tailed test
15. H_0: $p \leq 0.75$; H_a: $p > 0.75$; right-tailed test

11·2
1. H_0
2. Type I
3. Type II
4. α
5. β

6. Yes, you made the error of accepting H_0 when it is false. This error is called a Type II error.
7. No error was made; you decided to reject H_0 when it is false.
8. Yes, you made the error of rejecting H_0 when it is true. This error is called a Type I error.
9. Yes, you made the error of accepting H_0 when it is false. This error is called a Type II error.
10. No error was made; you did not accept H_0 when it is false. Thus, you avoided making a Type II error.

11·3
1. z
2. t
3. z
4. H_0
5. sample

11·4
1. **1.** $H_0: \mu = 22$ (the claim); $H_a: \mu \neq 22$ (two-tailed test)
   2. $\alpha = .05$
   3. Reject H_0 if either $z < -1.96$ or $z > 1.96$
   4. T.S. $= z = \dfrac{\bar{x} - \mu_0}{\dfrac{\sigma}{\sqrt{n}}} = \dfrac{25 - 22}{\dfrac{8}{\sqrt{50}}} = 2.65$
   5. Since T.S. $= 2.65 > 1.96$, reject H_0 and accept H_a.
   6. The sample data provide sufficient evidence at the $\alpha = .05$ level of significance to overturn the null hypothesis (the claim). Therefore, at the $\alpha = .05$ level of significance, you can conclude that the mean of the given population is not 22.
2. **1.** $H_0: \mu \geq 28$ (the conjecture); $H_a: \mu < 28$ (left-tailed)
   2. $\alpha = .01$
   3. Reject H_0 if $z < -2.33$.
   4. T.S. $= z = \dfrac{\bar{x} - \mu_0}{\dfrac{s}{\sqrt{n}}} = \dfrac{26.7 - 28}{\dfrac{6}{\sqrt{40}}} = -1.37$
   5. Since T.S. $= -1.37 \not< -2.33$, fail to reject H_0.
   6. The sample data fail to provide sufficient evidence at the $\alpha = .01$ level of significance to overturn the null hypothesis (the conjecture) that the mean is at least 28.
3. **1.** $H_0: \mu \leq 300$; $H_a: \mu > 300$ (the claim) (right-tailed)
   2. $\alpha = .05$
   3. Reject H_0 if $z > 1.645$
   4. T.S. $= z = \dfrac{\bar{x} - \mu_0}{\dfrac{s}{\sqrt{n}}} = \dfrac{301 - 300}{\dfrac{37}{\sqrt{100}}} = 0.27$
   5. Since T.S. $= 0.27 \not> 1.645$, fail to reject H_0.
   6. The sample data fail to provide sufficient evidence at the $\alpha = .05$ level of significance to overturn the null hypothesis. Therefore, at the $\alpha = .05$ level of significance, the claim that the mean is greater than 300 is not supported by the data.
4. **1.** $H_0: \mu \leq 50$ (the conjecture); $H_a: \mu > 50$ (right-tailed)
   2. $\alpha = .01$
   3. Reject H_0 if $z > 2.33$
   4. T.S. $= z = \dfrac{\bar{x} - \mu_0}{\dfrac{s}{\sqrt{n}}} = \dfrac{58 - 50}{\dfrac{15}{\sqrt{36}}} = 3.2$
   5. Since T.S. $= 3.2 > 2.33$, reject H_0 and accept H_a.
   6. The sample data provide sufficient evidence at the $\alpha = .01$ level of significance to overturn the null hypothesis (the conjecture). Therefore, at the $\alpha = .01$ level of significance, you can conclude that the mean of the given population is greater than 50.
5. **1.** $H_0: \mu \leq 120$; $H_a: \mu > 120$ (the claim) (right-tailed)
   2. $\alpha = .05$
   3. Reject H_0 if $z > 1.645$
   4. T.S. $= z = \dfrac{\bar{x} - \mu_0}{\dfrac{s}{\sqrt{n}}} = \dfrac{123 - 120}{\dfrac{25}{\sqrt{225}}} = 1.8$

5. Since $T.S. = 1.8 > 1.645$, reject H_0 and accept H_a.
6. The sample data provide sufficient evidence at the $\alpha = .05$ level of significance to overturn the null hypothesis. Therefore, at the $\alpha = .05$ level of significance, you can conclude that the mean of the given population exceeds 120.

6. **1.** $H_0: \mu = 250.00$ (the claim); $H_a: \mu \neq 250.00$ (two-tailed test)
   2. $\alpha = .05$
   3. Reject H_0 if either $z < -1.96$ or $z > 1.96$
   4. $T.S. = z = \dfrac{\bar{x} - \mu_0}{\frac{s}{\sqrt{n}}} = \dfrac{234.85 - 250.00}{\frac{95.23}{\sqrt{100}}} = -1.59$
   5. Since $T.S. = -1.59 \not< -1.96$, fail to reject H_0.
   6. The sample data fail to provide sufficient evidence at the $\alpha = .05$ level of significance to overturn the null hypothesis (the claim) that the average donation from contributors to the charity is \$250.00.
   p-value $= 2 \cdot P(Z \leq -1.59) = 2 \cdot 0.0559 = 0.1118$

7. **1.** $H_0: \mu \geq 45$ (the manufacturer's claim); $H_a: \mu < 45$ (left-tailed)
   2. $\alpha = .05$
   3. Reject H_0 if $z < -1.645$
   4. $T.S. = z = \dfrac{\bar{x} - \mu_0}{\frac{s}{\sqrt{n}}} = \dfrac{39 - 45}{\frac{8}{\sqrt{80}}} = -6.71$
   5. Since $T.S. = -6.71 < -1.645$, reject H_0 and accept H_a.
   6. The sample data provide sufficient evidence at the $\alpha = .05$ level of significance to overturn the null hypothesis (the manufacturer's claim). Therefore, at the $\alpha = .05$ level of significance, you can conclude that the average life of the manufacturer's batteries is less than 45 months.
   p-value $= P(Z \leq -6.71) < 0.0002$ (using -3.49, the least z-value in Table B)

8. **1.** $H_0: \mu \leq 2300$ (the claim); $H_a: \mu > 2300$ (right-tailed)
   2. $\alpha = .05$
   3. Reject H_0 if $z > 1.645$
   4. $T.S. - z = \dfrac{\bar{x} - \mu_0}{\frac{s}{\sqrt{n}}} = \dfrac{2400 - 2300}{\frac{930}{\sqrt{500}}} = 2.40$
   5. Since $T.S. = 2.40 > 1.645$, reject H_0 and accept H_a.
   6. The sample data provide sufficient evidence at the $\alpha - .05$ level of significance to overturn the null hypothesis (the claim). Therefore, at the $\alpha = .05$ level of significance, you can conclude that the true mean caloric intake of all adults in the United States is greater than 2300 calories.
   p-value $= P(Z \geq 2.40) = 1 - 0.9918 = 0.0082$

9. **1.** $H_0: \mu = 100,000$ (newsletter listing); $H_a: \mu \neq 100,000$ (two-tailed test)
   2. $\alpha = .01$
   3. Reject H_0 if either $z < -2.576$ or $z > 2.576$
   4. $T.S. = z = \dfrac{\bar{x} - \mu_0}{\frac{s}{\sqrt{n}}} = \dfrac{120000 - 100000}{\frac{47000}{\sqrt{50}}} = 3.01$
   5. Since $T.S. = 3.01 > 2.576$, reject H_0 and accept H_a.
   6. The sample data provide sufficient evidence at the $\alpha = .01$ level of significance to overturn the null hypothesis (the listing in the realtor's newsletter). Therefore, at the $\alpha = .01$ level of significance, you can conclude that the average price of a house in the given metropolitan area is not \$100,000.
   p-value $= 2 \cdot P(Z \geq 3.01) = 2(1 - 0.9987) = 0.0026$

10. **1.** $H_0: \mu \geq 110$; $H_a: \mu < 110$ (administrator's concern) (left-tailed)
    2. $\alpha = .01$
    3. Reject H_0 if $z < -2.33$
    4. $T.S. = z = \dfrac{\bar{x} - \mu_0}{\frac{\sigma}{\sqrt{n}}} = \dfrac{105 - 110}{\frac{9.5}{\sqrt{35}}} = -3.11$
    5. Since $T.S. = -3.11 < -2.33$, reject H_0.

6. The sample data provide sufficient evidence at the $\alpha = .01$ level of significance to overturn the null hypothesis. Therefore, at the $\alpha = .01$ level of significance, the data indicate that the mean weight of all newborn baby boys born at the local hospital is less than 110 ounces.

p-value = $P(Z \leq -3.11) = 0.0009$

11. Since $0.0009 < 0.05$, reject H_0 and accept H_a.
12. Since $0.1118 > 0.05$, fail to reject H_0.
13. Since $0.0499 < 0.05$, reject H_0 and accept H_a.
14. Since $0.0501 > 0.05$, fail to reject H_0.
15. Since $0.02 < 0.05$, reject H_0 and accept H_a.

11·5

1. **1.** H_0: $\mu = 22$ (the claim); H_a: $\mu \neq 22$ (two-tailed test)
   2. $\alpha = .05$
   3. Reject H_0 if either $z < -2.131$ or $z > 2.131$
   4. T.S. $= t = \dfrac{\overline{x} - \mu_0}{\dfrac{s}{\sqrt{n}}} = \dfrac{25 - 22}{\dfrac{8}{\sqrt{16}}} = 1.5$
   5. Since T.S. $= 1.5 \not> 2.131$, fail to reject H_0.
   6. The sample data fail to provide sufficient evidence at the $\alpha = .05$ level of significance to overturn the null hypothesis (the claim) that the mean of the population is 22.

2. **1.** H_0: $\mu \geq 28$ (the conjecture); H_a: $\mu < 28$ (left-tailed)
   2. $\alpha = .05$
   3. Reject H_0 if $t < -1.711$
   4. T.S. $= t = \dfrac{\overline{x} - \mu_0}{\dfrac{s}{\sqrt{n}}} = \dfrac{26.7 - 28}{\dfrac{6}{\sqrt{25}}} = -1.083$
   5. Since T.S. $= -1.083 \not< -1.711$, fail to reject H_0.
   6. The sample data fail to provide sufficient evidence at the $\alpha = .05$ level of significance to overturn the null hypothesis (the conjecture) that the mean μ is at least 28.

3. **1.** H_0: $\mu \leq 300$; H_a: $\mu > 300$ (the claim) (right-tailed)
   2. $\alpha = .10$
   3. Reject H_0 if $t > 1.345$
   4. T.S. $= t = \dfrac{\overline{x} - \mu_0}{\dfrac{s}{\sqrt{n}}} = \dfrac{301 - 300}{\dfrac{37}{\sqrt{15}}} = 0.105$
   5. Since T.S. $= 0.105 \not> 1.345$, fail to reject H_0.
   6. The sample data fail to provide sufficient evidence at the $\alpha = .10$ level of significance to overturn the null hypothesis. Therefore, at the $\alpha = .10$ level of significance, the claim that the mean of the population is greater than 300 is not supported by the data.

4. **1.** H_0: $\mu \leq 50$ (the conjecture); H_a: $\mu > 50$ (right-tailed)
   2. $\alpha = .01$
   3. Reject H_0 if $t > 4.541$
   4. T.S. $= t = \dfrac{\overline{x} - \mu_0}{\dfrac{s}{\sqrt{n}}} = \dfrac{58 - 50}{\dfrac{15}{\sqrt{4}}} = 1.067$
   5. Since T.S. $= 1.067 \not> 4.541$, fail to reject H_0.
   6. The sample data fail to provide sufficient evidence at the $\alpha = .01$ level of significance to overturn the null hypothesis (the conjecture) that the mean is no more than 50.

5. **1.** H_0: $\mu \leq 120$; H_a: $\mu > 120$ (the claim) (right-tailed)
   2. $\alpha = .05$
   3. Reject H_0 if $t > 1.729$
   4. T.S. $= t = \dfrac{\overline{x} - \mu_0}{\dfrac{s}{\sqrt{n}}} = \dfrac{123 - 120}{\dfrac{25}{\sqrt{20}}} = 0.537$
   5. Since T.S. $= 0.537 \not> 1.729$, fail to reject H_0.
   6. The sample data fail to provide sufficient evidence at the $\alpha = .05$ level of significance to overturn the null hypothesis. Thus, the claim that the mean of the population exceeds 120 is not supported by the data.

6. **1.** $H_0: \mu = 500$ (the claim); $H_a: \mu \neq 500$ (two-tailed test)
   2. $\alpha = .05$
   3. Reject H_0 if either $z < -2.064$ or $z > 2.064$
   4. $T.S. = t = \dfrac{\bar{x} - \mu_0}{\dfrac{s}{\sqrt{n}}} = \dfrac{480 - 500}{\dfrac{75}{\sqrt{25}}} = -1.333$
   5. Since $T.S. = -1.333 \not< -2.064$, fail to reject H_0.
   6. The sample data fail to provide sufficient evidence at the $\alpha = .05$ level of significance to overturn the null hypothesis (the claim) that the average score on the exam for all test takers is 500.

7. **1.** $H_0: \mu = 10$ (the claim); $H_a: \mu \neq 10$ (two-tailed test)
   2. $\alpha = .05$
   3. Reject H_0 if either $z < -3.182$ or $z > 3.182$
   4. $T.S. = t = \dfrac{\bar{x} - \mu_0}{\dfrac{s}{\sqrt{n}}} = \dfrac{11 - 10}{\dfrac{1.8}{\sqrt{4}}} = 1.111$
   5. Since $T.S. = 1.111 \not> 3.182$, fail to reject H_0.
   6. The sample data fail to provide sufficient evidence at the $\alpha = .05$ level of significance to overturn the null hypothesis (the claim) that the "heart healthy" sandwich has 10 fat grams.

8. **Note:** 2 hours = 120 minutes.
   1. $H_0: \mu \leq 120$ (the company's claim); $H_a: \mu > 120$ (right-tailed)
   2. $\alpha = .10$
   3. Reject H_0 if $t > 1.383$
   4. $T.S. = t = \dfrac{\bar{x} - \mu_0}{\dfrac{s}{\sqrt{n}}} = \dfrac{150 - 120}{\dfrac{30}{\sqrt{10}}} = 3.162$
   5. Since $T.S. = 3.162 > 1.383$, reject H_0 and accept H_a.
   6. The sample data provide sufficient evidence at the $\alpha = .10$ level of significance to overturn the null hypothesis (the company's claim). Therefore, at the $\alpha = .10$ level of significance, you can conclude that the true mean length of time, in minutes, for installing a bathtub by the company is more than 2 hours (120 minutes).

9. **1.** $H_0: \mu \geq 100$; $H_a: \mu < 100$ (focus of the administrator's study) (left-tailed)
   2. $\alpha = .01$
   3. Reject H_0 if $t < -2.539$
   4. $T.S. = t = \dfrac{\bar{x} - \mu_0}{\dfrac{s}{\sqrt{n}}} = \dfrac{95 - 100}{\dfrac{8}{\sqrt{20}}} = -2.795$
   5. Since $T.S. = -2.795 < -2.539$, reject H_0 and accept H_a.
   6. The sample data provide sufficient evidence at the $\alpha = .01$ level of significance to overturn the null hypothesis. Therefore, the hospital administrator can conclude that the true mean weight of all newborn baby girls born at the administrator's hospital is less than 100 ounces.

10. **1.** $H_0: \mu \leq 500$ (the consumer group's complaint); $H_a: \mu > 500$ (right-tailed)
    2. $\alpha = .10$
    3. Reject H_0 if $t > 1.533$
    4. $T.S. = t = \dfrac{\bar{x} - \mu_0}{\dfrac{s}{\sqrt{n}}} = \dfrac{520 - 500}{\dfrac{50}{\sqrt{5}}} = 0.894$
    5. Since $T.S. = 0.894 \not> 1.533$, fail to reject H_0.
    6. The sample data fail to provide sufficient evidence at the $\alpha = .10$ level of significance to overturn the null hypothesis (the consumer group's complaint) that the mean lifetime of this brand of incandescent light bulbs is no more than 500 hours.

11·6

1. $np_0 = (500)(0.05) = 25$ and $n(1 - p_0) = (500)(0.95) = 475$, so n is large enough.
2. $np_0 = (80)(0.18) = 14.4$ and $n(1 - p_0) = (80)(0.82) = 65.6$, so n is large enough.
3. $np_0 = (100)(0.40) = 40$ and $n(1 - p_0) = (100)(0.60) = 60$, so n is large enough.
4. $np_0 = (300)(0.75) = 225$ and $n(1 - p_0) = (300)(0.25) = 75$, so n is large enough.
5. $np_0 = (120)(0.01) = 1.2$, so n is too small.

6. **1.** $H_0: p \geq 0.05$; $H_a: p < 0.05$ (quality control guideline) (left-tailed test)
   2. $\alpha = .01$
   3. Reject H_0 if $z < -2.33$
   4. $\hat{p} = \dfrac{15}{500} = 0.03$; T.S. $= z = \dfrac{\hat{p} - p_0}{\sqrt{\dfrac{p_0(1-p_0)}{n}}} = \dfrac{0.03 - 0.05}{\sqrt{\dfrac{0.05(0.95)}{500}}} = -2.052$
   5. Since T.S. $= -2.052 \not< -2.33$, fail to reject H_0.
   6. The sample data do not provide sufficient evidence at the $\alpha = .01$ level of significance to overturn the null hypothesis. Therefore, the manufacturer likely will not be satisfied with the results of the test of hypothesis.

7. **1.** $H_0: p \leq 0.18$ (the claim); $H_a: p > 0.18$ (right-tailed test)
   2. $\alpha = .05$
   3. Reject H_0 if $z > 1.645$
   4. $\hat{p} = \dfrac{30}{80} = 0.375$; T.S. $= z = \dfrac{\hat{p} - p_0}{\sqrt{\dfrac{p_0(1-p_0)}{n}}} = \dfrac{0.375 - 0.18}{\sqrt{\dfrac{0.18(0.82)}{80}}} = 4.540$
   5. Since T.S. $= 4.540 > 1.645$, reject H_0 and accept H_a.
   6. The sample data provide sufficient evidence at the $\alpha = .05$ level of significance to overturn the null hypothesis. Therefore, at the $\alpha = .05$ level of significance, you can conclude that the true proportion of working women over the age of 60 in the metropolitan area exceeds 0.18.

8. **1.** $H_0: p \geq 0.40$ (station manager's hypothesis); $H_a: p < 0.40$ (left-tailed test)
   2. $\alpha = .05$
   3. Reject H_0 if $z < -1.645$
   4. $\hat{p} = \dfrac{34}{100} = 0.34$; T.S. $= z = \dfrac{\hat{p} - p_0}{\sqrt{\dfrac{p_0(1-p_0)}{n}}} = \dfrac{0.34 - 0.40}{\sqrt{\dfrac{0.40(0.60)}{100}}} = -1.225$
   5. Since T.S. $= -1.225 \not< -1.645$, fail to reject H_0.
   6. The sample data do not provide sufficient evidence at the $\alpha = .05$ level of significance to overturn the station manager's hypothesis (null hypothesis) that the percent of radio listeners in the area who listen to the manager's radio station is at least 40 percent.

9. **1.** $H_0: p \leq 0.75$; $H_a: p > 0.75$ (interior designer's belief) (right-tailed test)
   2. $\alpha = .05$
   3. Reject H_0 if $z > 1.645$
   4. $\hat{p} = \dfrac{240}{300} = 0.80$; T.S. $= z = \dfrac{\hat{p} - p_0}{\sqrt{\dfrac{p_0(1-p_0)}{n}}} = \dfrac{0.80 - 0.75}{\sqrt{\dfrac{0.75(0.25)}{300}}} = 2.00$
   5. Since T.S. $= 2.00 > 1.645$, reject H_0 and accept H_a.
   6. The sample data provide sufficient evidence at the $\alpha = .05$ level of significance to overturn the null hypothesis. Therefore, at the $\alpha = .05$ level of significance, you can concur with the interior designer that the proportion of assisted living residents who would prefer a blue hue on bedroom walls is greater than 0.75.

10. **1.** $H_0: p \geq 0.10$ (market researcher's prediction); $H_a: p < 0.10$ (left-tailed test)
    2. $\alpha = .10$
    3. Reject H_0 if $z < -1.28$
    4. $\hat{p} = \dfrac{6}{120} = 0.05$; T.S. $= z = \dfrac{\hat{p} - p_0}{\sqrt{\dfrac{p_0(1-p_0)}{n}}} = \dfrac{0.05 - 0.10}{\sqrt{\dfrac{0.10(0.90)}{120}}} = -1.826$
    5. Since T.S. $= -1.826 < -1.28$, reject H_0 and accept H_a.
    6. The sample data provide sufficient evidence at the $\alpha = .10$ level of significance to overturn the market researcher's prediction (null hypothesis). Therefore, at the $\alpha = .10$ level of significance, you can conclude that the percent of households that have no vehicle in the particular area is less than 10 percent.

1. **1.** $H_0: \mu_1 = \mu_2$ (no difference); $H_a: \mu_1 \neq \mu_2$ (two-tailed test)
   2. $\alpha = .01$
   3. $df = n_1 + n_2 - 2 = 77 + 125 - 2 = 200$
   Reject H_0 if either $t < -2.601$ or $t > 2.601$
   4. $s_p^2 = \dfrac{(n_1-1)s_1^2 + (n_2-1)s_2^2}{n_1+n_2-2} = \dfrac{(76)(15)^2 + (124)(20)^2}{200} = 333.5$

   $T.S. = t = \dfrac{(\bar{x}_1 - \bar{x}_2) - (\mu_1 - \mu_2)}{\sqrt{s_p^2\left(\dfrac{1}{n_1} + \dfrac{1}{n_2}\right)}} = \dfrac{(435 - 440) - (0)}{\sqrt{333.5\left(\dfrac{1}{77} + \dfrac{1}{125}\right)}} = -1.890$

   5. Since $T.S. = -1.890 \not< -2.601$, fail to reject H_0.
   6. The sample data fail to provide sufficient evidence at the $\alpha = .01$ level of significance to overturn the null hypothesis of no difference.

2. **1.** $H_0: \mu_1 \leq \mu_2$; $H_a: \mu_1 > \mu_2$ (right-tailed test)
   2. $\alpha = .10$
   3. $df = n_1 + n_2 - 2 = 38 + 29 - 2 = 65$
   Reject H_0 if $t > 1.295$
   4. $s_p^2 = \dfrac{(n_1-1)s_1^2 + (n_2-1)s_2^2}{n_1+n_2-2} = \dfrac{(37)(0.9)^2 + (28)(2.6)^2}{65} = 3.373$

   $T.S. = t = \dfrac{(\bar{x}_1 - \bar{x}_2) - (\mu_1 - \mu_2)}{\sqrt{s_p^2\left(\dfrac{1}{n_1} + \dfrac{1}{n_2}\right)}} = \dfrac{(8.4 - 7.8) - (0)}{\sqrt{3.373\left(\dfrac{1}{38} + \dfrac{1}{29}\right)}} = 1.325$

   5. Since $T.S. = 1.325 > 1.295$, reject H_0 and accept H_a.
   6. The sample data provide sufficient evidence at the $\alpha = .10$ level of significance to overturn the null hypothesis. Therefore, you can conclude that μ_1 is greater than μ_2.

3. **1.** Let μ_1 be the true average GRE quantitative score of students who applied in the past five years and μ_2 be the true average GRE quantitative score of students who applied more than five years ago. The hypotheses are:
   $H_0: \mu_1 \geq \mu_2$; $H_a: \mu_1 < \mu_2$ (left-tailed test)
   2. $\alpha = .05$
   3. $df = n_1 + n_2 - 2 = 38 + 44 - 2 = 80$
   Reject H_0 if $t < -1.664$
   4. $s_p^2 = \dfrac{(n_1-1)s_1^2 + (n_2-1)s_2^2}{n_1+n_2-2} = \dfrac{(37)(25)^2 + (43)(30)^2}{80} = 772.8125$

   $T.S. = t = \dfrac{(\bar{x}_1 - \bar{x}_2) - (\mu_1 - \mu_2)}{\sqrt{s_p^2\left(\dfrac{1}{n_1} + \dfrac{1}{n_2}\right)}} = \dfrac{(650 - 670) - (0)}{\sqrt{772.8125\left(\dfrac{1}{38} + \dfrac{1}{44}\right)}} = -3.249$

   5. Since $T.S. = -3.249 < -1.664$, reject H_0 and accept H_a.
   6. The sample data provide sufficient evidence at the $\alpha = .05$ level of significance to overturn the null hypothesis. Therefore, at the $\alpha = .05$ level of significance, the graduate recruiter can conclude that the true average GRE quantitative score of students who applied in the past five years is less than the true average GRE quantitative score of students who applied more than five years ago.

4. **1.** Let μ_1 be the true mean Internet sale amount and μ_2 be the true mean mail-order sale amount. The hypotheses are:
   $H_0: \mu_1 \leq \mu_2$; $H_a: \mu_1 > \mu_2$ (right-tailed test)
   2. $\alpha = .01$
   3. $df = n_1 + n_2 - 2 = 15 + 10 - 2 = 23$
   Reject H_0 if $t > 2.500$
   4. $s_p^2 = \dfrac{(n_1-1)s_1^2 + (n_2-1)s_2^2}{n_1+n_2-2} = \dfrac{(14)(18.75)^2 + (9)(14.25)^2}{23} = 293.4538$

   $T.S. = t = \dfrac{(\bar{x}_1 - \bar{x}_2) - (\mu_1 - \mu_2)}{\sqrt{s_p^2\left(\dfrac{1}{n_1} + \dfrac{1}{n_2}\right)}} = \dfrac{(86.40 - 75.20) - (0)}{\sqrt{293.4538\left(\dfrac{1}{15} + \dfrac{1}{10}\right)}} = 1.601$

5. Since $T.S. = 1.601 \ngtr 2.500$, fail to reject H_0.
6. The sample data do not provide sufficient evidence at the $\alpha = .01$ level of significance to overturn the null hypothesis. Thus, the data do not indicate that the true mean Internet sale amount exceeds the true mean mail-order sale amount.

5. Let μ_1 be the true average miles per gallon for Brand 1 and μ_2 be the true average miles per gallon for Brand 2. The hypotheses are:
1. $H_0: \mu_1 = \mu_2$ (no difference); $H_a: \mu_1 \neq \mu_2$ (two-tailed test)
2. $\alpha = .05$
3. $df = n_1 + n_2 - 2 = 5 + 8 - 2 = 11$
Reject H_0 if either $t < -2.201$ or $t > 2.201$
4. $s_p^2 = \dfrac{(n_1 - 1)s_1^2 + (n_2 - 1)s_2^2}{n_1 + n_2 - 2} = \dfrac{(4)(7.4)^2 + (7)(8.4)^2}{11} = 64.8145$

$T.S. = t = \dfrac{(\bar{x}_1 - \bar{x}_2) - (\mu_1 - \mu_2)}{\sqrt{s_p^2\left(\dfrac{1}{n_1} + \dfrac{1}{n_2}\right)}} = \dfrac{(29.5 - 31.6) - (0)}{\sqrt{64.8145\left(\dfrac{1}{5} + \dfrac{1}{8}\right)}} = -0.458$

5. Since $T.S. = -0.458 \nless -2.201$, fail to reject H_0.
6. The sample data fail to provide sufficient evidence at the $\alpha = .05$ level of significance to overturn the null hypothesis of no difference.

11·8

1. 1. If μ_1 is the true number of coughs in a four-hour period for the placebo population and μ_2 is the true mean number of coughs in a four-hour period for the treatment population, then, symbolically, the assertion "no difference" is written as $\mu_1 = \mu_2$ or $\mu_1 - \mu_2 = 0$, which is equivalent to $\mu_D = 0$. Thus, the hypotheses are:
$H_0: \mu_D = 0$ (no difference); $H_a: \mu_D \neq 0$ (two-tailed test)
2. $\alpha = .01$
3. $df = n_D - 1 = 5 - 1 = 4$
Reject H_0 if either $t < -4.604$ or $t > 4.604$
4. $T.S. = t = \dfrac{\bar{x}_D - 0}{\dfrac{s_D}{\sqrt{n_D}}} = \dfrac{20 - 0}{\dfrac{4}{\sqrt{5}}} = 11.180$
5. Since $T.S. = 11.180 > 4.604$, reject H_0 and accept H_a.
6. The sample data provide sufficient evidence at the $\alpha = .01$ level of significance to overturn the null hypothesis of no difference. Therefore, at the $\alpha = .01$ level of significance, you can conclude that the true mean of the population of all paired differences between placebo and treatment groups is not zero.

2. 1. If μ_1 is the true mean pre-assessment score, and μ_2 is the true mean post-assessment score, then, symbolically, the assertion "higher post-assessment scores" is written or $\mu_1 < \mu_2$ or $\mu_1 - \mu_2 < 0$, which is equivalent to $\mu_D < 0$. Thus, the hypotheses are
$H_0: \mu_D \geq 0$
$H_a: \mu_D < 0$ (higher post-assessment scores)
2. $\alpha = .05$
3. $df = n_D - 1 = 8 - 1 = 7$
Reject H_0 if $t < -1.895$
4. $T.S. = t = \dfrac{\bar{x}_D - 0}{\dfrac{s_D}{\sqrt{n_D}}} = \dfrac{-12.25 - 0}{\dfrac{5.007}{\sqrt{8}}} = -6.9199$
5. Since $T.S. = -6.9199 < -1.895$, reject H_0.
6. The sample data provide sufficient evidence at the $\alpha = .05$ level of significance to overturn the null hypothesis. Therefore, at the $\alpha = .05$ level of significance, you can conclude that the reading intervention produces higher post-assessment scores.

3. 1. If μ_1 is the true mean before weight and μ_2 is the true mean after weight, then, symbolically, the assertion "the low-fat one-month diet is effective" is written as $\mu_1 > \mu_2$ or $\mu_1 - \mu_2 > 0$, which is equivalent to $\mu_D > 0$. Thus, the hypotheses are:
$H_0: \mu_D \leq 0$
$H_a: \mu_D > 0$ (the diet is effective)

2. $\alpha = .10$
3. $df = n_D - 1 = 6 - 1 = 5$
   Reject H_0 if $t > 1.476$
4. $T.S. = t = \dfrac{\bar{x}_D - 0}{\dfrac{s_D}{\sqrt{n_D}}} = \dfrac{6.33 - 0}{\dfrac{5.785}{\sqrt{6}}} = 2.6803$
5. Since $T.S. = 2.6803 > 1.476$, reject H_0 and accept H_a.
6. The sample data provide sufficient evidence at the $\alpha = .10$ level of significance to overturn the null hypothesis. Therefore, at the $\alpha = .10$ level of significance, you can conclude that the low-fat one-month diet is effective.

4. 1. If μ_1 is the true mean number of panic attacks in one week for the placebo group and μ_2 is the true mean number of panic attacks in one week for the treatment group, then, symbolically, the assertion "the drug is effective against panic attacks" is written as $\mu_1 > \mu_2$ or $\mu_1 - \mu_2 > 0$, which is equivalent to $\mu_D > 0$. Thus, the hypotheses are:
   $H_0: \mu_D \le 0$
   $H_a: \mu_D > 0$ (the drug is effective against panic attacks)
2. $\alpha = .05$
3. $df = n_D - 1 = 7 - 1 = 6$
   Reject H_0 if $t > 1.943$
4. $T.S. = t = \dfrac{\bar{x}_D - 0}{\dfrac{s_D}{\sqrt{n_D}}} = \dfrac{9.714 - 0}{\dfrac{11.146}{\sqrt{7}}} = 2.3058$
5. Since $T.S. = 2.3058 > 1.943$, reject H_0 and accept H_a.
6. The sample data provide sufficient evidence at the $\alpha = .05$ level of significance to overturn the null hypothesis. Therefore, at the $\alpha = .05$ level of significance, you can conclude that the new drug is effective against panic attacks.

5. 1. If μ_1 is the true mean miles per gallon for Gasoline 1 and μ_2 is the true mean miles per gallon for Gasoline 2, then, symbolically, the assertion "no difference in performance between the two gasoline fuels" is written as $\mu_1 = \mu_2$ or $\mu_1 - \mu_2 = 0$, which is equivalent to $\mu_D = 0$. Thus, the hypotheses are:
   $H_0: \mu_D = 0$ (no difference); $H_a: \mu_D \ne 0$ (two-tailed test)
2. $\alpha = .05$
3. $df = n_D - 1 = 5 - 1 = 4$
   Reject H_0 if either $t < -2.776$ or $t > 2.776$
4. $T.S. = t = \dfrac{\bar{x}_D - 0}{\dfrac{s_D}{\sqrt{n_D}}} = \dfrac{-.34 - 0}{\dfrac{3.1045}{\sqrt{5}}} = -0.2449$
5. Since $T.S. = -0.2449 \not< -2.776$, fail to reject H_0.
6. The sample data do not provide sufficient evidence at the $\alpha = .05$ level of significance to overturn the null hypothesis of no difference.

11·9   1. 1. Symbolically, the assertion "the proportion p_1 of adults age 25 or older that have college degrees in population 1 is greater than the proportion p_2 of adults age 25 or older that have college degrees in population 2" is written as $p_1 > p_2$. Thus, the hypotheses are:
   $H_0: p_1 \le p_2$; $H_a: p_1 > p_2$ (right-tailed test)
2. $\alpha = .05$
3. Reject H_0 if $z > 1.645$
4. $\hat{p}_1 = 0.31$
   $\hat{p}_2 = 0.22$
   $\bar{p} = \dfrac{62 + 44}{200 + 200} = \dfrac{106}{400} = 0.265$
   $T.S. \ z = \dfrac{(\hat{p}_1 - \hat{p}_2) - (p_1 - p_2)}{\sqrt{\bar{p}(1 - \bar{p})\left(\dfrac{1}{n_1} + \dfrac{1}{n_2}\right)}} = \dfrac{(0.31 - 0.22) - (0)}{\sqrt{(0.265)(0.735)\left(\dfrac{1}{200} + \dfrac{1}{200}\right)}} = 2.039$
5. Since $T.S. = 2.039 > 1.645$, reject H_0 and accept H_a.

6. The sample data provide sufficient evidence at the $\alpha = .05$ level of significance to overturn the null hypothesis. Thus, at the $\alpha = .05$ level of significance, you can conclude that the proportion p_1 of adults age 25 or older that have college degrees in population 1 is greater than the proportion p_2 of adults age 25 or older that have college degrees in population 2.

2. **1.** Symbolically, the assertion "the proportion p_1 of middle school girls who work a summer job before entering high school is at least as great as the proportion p_2 of middle school boys who work a summer job before entering high school" is written as $p_1 \geq p_2$. Thus, the hypotheses are:

$H_0: p_1 \geq p_2$; $H_a: p_1 < p_2$ (left-tailed test)

2. $\alpha = .01$

3. Reject H_0 if $z < -2.33$.

4. $\hat{p}_1 = 0.12$

$\hat{p}_2 = 0.20$

$\bar{p} = \dfrac{21+30}{175+150} = \dfrac{51}{325} = 0.1569$

$T.S.\ z = \dfrac{(\hat{p}_1 - \hat{p}_2) - (p_1 - p_2)}{\sqrt{\bar{p}(1-\bar{p})\left(\dfrac{1}{n_1} + \dfrac{1}{n_2}\right)}} = \dfrac{(0.12 - 0.20) - (0)}{\sqrt{(0.1569)(0.8431)\left(\dfrac{1}{175} + \dfrac{1}{150}\right)}} = -1.977$

5. Since $T.S. = -1.977 \not< -2.33$, fail to reject H_0.

6. The sample data fail to provide sufficient evidence at the $\alpha = .01$ level of significance to overturn the null hypothesis that the proportion of middle school girls who work a summer job before entering high school is at least as great as the proportion of middle school boys who work a summer job before entering high school.

3. **1.** If p_1 = the true proportion of male adults 18 years or older in the United States who are smokers and p_2 = the true proportion of female adults 18 years or older in the United States who are smokers, then, symbolically, the assertion "the prevalence of smoking among male adults 18 years or older in the United States exceeds the prevalence of smoking among female adults 18 years or older" is written as $p_1 > p_2$. Thus, the hypotheses are:

$H_0: p_1 \leq p_2$; $H_a: p_1 > p_2$ (right-tailed test)

2. $\alpha = .05$

3. Reject H_0 if $z > 1.645$

4. $\hat{p}_1 = \dfrac{129}{516} = 0.2500$

$\hat{p}_2 = \dfrac{87}{484} = 0.1798$

$\bar{p} = \dfrac{129+87}{516+484} = \dfrac{216}{1000} = 0.216$

$T.S.\ z = \dfrac{(\hat{p}_1 - \hat{p}_2) - (p_1 - p_2)}{\sqrt{\bar{p}(1-\bar{p})\left(\dfrac{1}{n_1} + \dfrac{1}{n_2}\right)}} = \dfrac{(0.2500 - 0.1798) - (0)}{\sqrt{(0.216)(0.784)\left(\dfrac{1}{516} + \dfrac{1}{484}\right)}} = 2.70$

5. Since $T.S. = 2.70 > 1.645$, reject H_0 and accept H_a.

6. The sample data provide sufficient evidence at the $\alpha = .05$ level of significance to overturn the null hypothesis. Therefore, the health organization can conclude that the prevalence of smoking among male adults 18 years or older in the United States exceeds the prevalence of smoking among female adults 18 years or older.

4. **1.** If p_1 = the true proportion of adults 25 to 39 years old whose favorite hue is blue, and p_2 = the true proportion of adults 40 to 59 years old whose favorite hue is blue; then, symbolically, the assertion "adults 25 to 39 years old are less strong in their preference for blue as a favorite hue compared to the preference for blue as a favorite hue of adults 40 to 59 years old" is written as $p_1 < p_2$. Thus, the hypotheses are:

$H_0: p_1 \geq p_2$; $H_a: p_1 < p_2$ (left-tailed test)

2. $\alpha = .10$

3. Reject H_0 if $z < -1.28$

4. $\hat{p}_1 = \dfrac{292}{430} = 0.6791$

$\hat{p}_2 = \dfrac{180}{245} = 0.7347$

$$\bar{p} = \frac{292+180}{430+245} = \frac{472}{675} = 0.6993$$

$$T.S.\ z = \frac{(\hat{p}_1 - \hat{p}_2)-(p_1 - p_2)}{\sqrt{\bar{p}(1-\bar{p})\left(\frac{1}{n_1}+\frac{1}{n_2}\right)}} = \frac{(0.6791-0.7347)-(0)}{\sqrt{(0.6993)(0.3007)\left(\frac{1}{430}+\frac{1}{245}\right)}} = -1.51$$

5. Since $T.S. = -1.51 < -1.28$, reject H_0 and accept H_a.
6. The sample data provide sufficient evidence at the $\alpha = .10$ level of significance to overturn the null hypothesis. Therefore, adults 25 to 39 years old are less strong in their preference for blue as a favorite hue compared to the preference for blue as a favorite hue of adults 40 to 59 years old.

5. It is not appropriate to use the methods of this section to test the hypothesis. Since $n_1 \hat{p}_1 = (40)(.1) = 4 < 5$, this sample size is too small to conduct the test of hypothesis using the methods of this section.

12 Correlation analysis

12·1
1. is weaker than
2. is weaker than
3. is weaker than
4. is weaker than
5. is stronger than
6. is stronger than
7. is the same strength as
8. is the same strength as
9. is the same strength as
10. is stronger than

12·2

1. $r = \dfrac{n\sum xy - \left(\sum x\right)\left(\sum y\right)}{\sqrt{n\sum x^2 - \left(\sum x\right)^2}\sqrt{n\sum y^2 - \left(\sum y\right)^2}} = \dfrac{5(6399)-(177)(188)}{\sqrt{5(7475)-(177)^2}\sqrt{5(8118)-(188)^2}} = -0.22746 \approx -0.227$

2. $r = \dfrac{n\sum xy - \left(\sum x\right)\left(\sum y\right)}{\sqrt{n\sum x^2 - \left(\sum x\right)^2}\sqrt{n\sum y^2 - \left(\sum y\right)^2}} = \dfrac{5(38533)-(488)(439)}{\sqrt{5(52878)-(488)^2}\sqrt{5(42411)-(439)^2}} = -0.95741 \approx -0.957$

3. $r = \dfrac{n\sum xy - \left(\sum x\right)\left(\sum y\right)}{\sqrt{n\sum x^2 - \left(\sum x\right)^2}\sqrt{n\sum y^2 - \left(\sum y\right)^2}} = \dfrac{5(4806)-(56)(425)}{\sqrt{5(786)-(56)^2}\sqrt{5(36187)-(425)^2}} = 0.46359 \approx 0.464$

4. $r = \dfrac{n\sum xy - \left(\sum x\right)\left(\sum y\right)}{\sqrt{n\sum x^2 - \left(\sum x\right)^2}\sqrt{n\sum y^2 - \left(\sum y\right)^2}} = \dfrac{4(352)-(32)(52)}{\sqrt{4(376)-(32)^2}\sqrt{4(862)-(52)^2}} = -0.42838 \approx -0.428$

5. $r = \dfrac{n\sum xy - \left(\sum x\right)\left(\sum y\right)}{\sqrt{n\sum x^2 - \left(\sum x\right)^2}\sqrt{n\sum y^2 - \left(\sum y\right)^2}} = \dfrac{6(1918)-(23.5)(459)}{\sqrt{6(108.125)-(23.5)^2}\sqrt{6(36071)-(459)^2}} = 0.96901 \approx 0.969$

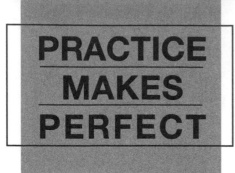
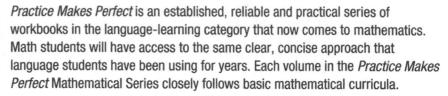